# Holding the Line

D1247878

# Holding the Line

## *Race, Racism, and American Foreign Policy toward Africa, 1953–1961*

GEORGE WHITE JR.

ROWMAN & LITTLEFIELD PUBLISHERS, INC.
*Lanham • Boulder • New York • Toronto • Oxford*

ROWMAN & LITTLEFIELD PUBLISHERS, INC.

Published in the United States of America
by Rowman & Littlefield Publishers, Inc.
A wholly owned subsidary of The Rowman & Littlefield Publishing Group, Inc.
4501 Forbes Boulevard, Suite 200, Lanham, Maryland 20706
www.rowmanlittlefield.com

PO Box 317
Oxford
OX2 9RU, UK

British Library Cataloguing in Publication Information Available

**Library of Congress Cataloging-in-Publication Data**

White, George, 1962-
   Holding the line : race, racism, and American foreign policy toward
Africa, 1953-1961 / George White, Jr.
      p. cm.
   Includes bibliographical references and index.
   ISBN 0-7425-3382-4 (hardcover : alk. paper) -- ISBN 0-7425-3383-2
(pbk. : alk. paper)
   1. United States--Foreign relations--Africa, Sub-Saharan.  2. Africa,
Sub-Saharan--Foreign relations--United States.  3. United States
--Foreign relations--1953-1961.  4. Africa, Sub-Saharan--Politics and
government--1884-1960.    I. Title.
DT38.5.W47 2005
327.73067'09'045--dc22                                    200501009

Printed in the United States of America

⊖™ The paper used in this publication meets the minimum requirements of American
National Standard for Information Sciences—Permanence of Paper for Printed Library
Materials, ANSI/NISO Z39.48-1992.

To Deseriee, my soulmate, my love, my friend, and my wife. Thank you for everything, but especially for reminding me that my life is worth saving.

# CONTENTS

# ACKNOWLEDGMENTS

As an apprenticing historian, I owe a tremendous debt of gratitude to so many people that writing this seems like an exercise in futility, apt to crash and burn and make more noise for what is not said than for what is. Yet, saying "thank you" is always a wonderful exercise. Because there is so much to say, I will begin at the beginning.

To begin, I must thank my family: my parents, George and Lois; my brothers, Anthony and Barron; my grandparents, aunts, uncles, cousins, nieces, nephews, and godchildren. Further, I must recognize my wife, Professor Deseriee Kennedy, and children, Noelle, Noah, and Nolani. In addition to the Foster-Whites, Perryman-Brooks, Wheelers, Barrons, and Wimpies, I also must thank the Kennedys, McCallas, and Geneces who have embraced me as one of their own. I thank my family because they are my first teachers.

Aside from family, there are numerous friends and acquaintances who deserve mention. I have been blessed by coming to know many beautiful people during my stays in towns as varied as Dallas, Boston, Los Angeles, and Philadelphia. However, one bunch deserves special recognition: the Nubian Study Group. Many thanks to Jetty, Lionel, and the rest of the guys for helping me reclaim my love of history and encouraging me to return to school.

Perhaps the most critically important group in this leg of my journey is the collection of humanists who shepherded me through graduate school, both teachers and students. Thanks to all my fellow neophytes at Temple, from Olivia, Khepri, Gary, and Stephanie to Will, Peniel, and John. Thank you Phoebe Hadden, Richard Immerman, Wilbert Jenkins, Teshale Tibebu for painstakingly reviewing and massaging my dissertation and molding my intellect. And thank you Dieu Nguyen for being a wonderful mentor and sounding board. All of you helped me to be a better scholar than I imagined possible.

My colleagues at the University of Tennessee also have provided invaluable support in numerous ways, especially Kathleen Brosnan, Penny Hamilton, Kim Harrison, Catherine Higgs, and Kurt Piehler. More importantly, I thank Cynthia Fleming—my first boss at the University of Tennessee when she served as director of the African and African American Studies Program—for her courage, insight, and confidence in my abilities. I especially appreciate all of the effort, advice, and equanimity of Anne Galloway, program secretary for African and African American

Acknowledgments

Studies, as she waded through several drafts of this manuscript and typeset this version.

As I continue to navigate the waters of professional scholarship, I am indebted to many whom have influenced my work either through their own research or by critical, thought-provoking comments regarding mine. Among the former, I must acknowledge pioneers like Derrick Bell, Sumi Cho, W. E. B. DuBois, Cheryl Harris, Gerald Horne, Robin D. G. Kelley, Rayford Logan, and Brenda Gayle Plummer. Of the latter, I thank my more immediate colleagues Carol Anderson, Andy DeRoche, Cary Fraser, Amy Staples, and Aida Sy-Wonyu for their time, thoughtfulness, and patience.

One of the most exciting periods of my early career as an academic was my service as the second Geraldine R. Dodge Postdoctoral Fellow at the Rutgers Institute on Ethnicity, Culture, and the Modern Experience. Personally, I learned so much from working with Lori Barcliff Baptista, Clement Price, and Charles Russell that words fail to answer even simple questions. Professionally, I blossomed because they supported   a number of research trips, read drafts of scholarly articles, teased me (Eisenhower HAD a policy toward Africa? That must have been a fifteen-page dissertation!), and allowed me to participate in the Institute's faculty colloquia. Thank you all for being friends and templates of a higher order.

As a novice, I also have benefitted immeasurably from the kindness (nay, pity) of many archivists across the country. Two who bear special mention are Herb Pankratz and David Haight at the Eisenhower Presidential Library and Museum in Abilene, Kansas. Thank you for your indulgence and persistence through my fumbling requests and clumsy questions.

Finally, I need to "big up" my "peeps" from East Knoxville: Tim, Tracy, Kenny, Derrick, Brett, Nippy, Paul, Rocky, DeVon, Stewart, Marvetta, the Kirks, the Jacksons, the Branners, Ms. Coleman, Linda Parris-Bailey, Umoja and Nkechi, and the rest of the crew. I also must thank all of the students whom I have taught at Temple University and the University of Tennessee, for you have taught me as well. To everyone named and unnamed on these pages, thank you for all you have meant to me. As I begin this book and "skirmish with disaster"—in the words of poet Meena Alexander—please know that I love you and intend to make you proud.

# CHAPTER ONE

# THE GHOSTS IN THE SHELL

Near the end of the Eisenhower administration, bones were crying in the Congo. As a result, the credibility of the United Nations shrank in the minds of many of the world's citizens. Developments in other parts of Africa also stirred official concern in Washington. The White House watched as the Afrikaners worked to build a racial Iron Curtain in southern Africa. Eisenhower officials cringed as pro-Western Ethiopia accepted a loan from the Czech Republic and voted at the United Nations to recognize Communist China. Adding to the anxiety, neutralist Ghana entertained accepting the offer of a development grant from the Soviet Union. With a Communist presence slowly forming in Africa, the recent revolution in Cuba, and the humiliating public exposure of the U-2 spy plane flights, the champion of the Free World seemed to be "swaying between atomic and spiritual disintegration."[1] This book explores how the United States came to such a pass.

In his oft-quoted, but truncated, statement, W. E. B. DuBois predicted the problems discussed herein. In his 1903 publication *The Souls of Black Folk*, the eminent scholar remarked that "the problem of the twentieth century is the problem of the color line—the relation of the darker to the lighter races of men in Asia and Africa, in America and the islands of the sea."[2] This book examines those very relations, rooted in American soil and extending to the African continent, which DuBois hailed. By analyzing how the Eisenhower administration cleaved to that color line, this book seeks to illuminate those needs and desires, which thrummed beneath the surface of American diplomacy toward Africa.

## Whiteness and Its Manifestations

On December 4, 2002, American media outlets reported that Senate Majority Leader Trent Lott remarked in a tribute to retiring Senator Strom Thurmond that had the rest of the country followed Mississippi's lead and supported Thurmond's bid for the White House as the Dixiecrat candidate in 1948, the nation "wouldn't have had all these problems over all these years." People from across the political spectrum interpreted Lott's remarks as a reference to racial segregation and contemporary race relations. Lott's comments surprised many, though close observers noted that he had made similar remarks throughout his tenure in the U.S. Senate. Amid the political firestorm caused by his statement, Lott apologized. During one televised apology, Lott explained that his remarks actually referred to Thurmond's strong anti-Communism, among other things, rather than nostalgia for the era of Jim Crow. However, billboards linking Dr. Martin Luther King Jr. to Communism dotted the South during President Eisenhower's second term, belying the distinction made by Lott.[3]

With contemporary America as a mirror, this book offers a break from the consensus on the Cold War by addressing Whiteness, its symptoms, and its impact on U.S. foreign relations. Whiteness describes the complex of associations, assumptions, and immunities attributed to people who are identified as White.[4] This complex of beliefs and impressions corresponds to every positive human trait. It is relativistic, mutable, imprecise, and resilient because it is based on constructed meanings rather than on fixed biological or genetic evidence.[5] Since Whiteness is learned though never named, it acts as a hegemonic force, making White people appear to be not only *better* than others but *normal*.[6] Although Whiteness as manifested in Eisenhower administration foreign policy is the locus of this work, this does not suggest that the actions of people of African descent are irrelevant. Indeed, the challenges posed by Africans and African Americans bring the ephemeral nature of Whiteness into much sharper focus.

The very real material, social, and psychic advantages which emerge from Whiteness collectively create White privilege. White privilege allows Whites, for instance, to define the world and its phenomena, to project themselves as the standard by which other people should be judged, and to determine the nature and scope of justice. Whiteness and White privilege manifest themselves in numerous ways, but for the purposes of this book, we will explore five of these manifestations: White innocence and entitlement, along with Black erasure, self-abnegation, and insatiability.

White innocence pertains to the idea that White people are inherently pious, just, and law-abiding, among other things. White innocence also provides self-absolution for the actions of Whites. Any White person or group of White people who acts in contradiction to this notion are considered individually deviant, and their acts do not impugn the character of the entire White collective. In addition to being exculpative, White innocence mocks any critique of White behavior because White innocence incorporates the idea of a purity of purpose and intent, as well as sanctity of essence.

White entitlement refers to the notion that Whites, because of the characteristics attributed to them, deserve a disproportionate share of power, resources, and esteem. For example, White entitlement was the motivating force behind the idea of Manifest Destiny, that because White people were Christian, civilized, industrious, and freedom-loving—especially in relation to Native Americans, the argument went—God had determined that they should sweep across the North American continent and lay claim to lands occupied by other peoples.[7] Similarly, White entitlement was the engine behind Alan Bakke's claim that he had been racially discriminated against by the admissions policy of the University of California-Davis medical school, leading to his landmark lawsuit, even though thirty-six White students admitted to the medical school had lower college GPAs than his and five students had been admitted because their parents either had attended or made donations to the institution.[8]

Black erasure is the ability of Whites to dismiss the accomplishments or desires of Black people. In the White Supremacist imagination, Black people are the antithesis of White people. Therefore, it is difficult for many Whites to believe that Blacks can accomplish things which Whites take for granted. Many Whites maintain these beliefs even in the face of evidence to the contrary. Black erasure can happen at any time, as former New York Supreme Court Justice Bruce Wright noted when recalling an emergency trip to the hospital for what his clerks feared was a heart attack.

> In the emergency room . . . I was placed in a curtained-off area where there were two beds . . . On one was a white man, obviously one of the poor derelicts now and then brought in from the Bowery. He appeared to be in a state of joyous alcoholic bewilderment. He needed a shave; neither his soiled sneakers nor his socks matched; he drooled a bit and sang softly in garbled syllables . . . As I watched from my bed, I felt pangs of pity . . . I felt guilty for being dressed in a three-piece suit and clean shirt. I heard a nurse outside the curtained area say, "Hurry, doctor, we have a judge who is ill." A white doctor parted the curtain, paused at the entrance, looked at me and then at the white derelict. He hurried to the side of the white man, lifted his wrist, as though to test his pulse, and said, "Judge, what seems to be the matter?"[9]

Black erasure becomes important when Blacks demonstrate or assert their competence, intelligence, righteousness, or courage, among other traits, because these demonstrations destabilize the comfortable, intoxicating delusion of Whiteness. Further, Black erasure insures that the undeniably positive actions of a single Black person or discreet group of Blacks cannot be used to enhance the character of the entire Black collective.[10]

Black self-abnegation also refers to the dismissal of Black humanity, needs, and goals. The difference is that in this instance Whiteness requires that Blacks do this themselves. Thus, it is not enough that Whites assign Blacks a place at or near the bottom of the cultural hierarchy or near the last rung of the ladder of social relevance; Blacks must agree that such a designation is correct or, at least, accept it.

Finally, Black insatiability refers to the White belief that Black expectations are unreasonable. Black insatiability emerges, in part, from stereotypes of Blacks as being undisciplined and lacking self-restraint. It also emerges from the belief that most Blacks are content with their lot in life, implying that Black activists are merely requesting things they do not need or should not have. The belief in Black insatiability surfaces as Blacks make demands for better jobs, increased access to political power, or racial justice in other forms. The belief in Black insatiability serves as a justification for White recalcitrance. The White fear is that if Whites concede one demand by Blacks, only more demands will follow, thereby unfairly toppling White privilege and entitlement. In some ways, Black insatiability acts as the obverse of White entitlement: by seeking that which Whites have earned and deserve, Blacks simply are asking too much.[11]

The varying elements of Whiteness and White privilege operate consistently, though some recede in force as others expand.[12] For instance, Black insatiability becomes prominent only when Black people assert a demand which requires Whites to surrender unwillingly some material or psychic resource.[13] These elements, among others, are the animating force for the invisible shroud that envelopes people identified as White; these elements are some of the ghosts within the shell of Whiteness.[14] When non-Whites identify and confront these ghosts, Whiteness loses its esteem and strength. In such an environment, Whites retreat to a sanctuary within which Whiteness can be redeemed.

The need for racial sanctuary frequently stems from successful challenges to White hegemony. These challenges can take many forms, whether they be proof of Black genius or the exposure of the corruption and brutality of White power. These challenges are successful when they rupture the consensus on White innocence or, in turn, Black deviance. It is within a racial sanctuary that Whiteness can be repaired and transformed so that it may continue to function in its wraith-like manner, unassailable because it returns cloaked by normalcy. The following pages examine just such a sanctuary.

Although this piece will focus on a narrow historical moment, modern Europe and its progeny—America, for example—were always affected by notions of race which resulted in a systematic attempt to control and dominate all interaction between people perceived as White and those classified as non-White. Thus, from inception all the benefits of the relationship between Europeans and Native Americans and Africans flowed toward the Europeans, while all the burdens of the relationship moved in reverse. Because this nation's development and expansion relied upon this stream of benefits and burdens, it is logical to assume that its ascendance to global prominence rested on this same formula.[15]

Given this overarching framework, American slavery was an organizational scheme within the larger power configuration of White Supremacy. Furthermore, as the larger power configuration, White Supremacy could exist without slavery. To bring the point closer to home, overt, state-sponsored racial segregation was an organizational scheme within the larger power configuration of White Supremacy. As the experiences of generations of African Americans living outside the segregated South attest, White Supremacy existed without de jure segregation.[16] Accordingly, Black resistance to de jure segregation in the United States and the concomitant push toward independence in Africa were successful, hard-fought challenges to existing organizational schemes. Unfortunately, both were accomplished without altering significantly the flow of benefits and burdens between White and non-White people. This outcome—illustrated by overwhelming evidence of continuing racial disparities, the popular defense of such disparities, and attacks on contemporary critics of racism—reflects the power of White Supremacy and its ability to protect White privilege.[17]

The Cold War provided the perfect environment for the preservation of Whiteness. The Eisenhower administration's objective was to hold the line during the tumultuous transformations of the 1950s so that the global stream of benefits and burdens would not change course. The Eisenhower White House sought to manage the pace of Continental change in order to ensure that the larger power configuration of White Supremacy withstood the abolition of traditional, but secondary, organizational schemes. The evaluation of available diplomatic options by the administration began with its perceptions of people of color. More specifically, to navigate the African terrain of the 1950s, members of the administration relied upon mental maps and social scripts developed at home.[18]

## Whiteness in the International and Domestic Context: A Sampler

Over the centuries, Whiteness has manifested itself in numerous ways. Two poignant examples for the purposes of this study pertain to relations between Haiti and the United States and the relationship between the federal government and the litigants in the *Brown v. Board of Education* case. Whereas Haiti serves as a template for America's informal colonization of people of African descent, the *Brown* case foreshadowed the role the Eisenhower administration played in the international drama of decolonization and African nation-building.

### Haiti: A Model of Noncolonial Imperialism

From the moment of its conception, the leaders and decision-makers of the United States have fretted over Haiti. Although the slave revolt which effectively expelled the French from the island ultimately delivered to Thomas Jefferson the land that became known as "The Louisiana Purchase," few Whites were sanguine about developments in the Carribean.[19] Haiti was the only nation in the Western Hemisphere which was controlled by dark-skinned peoples. Furthermore, Haiti came into being as an independent nation through slave rebellion. As such, Haiti was an unnerving example of what slaves could achieve.[20] Finally, Haitian people contemplated a future independent of foreign domination.[21] These factors caused great concern in nineteenth-century Washington.

Scholars like Brenda Gayle Plummer, Rayford Logan, and Anna Julia Cooper have authored fascinating histories of Haiti and Haitian-American relations.[22]

Reduced to its essentials, the story of these relations is one of constant vacillation between hostility and indifference. More importantly, the story reveals the way in which American racial views manifested themselves in diplomacy with an emerging state dominated by people of African descent.[23]

The U.S. government refused to recognize independent Haiti for decades. In addition to French diplomatic pressure, White politicians refused to take seriously a non-White republic, especially given the prevailing beliefs regarding Black inferiority.[24] According to one scholar, "to many [W]hites, they had only fortuitously slipped the yoke. Their freedom and pretensions to nationhood were specious, and only force of arms guaranteed their preposterous claims to sovereignty."[25] A story that circulated through Washington about an American ambassador's reaction to seeing his Haitian counterpart in the court of Louis Napoleon illustrates this point: "The American minister, Mr. Mason . . . was sleeved by an Englishman . . . who pointed to [the Haitian ambassador], and said, 'What do you think of him?' Mr. Mason said 'I think, clothes and all, he is worth $1,000.'"[26] During the 1862 congressional debates regarding recognition of Haiti, opponents warned that recognition would lead to the intermingling of Blacks and Whites and the appearance of racial parity. Thus, Democratic representative Charles Biddle of Pennsylvania argued against recognition because "racial equality might 'be a philosophic idea, an English idea, but it is eminently un-American.'"[27]

Notwithstanding prevailing racist opinions, the Congress voted to recognize Haiti, no doubt in part because of President Lincoln's support for plans to use the island as a haven to which American Blacks could be resettled.[28] Near the turn of the century, German and French business interests in Haiti were the leading segment of a varied foreign capitalist community which included British, Syrian, Lebanese, and Italian firms.[29] Americans especially feared the German presence; Bismark appeared intent on gaining a foothold in the West Indies in order to control or gain access to the proposed isthmian canal.[30] Civil unrest which resulted from a confluence of unequal wealth distribution, antiforeign sentiment, and government corruption/collaboration with foreign interests made Haiti a cauldron of international activity.[31] Thus, American President Theodore Roosevelt invoked the Monroe Doctrine with respect to Haiti in order to deter increasing Franco-German influence throughout Latin America.[32]

Attacks on foreign businessmen and property reached such a level that German and French officials on the island requested warships from their respective homelands to restore order.[33] Despite their struggles with the Germans and the French, Haitian officials repeatedly rebuffed American overtures of assistance. Haiti was more interested in maintaining its sovereignal integrity than in being a pawn in Atlantic power politics.[34] American arrogance grew to the point that U.S. Marines eventually made landfall at Haiti's urban center in 1915, beginning "a military occupation of Haiti that lasted two decades."[35]

Ostensibly, the invasion was a humanitarian endeavor. As one American official stated, "the government of the United States is seeking to make its relation to Haiti beneficial to the Haitian people. It has no other aim but to establish peace and stability."[36] The rationale for the invasion, freedom for Haiti, was a clear mix of Progressivist reformism and White Supremacy, which emphasized the American duty to teach Haitians "the intelligence and the civic spirit which are absolutely essential in a democracy."[37] Colonel Littleton Waller, a member of the U.S. military establishment in Haiti, took for granted the success of the occupation because he "knew the nigger and how to handle him."[38] Col. Waller probably felt comfortable in his smugness, given his years in a segregated Army and fighting in Cuba and the Phillippines.[39] The fact that Haitians were a heterogenous group of people quite different from African Americans did not bother Waller: "The Haitians 'are niggers in spite of the thin varnish of education and refinement,' he claimed. 'Down in their hearts they are just the same happy, idle, irresponsible people we know of.'"[40]

The placement of an American shadow government in Haiti resulted in the implementation of several policy goals. First, American occupation meant the subordination of Haitian desires to the interests of the United States. Second, American agriculturalists, bankers, and financial speculators could better exploit Haitian natural resources and the Haitian people, both as a supply of cheap labor and a market for American goods. Third, the American occupation accomplished one of the goals of the Monroe Doctrine: the termination of European influence in Haitian political and economic affairs. The legacy of fiscal austerity, military tyranny, favored status for foreign investors (primarily American), and depressed wages and living conditions remains with Haiti today.[41]

Woodrow Wilson's State Department searched for a leader to replace the assassinated president. The Haitian legislature, under coercion from U.S. Marines, elected Sudre Dartiguenave president and promulgated an American-Haitian treaty that legalized the occupation. The U.S. Senate ratified the treaty in February 1916 without comment. The next legislative task was a revision of the Haitian constitution. A key component of the indigenous constitution that bothered foreign powers was the "traditional refusal to allow foreign ownership of land." When the Haitian legislature refused to approve a revised document that had been drafted by the State Department, American occupation forces suspended the body for twelve years. A chimera plebiscite was held in which less than 5 percent of the electorate participated and approved the U.S.-crafted constitution.[42] Whiteness manifested itself in many other ways as well.

The American supervisors in Haiti revived the hated corvee' (forced labor) system and instituted curfews, press censorship, and intensive surveillance. They also imported their racial caste system: "Newly arrived U.S. personnel insisted on racial segregation and introduced it into hotels, restaurants, and clubs."[43]

Militarily, American occupation leaders immediately disbanded the nation's army and hoped to use the Haitian police to maintain order. The *Gendarmerie d'Haiti* was conceived of more as a stabilizing, coercive force than an army: "The most important of all the Treaty Services was the Gendarmerie d'Haiti. This one of the treaty services virtually controlled the Government and operated the other agencies." Thus, the Garde d'Haiti (as it was renamed in 1928) became the dominant force in Haitian life.[44] Within months of its organization, the Gendarmerie faced its stiffest test against a rebellion led by Charlemagne Peralte.

American officials initially left to the Gendarmerie the task of confronting the rebels. Because they conducted themselves in such desultory fashion, the Gendarmerie was replaced by the American military. Relying on an approach once recommended to Napoleon,[45] the Marines suppressed the rebellion by not bothering to distinguish between guerillas and innocents. In a manner similar to later military efforts, the "search and destroy" missions of American armed forces resulted in the deaths of at least 3,000 Haitians, mostly noncombatants, by 1920.[46] After the pacification campaign, the Gendarmerie was revitalized and resumed its predatory relationship with the Haitian peasantry, including the supervision of tax collection.[47]

When American troops left Haiti in 1935, American hegemony had simply been strengthened: "A new treaty abrogated all functions of the protectorate except those relating to financial administration, alienation of land, the avoidance of entangling alliances, and law and order. These exceptions were, of course, among the essential aspects of government."[48] Despite official statements of altruism,[49] private citizens of and entities from the United States controlled much of the Haitian economy.[50] Accordingly, they held sway over Haitian political aspirations. Such control led to agricultural and economic disaster just a few years later.

As the United States was swept into World War II, it looked for ways to boost its supply of critical materials. Japanese expansion throughout Southeast Asia crimped Allied rubber supplies. Consequently, American officials approached the Haitian government with regard to using the island's best farmland for rubber cultivation.

Haitian President Elie Lescot sponsored a bilateral development venture known as the *Societe Haitiano-Americaine de Developpement Agricole* (SHADA) whose primary objective was the cultivation of an indigenous vine rubber, cryptostegia.[51] The Lescot government secured a $5 million loan from the Export-Import Bank, which was then provided to SHADA.[52] The project was led by North Americans supposedly expert in tropical cultivation.[53]

SHADA exercised near dictatorial control in rural Haiti. Although Lescot made a half-hearted attempt at exempting small farmers from dispossession, "SHADA . . . held rights to prime land, acreage best suited for food crop production."[54] Government seizure of peasant land provided SHADA with nearly 330,000 acres or 21.5 percent of the total cultivated area of Haiti. In the process, roughly 40,000 Haitian families were evicted from their lands, some with no more than 48 hours notice, and watched their crops be destroyed.[55]

Despite tremendous advantages—financing provided by an American-controlled institutiton and guaranteed by the Haitian government; a supply of cheap, intimidated labor; nearly unrestricted access to land and logistical infrastructure; no competition; and military protection—SHADA was an abject failure.[56] SHADA exported no rubber from Haiti.[57] As a result of SHADA's policy of razing farmland

and hiring workers who otherwise would be engaged in staple food production, the Haitian people endured staggering food shortages. Although some officials in the Roosevelt administration hoped to use American funds to assist dislocated peasants who were returning to their lands, "vehement opposition from the Office of Wartime Economic Affairs prevented assistance from reaching the peasantry."[58] The environmental devastation alone further inhibited the ability of the nation to feed itself.[59]

Standing alone, SHADA is a prime example of Black self-abnegation by Haitian leadership. Yet, it is important to note that the American preference was to use Haitian troops to quell Black insurrection. From the moment of American occupation, U.S. officials had conceived of the Haitian police as a tool of social control.[60] Further, the Americans imposed a military-enforced censorship on the island's press to maintain the false impression that the masses of Haitians were content under the occupation.[61] Moreover, the Good Neighbor Policy of Franklin D. Roosevelt undermined Haitian economic diversification. For instance, the Haitian tourism industry faltered in the 1930s and 1940s in no small part because of Washington's demands: "The White House and the State Department obliged Haiti to place debt service above allocating funds for national development."[62]

In regard to the politics of Black insatiability, the U. S. continually ignored or minimized Haitian concerns. In October 1937 Rafael Trujillo, leader of the neighboring Dominican Republic and a staunch U.S. ally, sent Dominican National Guard units to the Haitian-Dominican frontier, where they slaughtered fifteen to twenty thousand Haitian migrant workers. Despite vehement protests by the Haitian foreign minister, the Haitian military, and even the U.S. Ambassador to Haiti, the Roosevelt administration held to a policy of "neutrality." Six years later, when President Lescot informed Roosevelt of an assassination plot created by Trujillo, the American response was cold. After two months' delay, FDR responded by saying that, though saddened by the news, he was relieved to know that Lescot had done "nothing to disturb the continental solidarity which is so necessary in the present struggle."[63]

Although the Haitian experience was not an exact model for decolonization—in the sense that the Eisenhower administration either deliberately included personnel from pervious administrations who had dealt with Haiti or sought to duplicate the same process in Africa—it stands as an important example of "quasi-colonialism" involving a nation heavily populated by people of African descent.[64] The veneer of self-governance makes Haiti an instructive example precisely because it reveals the ability of the American government to control informally a burgeoning nation. Additionally, it reveals the consensus on the inferiority of Africans and the concomitant entitlement of Whites to place Black aspirations within a White-defined international context and to provide the appropriate stewardship for Black political development. Thus, American elites knew that a better way of maintaining European economic growth—and, ultimately, American dominance—could be achieved by abandoning the colonial structure for a facade of independence.[65]

### The Eisenhower Administration and the Brown(ing) of America

The advent of the Cold War coincided with the galvanizing of forces within the Black community that led to the most recent period of sustained, mass Black protest. As with so many other periods in American history, the distinctions between American ideals and practices revealed themselves starkly. African American activists, international critics, and media placed this schism on full, global display. For its part, the Eisenhower administration's desire to balance the interests of Blacks and the expectations of Whites provided the domestic root for what Thomas Noer referred to as the White House's "middle ground" foreign policy in Africa.[66] Additionally, the White House's efforts to silence global criticism of American race relations foregrounded the extension of the racial sanctuary into the realm of international affairs.

Lynching of Blacks was so commonplace immediately after World War II that the NAACP's January 3, 1947, report referred to 1946 as "one of the grimmest years in the history of the [organization]."[67] Part of the Black response to these conditions was to appeal to the United Nations; one appeal was from the National Negro Congress (NNC) and another from the NAACP. Marxist media outlets castigated American racism and widely circulated stories typical of the ones serving as the basis of these appeals. Even stalwart international conservatives lamented the poor state of American race relations.[68]

The reality of America's racially segregated public schools was a linchpin in many powerful critiques of Western democracy.[69] Shortly before 1954, several education cases gained notoriety as the legal vanguard against the separate-but-equal doctrine articulated in *Plessy v. Ferguson.*[70] However, none of them had actually overturned the *Plessy* standard. The case which would in fact toll the death knell for *Plessy* was *Brown v. Board of Education.*[71]

As they had in other lawsuits, federal government attorneys championed the interests of racial tolerance through the filing of *amicus curiae* briefs.[72] However, major differences existed between the briefs and arguments of Justice Department attorneys under Truman and, later, Eisenhower. The 1952 amicus brief in *Brown*, the longest such filing by the Truman Justice Department, laid out both the distressing international situation facing the U. S. and the grim detail of Black life in America. These pages contained the transcendent statement linking racial segregation and American diplomacy: "It is in the context of the present world struggle between freedom and tyranny that the problem of racial discrimination must be viewed . . . Racial discrimination furnishes grist for the Communist propaganda mills, and it raises doubts even among friendly nations as to the intensity of our devotion to the democratic faith.[73]

By 1953, Eisenhower had replaced Truman in the White House, and the Supreme Court issued an order setting *Brown* and its companion cases for reargument. The order invited the new attorney general, Herbert Brownell, to file a second brief.[74] Indeed, the change in government support, which many advocates of Black civil rights feared, manifested itself in the Eisenhower Justice Department's amicus brief. The attitude of the government lawyers, articulated in the 1953 brief, signaled a subtle transformation in the government's position with regard to race relations. Under Democratic control, the Justice Department primarily acted as an advocate for Black plaintiffs. Under Republican leadership, the Justice Department adopted a noncommittal stance as a "racial referee," managing what it considered to be potentially destabilizing social change.[75]

On December 8, 1953, the Supreme Court held oral reargument in *Brown I*. Assistant Attorney General J. Lee Rankin opened his presentation by informing the Court that the Justice Department considered it their duty to answer the Court's questions objectively, as "someone who had no personal interest in the case."[76] Rankin forcefully argued that the state-enforced racial segregation of public schools was a violation of the due process clause of the Fourteenth Amendment to the Constitution.[77] Then Rankin confessed that the "problem about the questions that the Court presented that gave us the greatest trouble was the question of relief." Eventually, Rankin gave the government's recommendation for a solution: "We suggest a year for the presentation and consideration of a [desegregation] plan, not because that is an exact standard, *but with the idea that it might involve the principle of handling the matter with deliberate speed.*"[78] Accordingly, the Eisenhower Justice Department asserted that the vindication of Black constitutional rights was secondary to White privilege and power.

On May 17, 1954, the Supreme Court ruled that state-sponsored racial segregation in public education was a violation of the Constitution.[79] Roughly a year later, the Court prepared to tackle the question of relief. The Justice Department's first brief in the remedy phase of the case averred that the national interest was best served by a Supreme Court order which balanced the desires of the Black litigants with the concerns of the White leaders in the affected school districts.[80] Despite clear evidence of White resistance to the idea of racially integrated schools, the Justice Department saw no need for the Court to issue an injunction against the wrongdoers.[81]

The government asserted that school administrators needed public support and acceptance in order to integrate public schools. The heart of the matter, for the Justice Department, was the need to ensure a smooth alteration of the prevailing system:

> There is . . . a general recognition of the need for thoughtful advance preparations to resolve the problems of desegregation with as few disruptions as possible. If any lesson can be derived from past experiences in ending segregated school systems, *it is the importance of public confidence in the ability of school administrators to accomplish the adjustment without, in the process, losing sight of or sacrificing the basic and continuing educational needs of all the children affected.*[82]

This line of reasoning continued at the oral arguments. On April 13 and 14, 1955, the Supreme Court heard oral arguments from Thurgood Marshall of the NAACP, representatives of six southern states, and the solicitor general of the United States, Simon Sobeloff.[83] In short, the NAACP argued that the plaintiffs were entitled to immediate vindication of their constitutional rights, while the states discussed the onerous burdens for the various school districts that arose from the Court's May 17, 1954, order. In addition, the attorneys for the various states suggested that the masses of Whites would comply with the Court's order, and as a result, they would be more willing to support school integration if the Court did not impose a deadline for compliance.[84] Against this backdrop, the Justice Department posed as the voice of temperance.

Arguing that the plaintiffs in *Brown* were in fact the vanguard of non-White students who would be absorbed by an integrated school system, Solicitor General Sobeloff indicated that the Court could best balance the competing needs and ensure the public interest through a gradual approach.[85]

Allowing that the vindication of constitutional rights should not "depend upon a public opinion poll," Sobeloff indicated that an "effective gradual adjustment" was the best remedy in *Brown*: "*Local sentiment, local conditions, are not being overridden*; but neither is action paralyzed because of an assertion of a local feeling."[86] Shortly before recess, Sobeloff concluded that if the Court issued a decree calling for gradual integration of Southern schools, "you can have the flexibility *which the defendants rightfully ask for*, and at the same time give the plaintiffs assurances against abuse."[87] Sobeloff continued his crusade for moderation and White privilege.[88]

Central to the government's argument were three notions: (1) that the concerns of White parents, administrators, and legislators were, at least, equivalent to the constitutional rights of the Black plaintiffs; (2) that school administrators in the various states would make a good faith attempt to produce promptly their desegregation plans; and, (3) that state officials were entitled to a malleable Court order. Sobeloff argued "that the prestige of this Court is such that people will be disposed to abide by the law and not invent spurious reasons for delay."[89] Subsequently, the Court issued its order in *Brown II* which, following the government's lead, directed the lower federal courts to oversee the desegregation of public schools with all deliberate speed.[90]

Clearly, a central factor in the success of 1940s and 1950s civil rights litigation was the exigency of the Cold War. Of note is the fact that the Eisenhower administration, guided by the unspoken rules of racial conduct, was indisposed to make Whites uncomfortable on behalf of Blacks, even Black children. Indeed, the language of the Eisenhower Justice Department reflected a sense of expediency and situational ethics. Bringing to mind the central thesis in Cheryl Harris's seminal work, "Whiteness As Property," the Justice Department argued for a Supreme Court ruling that protected the interests and expectations of a White public forced to alter the prevailing consensus on Black subordination.[91] Thus, for the Eisenhower White

House, the best means to serve the ends of justice in this particular circumstance was to salvage the nation's reputation while protecting White skin privilege.

Harris remarked that "to its credit, the Court not only rejected the property right of whites in officially sanctioned inequality, but also refused to protect the old property interest in whiteness by not accepting the old argument that the rights of whites to disassociate is a valid counterweight to the rights of Blacks to be free of subordination imposed by segregation."[92] Yet, the Court, partly in response to the arguments of government attorneys, allowed Whites to determine how best to redress the harm they had caused to the Black plaintiffs. By privileging Whiteness in this manner, the government and the Court allowed for the transformation of racial subordination, the maintenance of White Supremacy, and the rehabilitation of the White image: "*Brown I*'s dialectical contradiction was that it dismantled an old form of whiteness as property while simultaneously permitting its reemergence in a more subtle form."[93] The immediate response to this privileging of Whiteness came in the form of the Parker Doctrine, "pupil placement" programs, "freedom of choice" plans, the infamous Southern Manifesto, and other means of frustrating the spirit, if not the intent, of *Brown I*.[94]

Legal scholar Sumi Cho proffers a way of understanding *Brown* that augments the arguments about the power and adaptability of White Supremacy. For Cho, racial redemption, "a psycho-social and ideological process through which [W]hiteness maintains its fullest reputational value," was at the heart of the *Brown* decision.[95] Through its 1954 ruling, the Supreme Court repudiated a long-standing form of White Supremacy without attacking Whiteness: "*Brown I*'s engagement of the most extreme forms of American apartheid demonstrates the burial function of racial redemption through the techniques of silence, euphemism and contradiction."[96] In its opinion, the Court failed to condemn the racist underpinnings of *Plessy* (Whiteness as a normative value entitled to respect and protection) and accepted the idea that White skin privilege was not the basis of segregation.[97] The euphemisms and obfuscations of the Eisenhower legal team helped the Court conceal the roots of racial subordination in its ruling in *Brown II* and repair the reputation of a "White" nation as one committed to fairness and equality. However, the silencing of Black cries for justice was insufficient. The government and the Court subtly insisted that Blacks willingly accept this subordination.

As mentioned previously, one manifestation of White Supremacy has been the demand for Black self-abnegation. In *Brown*, however, the Black plaintiffs revealed that they were unwilling to sacrifice their concerns for the survival of White Supremacy. Thurgood Marshall and other lawyers for the NAACP refused to relent and continued to press the Supreme Court for an injunction. Therefore, government attorneys and the Court were left to give primacy to White concerns, absolve the government of its participation in racial subjugation, and reject African American historical memory. By consistently following this tack, the government and the Court told the plaintiffs and their lawyers that the disappointing result in *Brown II* was the best remedy they could hope to receive.

An integral part of the plaintiffs' cases had been testimony about the perniciousness of racial hostility in their home states.[98] Although *Brown I* renounced racially segregated schools, it failed to discuss the personal and community histories that described the evolution and maintenance of segregated institutions. The Justice Department glossed over this reality in its briefs and oral arguments. Thus, it was left to Marshall and his team to raise the issue with the Court in oral argument during the remedy phase of the case.[99]

On several occasions, the NAACP legal team countered southern demands and federal assurances of the South's "good faith." For instance, Marshall addressed the statements of White lawyers from Florida with direct proof of the state's recalcitrance by, among other things, pointing to the fact that the state continued to refuse to admit a Black student to the University of Florida Law School in clear defiance of Supreme Court rulings from 1950: "that has taken them five years, and they have not gotten around to that yet. I think it is quite pertinent to consider how long it would take, without a forthright decree of this Court, to get around to the elementary and high schools."[100]

Marshall continued by directly refuting the claims of the lawyers from Arkansas, Oklahoma, South Carolina, and Texas. Perhaps because he was a native of Maryland, Marshall made a special plea regarding "good faith" in the Upper South:

> And it is significant that the Attorney General of Maryland, in asking for time—for unlimited time—based it on the fact that they were making such "terrific progress on race relations," to the point that this year—last year, 1954—they abolished the scholarship provision to send Negroes out of the State—which was declared unconstitutional by this Court in 1938, and by the Courts of Appeals of Maryland in 1936—so that it took them 16 years to catch up with the law of their own Court of Appeals, and the law of this Court; and [they] use that as the basis for saying that, because of their good faith, we should [let them] work the problem out.[101]

Through the use of pronouns such as "we" and "our," Marshall rejected the notion that African Americans were separate and distinct from the American body politic and that desegregation was a "private" interest relevant only to Blacks. Marshall further rejected the construction of the remedy question as a balancing between equally legitimate "rights."[102] Also compelling for Marshall was the notion that the government and defendants were arguing for a novel approach to constitutional jurisprudence—piecemeal enforcement of a constitutional right:

> And Texas went so far as to bring in maps to show that [desegregation] would operate from one area to the other in a different fashion. I am sure that the State of Texas does not even administer their own constitution in varying areas of various sections of the country, but they want the Federal Constitution [to be administered that way].[103]

Because the federal government moved the legislative and administrative concerns to center stage, Marshall and the NAACP were trapped in a running battle with multiple fronts.

Trina Grillo and Stephanie Wildman, among others, have argued that comparisons between different forms of oppression often can be dangerous because "the significance of race [is] marginalized and obscured and the different role that race plays in the lives of people of color and [W]hites [is] overlooked."[104] In *Brown*, the comparison between the plaintiffs' constitutional rights and the defendants' administrative burdens obscured the significance of race throughout the proceedings. The government attorneys' insistence on antitrust or nuisance litigation as the appropriate analogy for the Court to use in understanding the "gradual relief" argument was their attempt at "taking back the center" from the Black plaintiffs.[105] The phenomenon of "taking back the center" was significant as well for its relation to the necessary construction of "innocent" Whiteness.

The notion of White innocence resonates from both the attorneys' arguments and the rulings of the Court. Like Sobeloff's statement in oral argument, the following claim from one of its 1955 amicus briefs exemplified the government's claim of White innocence: "We do not believe that there is warrant for presuming that responsible officials and citizens will tolerate violations of the Constitution."[106] In oral argument, defense attorney John W. Davis "lectured the Court on the non-racist nature of segregation" and likened the ruling in *Brown I* to a "return to an experiment" from "the tragic era" of Reconstruction.[107] Legal scholar Thomas Ross indicates that the Court greeted these assertions of the absence of racism with a "howling silence."[108] Ross also notes that "had the Court in *Brown I* spoken of the racism that motivated the segregation laws, the delay in *Brown II* would have been more difficult to justify."[109] The defendants pressed harder in the relief phase of the case.

Lawyers for the affected states not only repeated their claims of innocence but also revealed significant militancy with regard to compliance. One of the objections to desegregation listed by Virginia lawyers was the supposedly "low health standards" of Blacks, which Marshall suggested did not bother Whites when the mothers of these alleged unclean children were cooking their meals and washing their clothes.[110] More specifically, Emory Rogers from Clarendon County, South Carolina, addressed the Court with such a pugnacious attitude that some observers believed that Chief Justice Warren might have charged him with contempt.[111] Rogers requested that the Court issue an "open decree," meaning that the ruling would not specify when and how desegregation would occur. During an aggressive exchange between Rogers and Warren, the attorney stated what many other lawyers probably were thinking: that the segregationists would not make an "honest" attempt to abide by a Court order mandating desegregation "because I would have to tell you that right now we would not conform—we would not send our white children to the Negro schools."[112] As Richard Kluger noted, "to Earl Warren, this was close to heresy."[113] Yet, these rebels benefitted from their combativeness.[114]

Sumi Cho remarks that "the Chief Justice, writing for the Court in *Brown II*, described the [pro-segregation] presentations as 'informative and helpful' in considering the 'complexities' of transitioning to a public education system free of racial discrimination."[115] In this manner, the Chief Justice masked the South's palpable anger toward the Court's rendering in *Brown I*. Absolving Whites of any responsibility for racial subjugation on either the federal or state level was necessary to maintain the myth of "fairness" in the decree, as well as the myth of the color-blind "traditions" of American society. It also hid the structural inequalities inherent with White Supremacy, like the estimated $2 billion necessary to equalize southern Black schools with their White counterparts.[116] Therefore, the Court's behavior forced Blacks to accept the shortcomings of *Brown II*.

While the nation reaped the benefits of restored international esteem, the burden of enforcement shifted to Black shoulders already sagging under the weight of disappointment. Following the announcement of *Brown II*, Marshall called Carl Murphy, president of the *Baltimore Afro American*, to discuss the ruling. Though both men were excited about the constitutional basis for the Court's decision, they conceded the limited nature of the remedy, and Marshall acknowledged that the NAACP's challenge would be to seek implementation on a state-by-state basis. Thus, instead of the Court directing the defendants to behave in a manner indicative of their guilt, the Justices left it to the plaintiffs to compel White conformity to the new reading of the Constitution.[117]

The Justice Department's characterizations of the significant issues in *Brown* fit neatly into the paradigm of Black insatiability; not only were the plaintiffs' demands for immediate enrollment in White schools "extreme," the "orderly transition" to desegregated schools was a cognizable legal "principle" to which the defendant states were entitled.[118] Adding to this refrain were the assertions by attorneys for the southern states, refuted by Marshall, that desegregation of schools was best left to local officials because desegregation in general was proceeding in a satisfactory manner. Taking these dubious claims at face value, the Court reasoned that Black demands for an immediate vindication of "present and personal" constitutional rights was simply asking for too much, too soon. The Court echoed Sobeloff's praise of segregationists in its opinion in *Brown II* and reinterpreted the open defiance of southern states as receptiveness: "The [pro-segregationist] presentations [at oral argument] demonstrated that substantial steps to eliminate racial discrimination in public schools have already taken place."[119]

Through its efforts, the Eisenhower administration helped manufacture the fraudulent commitment to racial justice embodied in *Brown I* and *Brown II*. By aiding the impression that Black plaintiffs had received their reward, government attorneys chided Blacks for demanding a solution that was not "intelligent," "orderly," or "effective." From this perspective, Blacks were asking too much and the government had to safeguard the interests of several states and their school systems. In this regard, the gradualist approach created "due process" for Whites who might have been deprived of their property, the race-based interests and expectations that they should control the structural aspects of public education.[120] Accordingly, the implicit characterization of Blacks as voracious, self-interested political grandstanders helped justify the Court's weak remedy and foreshadowed the administration's approach to the African struggle for independence. As would happen in Africa, the Eisenhower administration's politics of Black insatiability rationalized limited, qualified support for Black self-determination and maintenance of White privilege.

## The Eisenhower Administration's Views of "Colored People"

Historians and other researchers have noted the negative racial attitudes of the Eisenhower administration toward people of color. For instance, Thomas Noer wrote that, as president, Eisenhower "reportedly objected to inviting 'those niggers' to diplomatic receptions and regularly, if unwittingly, insulted African leaders by appearing uninterested in their problems and uninformed about their nations."[121] Another set of scholars have noted that the administration officials who orchestrated the overthrow of the democratically elected government in Guatemala characterized its deposed president as "a weak individual who was simply his wife's puppet."[122] In writing about American foreign policy toward China, Gordon Chang asserted that the members of the Eisenhower administration "had grown to maturity during years when Asians tended to be identified as both inferior and insidious."[123] Although some would dispute the aforementioned statements, these assessments fit with the historical racial bent of American diplomacy.[124]

A necessary point of departure is the recounting of the personal feelings and statements of members of the Eisenhower administration. Their individual assessments of non-Whites provide one perspective from which to assay the saturation of racial animus into the diplomacy crafted by decision-makers and their advisors. For example, American efforts to restrain China are understood more fully when one acknowledges that:

> the President believed that the Chinese valued life less than Westerners. In his memoirs he openly invokes the specter of the Yellow Peril: he and Dulles had kept a sharp eye on the Chinese because they were a "smart people . . . tremendous in number, and their leaders seem absolutely indifferent to the prospect of losing millions of people." In contrast, "among Western statesmen, human life is weighed carefully—to understate our attitude." To Eisenhower the difference between the West and the East was obvious and intrinsic.[125]

Apparently, the value of life cheapened in many instances. The president's statement obscures the reality that he "actively embraced covert actions in regions . . . where the risk of triggering a general war was negligible and few political constraints applied." It should be noted that these places were neither vital to American interests nor venues where the United States directly engaged the Soviet Union.[126] In other words, Washington risked being adventurous in nearly all Third World countries and colonies, areas heavily populated by non-White people. Moreover, Eisenhower distinguished between the Soviets and the Chinese by claiming that "no matter what differences in culture and tradition, values and language, the Russian leaders were human beings, and they wanted to remain alive."[127]

For his part, John Foster Dulles echoed the president's suspicious sentiments. A low-level State Department official conceded that Dulles was condescending to Asian officials. He reasoned that Dulles talked down to his Asian peers because Dulles's mind was too quick for "the average Oriental, who is accustomed to being more circuitous about his explanations and his reasoning."[128] Furthermore, Dulles was convinced that "the Oriental mind . . . was always more devious" than its Occidental counterpart. According to Paul Linebarger, the administration's expert on Asian political behavior, "the Chinese were fixated with honor and face and were too irrational to take seriously the threat of nuclear weapons." Since the Chinese were supposedly hysterical, irrational, and fanatical, they were a more dangerous foe than the Soviets, who "at least were a comprehensible, European adversary."[129]

Although it may seem obvious, it is worth noting that the views of the Eisenhower administration were shaped largely by White, elite males. The inner circle of government officials was exclusively White, so much so that the attendance at a Cabinet meeting by an African American was a noteworthy event.[130] Of course, the list of invitees to the president's numerous stag parties consisted of wealthy and powerful men.[131] These were men with a great deal more status than most White people and certainly with more to lose than psychic resources if White hegemony collapsed.

With regard to people of African descent in the United States, there were few direct statements or observations. Generally, Blacks were the subject of conversations in situations in which major problems were discussed.[132] As such, Blacks were associated with controversy and anxiety. Importantly, their concerns were regarded as secondary to the significant issues facing the nation.[133] Rarely are Blacks or "Black issues" raised in a positive context. Even on these occasions, Blacks form more of the backdrop than the centerpiece of political discussions.

In a conversation with one of his assistants, the president entered into a discussion about blood banks in the United States. When the conversation turned to the acceptability of blood from African Americans, Eisenhower remarked "there is no different (sic) in the blood [of Whites and Blacks]—except that Negroes have a tendency to faint at high altitude."[134] The experiences of the African American pilots known collectively as the Tuskegee Airmen clearly refuted this shibboleth.[135]

Eisenhower slights Blacks not only through the use of stereotypes but by omission as well. In a long letter to a friend, the President discussed, among many other things, the problem of the *Brown* decision. In describing his disappointment in the initial Supreme Court decision, as well as his own *gradualist* strategy for desegregation, Eisenhower says that "my approach to the many problems has been dictated by several obvious truths." The President then lists the four truths, which pleaded for a slow evolution of race relations:

> (a) Laws are rarely effective unless they represent the will of the majority . . . (b) When emotions are deeply stirred, logic and reason must operate gradually and with consideration for human feelings or we will have a resultant disaster rather than human advancement . . . (c) School segregation itself was . . . completely constitutional until the reversal of the decision was accomplished in 1954 . . . As a result, the social, economic and political patterns of the South were considered by most [W]hites, especially by those in that region, as not only respectable but completely legal and ethical. (d) After three score years of living under these patterns, it was impossible to expect complete and instant reversal of conduct by mere decision of the Supreme Court.[136]

The human feelings to which Eisenhower refers are those of White southerners. The president ignored the human feelings or beliefs of Blacks.

Eisenhower also made noteworthy mention of Blacks in discussions regarding the burgeoning civil rights movement. During conversations or correspondence with Oveta Culp Hobby, Rev. Billy Graham, and Arthur Sulzberger, Eisenhower enunciated his fears regarding desegregation. He often stated that the pace of desegregation desired by American Blacks was too swift and that neither Whites nor Blacks were prepared for the consequences of such rapid change.[137] The president was repeating a long-standing canard in White Supremacist thought. If Blacks were unprepared—this line of reasoning held—it was because they were not sufficiently capable (intelligent, resourceful, hardworking, pious) to compete with Whites on an equal footing.[138]

Although Eisenhower was careful not to criticize publicly the Supreme Court's decision in *Brown v. Board of Education*, he was consistent in his private criticism of the legal challenge to segregation.[139] A week after sending federal troops into Little Rock, the president told one of his speech writers that the Supreme Court decision in *Brown* was wrong. This staffer, being an attorney, asserted that Black children were harmed by segregation and that the separate-but-equal standard was overruled because separate educational facilities were inherently unequal. Eisenhower responded: "I am thoroughly familiar with that argument, but I do not find it compelling."[140] Even this apologist was shocked when the president told him that "social equality of political and economic opportunity did not mean necessarily that everyone has to mingle socially—'or that a Negro should court my daughter.'"[141]

Although there are few direct references to Black women, Eisenhower probably tolerated them less than Black men. His treatment of the first lady of the Black press is instructive. Ethel Payne, a reporter for the *Chicago Defender*, annoyed

Eisenhower at a 1954 press conference. Payne asked the president "when he planned to ban segregation in interstate travel. Eisenhower barked back that he refused to support any special interest . . . After the incident, Eisenhower refused to recognize Payne during press conferences."[142] Beyond this specific incident, the president's construction of the undesirable consequences of racial integration is enlightening.

Eisenhower's articulated fears about Black males preying on his daughter or granddaughter repeated a centuries-old refrain of American bigots.[143] It is worth noting that the justification for White societal control of the imagined Black sexual predator also contained a severe condemnation of Black women. Many Whites asserted that the Black male craving for White women was caused by the immorality and inferiority of Black women. As a result, the contention that Black women were not real women meant that they deserved no protection from male violence and social terror.[144] This ideology manifested itself in the administration's failure to protect Autherine Lucy from White mobs at the University of Alabama in 1956.[145] In contrast to the generally coded discourse on American race relations, statements by Eisenhower and his advisers about Africans were explicit.

Eisenhower and his aids considered Africa a terribly primordial place and its indigenous population equally retrograde.[146] Accordingly, Eisenhower, John Foster Dulles, and others puzzled over the fact that Africans wanted independence. During a discussion regarding the Horn of Africa, Eisenhower wondered aloud why the Somalis "were so interested in running their own country when they were so primitive."[147] Not surprisingly, influential friends of the administration held similar views toward Central Americans.[148]

Vice President Richard Nixon, whom Gordon Gray, special assistant for National Security Affairs, referred to as the father of the administration's foreign policy toward Africa, admitted an obsession about Africa, though he hardly considered Africans fit to run their own affairs.[149] During a March 1960 National Security Council meeting, the president and vice president joined a discussion about NSC papers 5818 and 5920.[150] Gray prepared a briefing which articulated three objectives: (1) the maintenance of Free-World orientation and suppression of Communist influence in emerging nations and colonies; (2) orderly economic development and political progress toward self-determination for countries which cooperated with European metropoles and other free world nation-states; and (3) access to military and facility rights and strategic resources as may be required by U.S. national security interests. As the attendees discussed how to prioritize the objectives, Allen Dulles interjected that none of the emerging nations "had the capability of governing themselves." Eisenhower agreed, if Dulles excluded South Africa.[151]

This alleged backwardness exacerbated the problem of maintaining the emerging African states in a pro-Western posture. Though the president had fond recollections of Ethiopia's Aklilou Abde Wold and Togo's Sylvanus Olympio, his memoirs are peppered with disparaging remarks about African leaders.[152] For

Nixon, the thing that made Africa potentially the most explosive flashpoint in the Cold War was the fact that within the newly developed countries there existed no one who knew "how to administer their affairs effectively."[153] Clarence Randall, chairman of the Council of Economic Foreign Policy and perhaps the administration's most sympathetic expert on the continent, added that a significant impediment to economic development on the continent was that land was owned communally.[154]

Because of supposed African primitivism, the United States could not afford to allow Africans to manage finances or weapons. Given the administration's racial perspective, it was illogical to provide either resource to people who could not use them properly. As with Arabs and Native Americans, it was dangerous to leave these children to their own volition.[155] American planners worried about fostering an arms race in Africa.[156] Although the concern was occasionally couched in East-West terminology, the real worry was arming non-White men who could potentially fight White men. Indeed, Whites established and policed the international color line with violence; thus primitive resistance to Western guidance might mean that American weapons might one day be aimed at Americans and their allies.[157]

Simultaneously, Washington was averse to providing developmental aid beyond limited agricultural or educational funds. One of the constraints in this area was the desire to avoid any behavior that might alienate America's European allies.[158] A second concern was the breadth and the scope of African underdevelopment. Some officials believed that Africans had an insatiable appetite for modernization. The apprehension was that an Africa dissatisfied with the American-led pace of development might spurn the West in favor of the Soviet bloc. Thus, Maurice Stans, director of the Budget Bureau, remarked that it was tempting to consider first allowing the Soviets the dubious distinction of trying, and failing, to quench the continent's thirst for economic advancement.[159]

Less obvious is the variegated impact of U.S. diplomacy on African women. The American discourse on the need to modernize Africa contained a master narrative which feminized African men and buttressed the subordinate position of African women.[160] Politically responsible African leaders were exclusively men who respected and cooperated with the former colonial powers. Thus, the exclusion of African women from civic power was natural; if the men were too emotional, impressionable, and primitive to govern African nations, surely the women were less suited for leadership.[161] Washington's discourse on aid to Africa contained a hierarchy that placed America in a dominant, masculine position with respect to the dependent, infantile emerging nations.[162] Equally important was the American objective of maintaining African economic subordination to the West. Such a policy further eroded the economic position of African women by making them vulnerable to a male-centered state, male-dominated private enterprise, and male-orchestrated global capital.[163]

The parallels between the administration's views on continental and diasporan Blacks are not accidental. The consensus on White supremacy and corresponding Black inferiority was developed over centuries in a Western environment obsessed with race. According to this consensus, Blacks in America were unprepared for desegregation just as Blacks in Africa were unprepared for decolonization. The only way Blacks could prove that they were ready for independence was to make manifest a sincere loyalty and obedience toward America and the West. Because many would-be African nations either distanced themselves from the West or hoped to evade the East-West polarization, the Eisenhower administration considered their independence to be premature. Like American slaveholders a century earlier, the Eisenhower administration ridiculed but secretly feared Africans and justified their continued subservience as a means of development. At its base, the Eisenhower administration's policies toward Africa created the perfect construct of Black political illness, a diagnosis of African self-determination based on Black inferiority and Communist intrigue which warranted a cure of Western intervention.

An international racial sanctuary gained strength during this period. Given the symmetry between White views and treatment of Africans and African Americans, it is imperative to locate the development of this sanctuary within the United States. Changes in the treatment of people of African descent in the United States occurred without fundamental changes in the consensus on White Supremacy. Yet, White Americans used these changes to project across the globe an image of egalitarianism that redeemed Whiteness. Therefore, when American elite support for decolonization surfaced in the 1950s, it converged with the African interest in self-determination to create the appearance of an approaching era of global justice.[164]

The Cold War served as the international racial sanctuary. Washington articulated a worldview that cast global Communism as an evil force bent on enslaving the world. In contrast, official American doctrine cast the United States—and, by extension, the great or formerly great imperial powers—as the font of liberty, opportunity, and individual freedom. Furthermore, American officials openly supported decolonization abroad and pitched a new dawn of American race relations at home. This discourse erased the history and legacy of Europe as the scourge of the globe. Gone was the visage of the far-flung Western economic engine gorging itself on the fuel of the Atlantic slave trade. Gone was the image of dismembered Congolese hands, cut off by the Belgians for failure to meet rubber quotas. Gone were the stories of the mass slaughters, like the one perpetrated by the Germans against the Maji Maji a generation before the Jewish Holocaust. In the place of these skeletons stood the new, tidy, innocent countenance of the Free World.[165]

The notion of an unblemished West implied a happily subordinate Africa. In this Cold War construction of the world, Africans were a backward people gradually being led into modernization by the benevolent hand of the West. By this logic, Africans' primitive nature dictated a slow pace of development. As with the redeemed reputation of the White world, the racial sanctuary told a tale of Black Africa—a place where poverty was as natural as European wealth, a place of cultural depravity and deviance, a place where most people were content with Western guidance. Based on this construction, the only plausible explanations for

African radicalism were Black incompetence, insatiability, and blind hatred of Whites, fed by Communist propaganda. This redemption of Whiteness, like the 1957 billboard accusing Martin Luther King Jr. of receiving Communist training at the Highlander Center, among other things, refutes the notion that anti-Communism and race were wholly separate matters. A review and analysis of domestic race relations during the early Cold War reveals that, in many ways, they were indivisible, thus foreshadowing developments on the African continent.

# CHAPTER TWO

# AS THE SNAKE SHEDS ITS SKIN: EISENHOWER DIPLOMACY, AFRICAN DECOLONIZATION, AND NATIONALISM

Decolonization is best described as the process of an indigenous people losing the formal trappings of colonial domination in a transfer of the nominal instruments of sovereignal authority.[1] The process can be negotiated by peaceful means or by military means. On the African continent, the indigenous peoples relied on both forms to free themselves from the yoke of their imperial overseers.[2] For many Africans, decolonization meant an end to tyranny. However, to members of the American diplomatic and intelligence corps, decolonization was a means to a different end.

During the fall of 1955, John Cowles, the publisher of the *Minneapolis Star & Tribune*, entertained historian Arnold Toynbee as his personal guest. Cowles recounted this visit in a letter to the president. At dinner, Cowles asked Toynbee for his impressions of American foreign policy. Toynbee indicated that "the paramount problem is to prevent the presently uncommitted peoples from gravitating into the Communist orbit." Earlier, Toynbee had said that colonialism was a critical issue and that the United States needed to express "clear sympathy for independence." To Toynbee, decolonization was necessary to prevent the Communist orientation of the people throughout the Third World. Toynbee also favored Third World neutrality because, to him, the objective of policy should not be to coerce nations "to line up with the West," but to prevent their gravitation toward the Communist bloc.[3] Eisenhower was so excited by Cowles's letter that he invited Cowles to the White House to view two documents that reflected a similar viewpoint and planned to circulate the publisher's letter among his subordinates.[4]

Since the United States government had committed to a similar approach before the Cowles-Toynbee dinner conversation, it would be inaccurate to suggest that Toynbee's views influenced American strategy. What is fascinating about the exchange is the consanguinity of White elite ideas. As articulated by these and other elites, the objective of American foreign policy with regard to the majority of the world's population was to prevent them from aligning with the Communists.[5] Equally important, the conversation reveals the entitlement of Whites to dictate the political evolution of non-Whites.

Although many so-called Third World countries envisioned a political existence outside of the East-West dialectic, Eisenhower officials found this difficult to fathom and were determined to prevent such a progression.[6] U.S. support for decolonization meant support for Western stability by muting radical nationalism or other progressive political developments. The chief justification of American support for decolonization was not an idealistic impulse but the desire to maintain the exploitive relationship between the White and non-White worlds.

## The Policy Impetus for Decolonization

### European Reconstruction and NSC 68

With its roots in the wartime policies of the Roosevelt administration, Cold War diplomacy toward emerging states emphasized the need for imperial powers to support the political aspirations of their colonial subjects.[7] Although this approach angered America's allies,[8] it was based upon a desire to foster American and, by extension, Western political and economic dominance rather than any yearning to free millions of people of color from the yoke of White Supremacy.[9] Accordingly, the numerous compromises U.S. officials made with their European comrades, along with the expansion of American business interests, caused concern among supporters of African independence.[10]

As the Truman administration backed away from the wartime alliance with the Soviet Union, American officials were focusing on rebuilding the European continent. As a means of maintaining international dominance vis-à-vis Communism, the United States needed a potent Western Europe as an ally. In a March 1947 speech, the president requested $400 million for aid to Greece and Turkey and outlined the Truman Doctrine: the policy of the United States thereafter would be to support free peoples resisting domination by armed minorities or outside influences.[11] Within short order, a massive American financial assistance program to Europe, the Marshall Plan, was devised as a means of offsetting potential economic and political instability in Europe.[12]

One of the major economic problems in England and France was the dollar gap; Western European countries had too few dollars with which to purchase goods and materials from the United States. Although European leaders acknowledged the seriousness of the problem, they asserted that the people in European colonies seemed to be in the best position to close the dollar gap; "Britain, France, and the Netherlands . . . devised ambitious schemes to augment the production and export of raw materials and foodstuffs in those parts of the Third World over which they still exercised considerable influence."[13] The European states "squeezed and exploited their colonies in Africa (and also in Southeast Asia) in ways never seen before by means of a complex network of administrative controls."[14] Consequently, hopes for decolonization dimmed because European economic recovery rested upon increased exploitation of the labor and raw materials of Europe's colonies in Africa and other places.[15]

Its economic support for Europe notwithstanding, America's anticolonial rhetoric disturbed many on the other side of the Atlantic. The United States regularly recommended that its imperial allies make gradual reforms toward self-government as a means of muting the clamor for independence. As one American official stated, the United States was "essentially in the same boat as [the] French, also as [the] British and Dutch. We cannot conceive of setbacks to long-range interests [of] France which would not also be setbacks [to] our own."[16] For example, with regard to the situation in Vietnam, Americans and Europeans feared that the leadership of Ho Chi Minh would lead to internal strife and, perhaps, Communist domination of the area. Thus, American advisers offered the same advice to the French as they had to the Dutch with respect to Indonesia: "They argued that it was wise to make concessions in order to co-opt nationalist ferment, avoid military strife, raise production levels, and restore exports. Indochina and Indonesia might then be kept within the Western camp, to make their contribution to Western Europe's economic recovery."[17]

Despite economic advances in 1947-1948, European economies remained vulnerable. As the United States endured a recession and Great Britain puzzled over the collapse of its sterling reserve, CIA officers warned of the adverse effects on the rest of the European continent. The fear among many was that these financial problems might "restore the subversive capabilities of local Communist parties in Western Europe, impair Western rearmament programs, accentuate the divergent economic interests of the Western powers, and weaken their hand in dealing with the USSR."[18] The State Department turned its attention to the issue by creating a policy guide that would address European and global issues in more than strictly economic terms. National Security Council Memorandum 68 served as that guide.

NSC 68 was created by the State Department's policy planning staff. As director of policy planning, Paul Nitze's could use his office as a platform from which he could lobby for an intensified struggle against the suddenly more threatening specter of global Communism. The Soviet Union's detonation of a nuclear device in the summer of 1949 ended America's atomic monopoly.[19] The Communist triumph in China further dismayed Western observers.[20] These events increased Africa's significance for America and Western Europe.[21] Using the Soviet Union's atomic capability as a springboard, Nitze echoed Roosevelt-era strategists when he asserted that America's national interests were threatened because "any substantial extension of the area under the domination of the Kremlin would raise the possibility that no coalition adequate to confront the Kremlin with greater strength could be assembled."[22]

NSC 68 begins with a summary of world events from the preceding thirty-five years: two global wars, two popular revolutions, the collapse of five empires, and the precipitous decline of two others. As a result, global power had moved toward poles occupied by the United States and the Soviet Union. Because the Communists, "animated by a new fanatical faith," sought "to impose [their] absolute authority over the rest of the world, . . . this Republic and its citizens in the ascendancy of their strength stand in their deepest peril." NSC 68 further asserted that the principal purpose of the United States derived from the ideals set forth in the Constitution, while the purpose of the Soviet Union was absolute global domination.[23]

As conceived in NSC 68, one of America's principal goals was the development of a healthy international community, which meant a fully rehabilitated Western Europe. Because European reconstruction rested upon the maintenance of control over colonial subjects, NSC 68 implied that non-White nationalist sentiments had to be constrained. Without actually mentioning European colonies, NSC 68 clearly envisioned the need to modernize emerging nations and colonial peoples in order to maintain their subservience to the West.[24] The implications of NSC 68 were consistent with the Truman administration's designs on Africa. The Truman White House wanted African peoples to be allies of the United States. Yet, Africa's place in America's global strategy remained subordinate to Europe:[25] "A 1951 State Department directive, for example, emphasized that because 'Africa provides a sizable portion of the critical commodities now required by the Free World,' it was imperative to insure that Africa will remain . . . firmly fixed in the political orbit of the Free World."[26] This was based on a belief that if "'indigenous disturbances' created conditions favorable to Communism the political and economic interests of the United States would be best served by decolonization."[27] America's imperial anticolonialism was also informed by its historical experiences with non-White people in the Americas, especially in the West Indies.[28]

## Decolonization for Global Domination

The Eisenhower administration took a different approach to the issue of decolonization than the Truman administration did. Instead of openly acquiescing to imperial interests, Eisenhower hoped to forge a consensus with European powers to proceed cooperatively toward an abolition of colonialism. Yet, the Cold War meant that imperial interests became American interests.[29] One of the chief planning papers of the Eisenhower administration was National Security Council Memorandum 162/2. Although NSC 162/2 emphasized the use of nuclear weapons in a conflict against China or the Soviet Union, the drafters also acknowledged the problem of supporting European imperialism. NSC 162/2 conceived of a Third World liberated from the formal chains of colonialism. However, this conception was based principally upon the need to maintain Third World resources within the Free World structure in order to ensure success against international Communism.[30]

Although Eisenhower bureaucrats recognized the need for continued exploitation of the Third World by European imperialists, they noted that maintenance of a formal colonial relationship might erode the necessary political and economic bonds between First World and Third World. "By reason of their colonial experience," advised the State Department's policy planning staff, "these countries are apt to distrust Western motives almost as much as they distrust those of the Communists. They are ultrasensitive to policies or attitudes which seem to them to partake of colonialism or reflect on their sovereignty."[31] In order to maintain American global hegemony, Washington planners had to contend with issues of concern to Africans, nationalism, and non-alignment.

## American Conceptions of Neutrality

American policymakers disagreed about the value of neutrality. John Foster Dulles considered neutrality a short step from Communism.[32] Dulles's view exhibited a zero-sum game mentality described by a former U.S. ambassador: "I think Mr. Dulles' view might best be summed up in that he felt that anything which you allowed to fall into the Communist hopper was gone, and it was irretrievable . . . Any loss to the Communists, therefore, was two-fold. It was a loss of our own strength and addition to the strength of the Communists."[33] His perspective also reflected the prevailing mythology of Soviet omnipresence.

Like the preceding administration, the Eisenhower administration "attributed to the Russians a transcendent ability to shape events where in the most remote countries, and even where they did not initiate them they almost invariably knew how to exploit them, so that where Communists were not important, other groups could serve Soviet interests whether or not they intended to do so."[34] Not surprisingly, Dulles's opinion was consistent with NSC 68. The drafters of that document warned of the risks of nonalignment; a second priority was "that our allies or potential allies do not as a result of a sense of frustration or of Soviet intimidation drift into a course of neutrality eventually leading to Soviet domination."[35]

In the context of India, Eisenhower's perspective differed. Describing neutrality as a military rather than a moral issue, Eisenhower stated that he preferred certain countries to be neutral. In this case, India's neutrality alleviated any sense of obligation the United States might have had to aid that nation if it fell under political or military duress.[36]

Vice President Nixon, considered the father of the administration's Africa policy, also differed slightly with Foster Dulles's Manichaean view of the Cold War world.[37] Nixon, who had traveled throughout the continent during his vice presidency and directly participated in the preparation of policy papers and studies regarding the continent, thought the United States should encourage neutrality.[38] Yet, those who were tolerant of African neutrality maintained a narrow definition.

In discussing the necessary flexibility of American policy toward Africa, Under Secretary of State for Economic Affairs Douglass Dillon said that neutralism was tolerable as long as the country was "genuinely neutral—that is, friendly to the West and to free enterprise. But if they went as far as Guinea, neutralism could be undesirable."[39] Although "neutralism was better than Communism," America had to keep a close eye on neutral nations.[40]

## The White House and Black Nationalism

Rhetoric aside, President Eisenhower and his advisers generally frowned upon non-White nationalism. The president told journalists that he suspected Communist infiltration was widespread throughout the world, and his advisers feared that most leaders who claimed to be nationalists were disguised Communists or Communist sympathizers.[41]

The president viewed African nationalism with a particularly skeptical eye. In his memoirs, he remarked that "in flood force, the spirit of nationalism had grown in all Africa. The determination of the peoples for self-rule, their own flag, and their own vote in the United Nations resembled a torrent overrunning everything in its path, including, frequently, the best interests of those concerned."[42] This view was echoed by his staff during strategy sessions and the drafting of policy papers.

In 1955, the Planning Coordinating Group (PCG) produced a document titled "Psychological Aspects of United States Strategy." Colonel George Lincoln of the United States Military Academy penned the working paper on the Middle East and Africa. In reference to colonialism, Col. Lincoln wrote that "there is an old rule that it is better to go gracefully than to be kicked out. In retrospect, a great part of our problems in the world come from having our allies kicked out of their colonial areas, and this without having made preparation for a stable friendly government to follow." Recognizing the colonial issue as the United States' major problem with respect to Africa, Lincoln suggested that American officials faced contradictory concerns: "(1) our traditional anticolonialism; and (2) our strategic interest in our allies, bases, raw materials, etc. It is suggested that a doctrinaire adherence to either line is likely to be disastrous. A middle course is a better course."

Although convinced that the United States faced a difficult challenge in the coming decade, Lincoln remained cautiously optimistic. From his perspective, the challenge to U.S. diplomacy was to provide guidance to the independence movements in order to foster a gradual pattern of progress. If such careful management of the situation failed, "then a nationalism of a type we now little foresee or understand (witness the Mau Mau movement) may overflow the land.

This nationalism would be characterized by unpredictabilities, emotional as to policy, which would make the irrationality of some Arab politics seem like cold logic."[43]

NSC 5719/1 set out a U.S. policy for sub-Saharan Africa that remained relatively constant throughout the balance of Eisenhower's second term in office. Noting what it considered the essential ties between Europe and Africa, NSC 5719/1 recited America's interest in strengthening those ties: "that Africa South of the Sahara develop in an orderly manner towards self-government and independence in cooperation with the European powers now in control of large areas of the continent."[44]

Though largely concerned with maintaining a firm grip on the resources of Africa, the Eisenhower administration never lost sight of the strategic significance of the continent. Administration staffers soon replaced the generic statement of Africa's "limited military and strategic value" in the central planning document.[45] In the summer of 1958, the NSC Planning Board revised several paragraphs in NSC 5719/1. Paragraph 6 on the continent's strategic value was beefed up to reflect the importance of its "alternative air and sea routes to the Far East and . . . its strategic materials."[46] Because of conflict in the Middle East and a concern about intensified Communist activity in Africa, planners also enhanced the sections on military and strategic value and policy guidance.[47]

The drafters of NSC 5719/1 resigned themselves to the maintenance of America's middle-of-the-road position on decolonization. Flexible American policies for the continent were "designed to encourage an orderly development of the whole area based on a mutually advantageous accommodation between nationalism and the metropolitan powers." Despite the admitted limitations of such an approach, "it [was] the only logical and correct course of action to follow."[48] Such a rationalization was easy given American assessments of Africans.

In the eyes of American analysts, African self-determination was the manifestation of overwrought emotionalism. The rhetoric of the planning document reflected Col. Lincoln's view: "Premature independence would be as harmful to our interests in Africa as would be a continuation of nineteenth century colonialism, and we must tailor our policies to the capabilities and needs of each particular area as well as to our overall relations with the metropolitan powers concerned."[49]

Therefore, NSC 5719/1 suggested that the United States "support the principle of self-determination . . . consistently and in such a way as to assure that evolution toward this objective will be orderly; making clear, however, that self-government and independence impose important responsibilities which the peoples concerned must be ready and able to discharge." Although acknowledging that Africans naturally would act in their perceived best interests, the White elite consensus held that Blacks were too infantile for freedom: "To a considerable extent, the African is still immature and unsophisticated with respect to his attitudes towards the issues that divide the world today. The African's mind is not made up and he is being subjected to a number of contradictory forces. This pressure will increase in the future."[50]

Washington officials believed that the continent, given its incredible wealth of human and natural resources, was too important to lose to the Soviets. In a separate discussion of the economic potential of colonized areas, the discourse focused on the capacity of the metropoles to continue to exploit these resources.[51] One of the major worries was that Africans did not comprehend the seriousness of Soviet subversive abilities and objectives. This was one of the reasons the United States needed the African strongman on its side—to guarantee a pro-Western orientation of the emerging African states.[52] Although America needed to confront Soviet intrigues, it had "to combat Communist subversive activities to the extent that this can be done without assisting in [the] repression of responsible non-Communist nationalist movements."[53]

The assertions regarding Soviet designs on Africa were based upon both the American perception of a small but growing Communist presence in African labor unions and the non-White political groups of South Africa, as well as the allegedly inherent weaknesses of Africans themselves: "African students in Europe, furthermore, are assiduously cultivated by local Communists and many have been subverted. Soviet pretensions to being anti-colonial and non-European tend to be effective in Liberia and Ghana, and these governments are flattered by Soviet attempts to cultivate them."[54]

In addition to the concern that Communists were making inroads by ingratiating themselves with African leaders, the need to offset the Communist threat was based upon the assumption that Africans lived in desperate need of supervision. With regard to modern Africans who they considered "extremely primitive in many of their social outlooks," Eisenhower officials were convinced that "until some new loyalty is provided, the detribalized African will be an easy target for elements eager to exploit his traditional need for leadership and guidance."[55] Ultimately, because of the Africans' supposed childlike nature, American policymakers had to foment and then cement a pro-Western deference among African people.[56]

American officials engaged in a policy of encouraging decolonization, in part, as a means to liberate the Free World from the burden of its imperialistic legacy. At one 1958 NSC meeting, the president stated that he favored a quicker pace of change on the African continent than the metropoles were providing because "he would like to be on the side of the natives for once."[57] Nowhere do U.S. policymakers speak of African decolonization in terms of equality or independence, only in terms of responsibility and preparedness. The official discourse in support of decolonization was an attempt at distancing the United States from recalcitrant European powers, while maintaining a careful watch over the allegedly infantile Africans to ensure that the Africans respected the needs of the Europeans. In fact, some discussions focused on the need for multilateral economic or military action in order to avoid the appearance of siding with colonial powers.[58]

Although there are few direct references to Pan-Africanism, the Eisenhower administration's perspective on that philosophical and political phenomenon was similar to its view of nationalism. Administration officials considered Pan-Africanism a potentially dangerous philosophy because of its critique of the West (and, especially, capitalism) and its assumption that African peoples should act collectively because they shared a common fate.

## Tensions between Pan-Africanism and Responsible Nationalism

Official documents suggest that State Department planners were suspicious of Pan-Africanism. The drafters of NSC 5719/1 recognized that the metropolitan powers and independent states of Africa might be reluctant to work together. They hoped that an upcoming conference in Ghana might push the independent states toward closer cooperation with the West. As a safeguard, they looked for a role in such interarea conferences to prevent the balkanization of Africa and to serve as "an antidote to the blandishments of Egypt and the Soviets."[59]

Yet, as widespread independence became likely, Pan-Africanism took on a sinister luster. Although they acknowledged Kwame Nkrumah's proclamation of nonalignment and believed that the American ambassador in Accra had some influence on him, officials in Washington worried about Nkrumah's Pan-African Congress of 1958:[60] "Invitations will be extended to all African political movements with aspirations similar to those of the CPP without regard to the political status of their countries of origin. No planning [by OCB] will be done until after the conference . . . Such a nongovernmental Pan-African gathering would probably be heavily influenced by nationalist extremists and communist elements."[61] Washington was willing to tolerate regional intrastate formations if such groups could meet American definitions of neutrality, at the least. Shortly before the Accra Conference of Independent African States, Secretary of State Dulles sent a personal message to Nkrumah, which "expressed good wishes for the success of the Conference and United States willingness to support the constructive efforts of African states to achieve a stable, prosperous community."[62]

Eisenhower and his advisers had been concerned about collective action among Third World peoples since the announcement of the Bandung Conference of 1955. Although the administration did nothing to stop the conference, it hoped to: (1) diminish its significance by ignoring it; (2) offset any anti-West sentiment by encouraging the participation of pro-West states; and (3) encourage the growing rivalry between China and India.[63] The Eisenhower administration ignored the Bandung Conference precisely because it represented a clear challenge to the racial sanctuary that was the Cold War; many of the participants not only sought a new course away from the bilateralism of the Cold War, they also rejected Western anti-Communist doctrine and asserted that the primary challenges of the new period were the end of White domination of non-White peoples and the ability of colonized peoples to build states which served their interests. However, Washington applauded intrastate or regional cooperation, which Africans structured on Western norms. In 1960, Liberian President Tubman gave a speech signaling the need for increased regional cooperation amongst West African nations. NSC personnel looked favorably upon Tubman's speech because of its pro-West bent, but also, no doubt, in part because he "had informal U.S. assistance and advice in drafting the speech."[64]

As with Pan-Arabism, Eisenhower and his men feared that a single individual would build a cult of personality around himself and pull the rest of the continent's nations behind him. The president was convinced that such was Nkrumah's objective.[65] Thus, the problem for the administration was not simply that groups of Africans might act collectively; it was that such collective action might pull them away from their former colonial oppressors and weaken the Free World.[66]

When Portugal joined NATO in 1949, Salazar made clear to the other member states "that Portugal's participation in it did not signify acceptance of the liberal and democratic principles stated in NATO's charter."[67] Two years later, "the Portuguese government officially termed its colonies 'provinces,' integral parts of Portugal for which independence was unthinkable."[68] During the Eisenhower administration, the United States continued to acquiesce in the face of Portuguese intransigence. A March 1958 OCB Progress Report on NSC 5719/1 summarized the Portuguese position regarding its African provinces, its bitter resentment of American anticolonialism, and its perception of American bungling "in the Far East, South Asia, and the Middle East since the close of the war."[69]

After noting Portugal's limited effort to head off indigenous pressures for self-government, the report rationalized America's lack of vigor for decolonization: the supposed political and social immaturity of the people of Angola and Mozambique. Just as importantly, the OCB report indicated the growing potential for conflict as Portugal's colonial subjects observed developments in other parts of the continent.[70] Even as global hegemon, the United States was not omnipotent. Therefore, the relevant issue raised is the choice made by American officials: prioritize Portugal's claims above the desires of Portugal's African subjects, even though Portugal had little leverage because it was unlikely to aid global Communism. The United States chose what it considered to be the safest route.

The limits of American support for African independence shrank even further in regard to Pan-Africanists, largely because of their anti-West rhetoric. Given the consensus in the Eisenhower administration regarding the increasing strategic importance of sub-Saharan Africa, as well as its increasing vulnerability to Soviet subversion,[71] any criticism of global capitalism was treated as Communist-inspired. An episode regarding the Cameroun provides a pertinent example of American treatment of radical African nationalists. In August 1959, Dr. Felix Moumie of the Union des populations du Cameroun (the UPC) and Andre Marie M'bida of the Parti des Democrates Camerounais (the PDC) met in Conakry with American Ambassador John Morrow. Moumie handed to Morrow a joint communiqué from the UPC and PDC. Morrow offered no analysis of the communiqué so that it quickly could reach the State Department.[72]

The joint communiqué was the result of a meeting between Moumie and M'bida at the Monrovia Conference of Independent States. During the conference, the leaders of the UPC and PDC openly reviewed the crisis in their country. The joint communiqué criticized the French model of decolonization: "[The UPC and PDC] deplored the extremely serious situation that prevails in their country owing to France's intention to integrate Cameroun, manu militari, into the French Community, with the help of some Camerounians who are in her pay." Noting that the French used U.S. weapons to control Camerounians, the two leaders sought "American public opinion in particular to put pressure on the American government to stop lending its support to a policy that can only adversely affect the good relations that should exist between the American people and the Cameroun people."[73]

The leaders condemned the U.S. government for secretly hosting their opponent, Ahmadou Ahidjo, a few days before the Monrovia Conference, where, according to Moumie and M'bida, the parties discussed the need to bind "the Cameroun people, hand and foot, to French expansionist policy." "Determined to place and always keep the struggle of the Cameroun people in its proper African framework," Moumie and M'bida lauded the support they received at the Monrovia Conference. Noting that the majority of the people of the Cameroun supported their position, they highlighted the fact that both parties agreed to the need for a peaceful and democratic resolution of the current crisis.[74]

The joint communiqué stressed the applicability of the U.N. Charter and the Universal Declaration of the Rights of Man. Moreover, Moumie and M'bida demonstrated an understanding of the shifting politics of the United Nations and "non-interference in domestic affairs." They urged the American government and people to acknowledge that their struggle was not "a domestic matter within the French Community," but "a struggle between the French Community and its supporters on the one hand, and the desires of the Cameroun people, on the other hand, who yearn to be truly free, as does all of Africa."[75]

The UPC and PDC encouraged U.S. and U.N. support for a seven-part peace plan, which included a request for a U.N.-supervised plebiscite before independence that would be adopted by resolution at the Monrovia Conference. Moumie and M'bida appealed to French citizens in France and Africa to support such a peaceful, binding resolution. Leaving no stone unturned, they issued their call for peace to foreign business interests: "The best guaranty for their capital is

to be found, not in a policy of war but in political stability." In closing, they
appealed to France's allies, in particular the United States:

> [The United States and other French allies must] stop supporting French
> colonialist policy, as such support can only set the African peoples in general,
> and the people of Cameroun in particular, against these States, because, for the
> people of Cameroun as well as for all African peoples, the hour of decision has
> arrived, and it is necessary that each State define its future position in relation
> to the African Continent, taking into account the wishes of the peoples
> concerned.[76]

In his transmittal letter covering both the Morrow dispatch and the Moumie-
M'bida joint communiqué, John Calhoun wrote: "as in the past the Department
recommends against a Presidential reply to this exiled, Communist-influenced
politician."[77] Relying on interviews of former Cameroon politicians, indigenous
political documents, and other research by African historians, Richard Joseph
confirmed the contentions of Moumie and M'bida: "In 1959 the United Nations
took the unprecedented step of agreeing to end Cameroon's trusteeship without
requiring new elections, thereby permitting the French to complete the
devolution of power onto the government of [Ahmadou] Ahidjo . . . [This]
abnormality . . . resulted in the establishment of a highly repressive political-
military apparatus during . . . Ahidjo's two decades in power. Ironically, the
American effort to bind Africa to the West undermined the development of
democracy in a country which had prepared for Western-style constitutional
government as early as 1947."[78]

White suspicions about Pan-Africanism were also fueled by conservative
Africans. In the fall of 1959, President Eisenhower met with a delegation from
the French Community headed by Felix Houphouet-Boigny, prime minister of
the Ivory Coast. The president applauded Houphouet-Boigny's gradualist
approach to independence, as well as his anti-Communism:[79] "Communism is
excluded from the Ivory Coast, said Mr. Houphouet-Boigny, and even badly-
needed technicians sent by France are not admitted if they are Communists."[80]
Eisenhower was especially heartened to hear the Ivorian's views on African
development.

With reference to Pan-Africanism, Mr. Houphouet-Boigny said that such a
concept was utopian and only a useful propaganda device. He stated that his
principal fears lay in the so-called Afro-Asian bloc because Asia had nothing
tangible to offer Africa in its quest for social and economic improvement. The
future of Africa was with the West.[81] Eisenhower "agreed wholeheartedly . . .
that the larger entities in Africa cooperating closely with the West was
preferable to a series of small independent states; the President also agreed that
continent-wide federation could not be achieved at this time."[82]

## Conclusion

To paraphrase Anna Julia Cooper, non-White labor remained the wheel of Western power during the early Cold War.[83] The United States' push for decolonization was a defensive measure aimed at protecting the West rather than fostering freedom and self-determination for the Third World. The White House subscribed to the notion "that the best policy for the imperialists was to establish good relations with their assumed successors before they became embittered by years of friction and waiting."[84] Accordingly, African choices for viable self-determination found rhetorical support from Americans, even as those choices narrowed under Washington's dualistic, self-interested worldview.[85] President Eisenhower said as much in a 1960 National Security Council meeting which discussed America's multifaceted goals for the continent: "If we are unable to achieve our objective of maintaining the Free World orientation of the area and denying it to Communism, we would not want to proceed with our other objectives." In other words, if areas in Africa leaned toward Marxism, "we would not wish to undertake programs for their orderly economic development and political progress."[86]

Yet, the Eisenhower administration could not make known its desire to privilege the needs of the West above those of the Africans. As a result, the Eisenhower administration appealed to Africans in a manner that emphasized the promises of economic and political advancement that would inure from allegiance to the West and the global perception of African self-realization through cooperation with the West. It constructed an image of the West that obliterated the genocidal legacy of imperialism, touted the altruism of Western nations, and emphasized the salience of Western characterizations of global issues and the requirement of Africans to adopt the resultant Western priorities.[87]

Through the rhetoric of the Eisenhower administration, decolonization became a beneficent gift from an innocent Free World to an undeserving continent. As in *Brown*, the Eisenhower administration reduced the needs of imperialists and the yearnings of Africa to morally equivalent political extremes. Having done so, the major obstacle for Washington was to ensure that Africa's Blacks expressed their gratitude by accepting this brand of decolonization and maintaining their fealty to the United States and its allies, without challenging their right to control the transformation.[88]

The Eisenhower administration's policy regarding African decolonization warped reality to fit the imperatives of Whiteness. To justify White privileges and entitlement, the nations of the world that grew to prominence through imperialist expansion and the subjugation of various non-White people became known as the Free World and their former subjects seeking freedom were led by extremists, Soviet puppets, or self-aggrandizers whose efforts imperiled the globe.[89] Within the context of the administration's policy papers, Africans were simply children and chattel that needed to be controlled and denied to the

Soviets. They were fit for independence when, like Haiti, they were prepared to act responsibly. They were not truly human.

The erasure of Third World personality meant that Africans were malleable entities who required constant supervision and guidance. The irony of this position was that American action or inaction retarded the development of responsible government.[90] This result is predictable based upon Walter Rodney's thesis regarding European culpability for the underdevelopment of the African continent.[91] The erasure also meant that the incredible diversity of African traditions, cultures, and experiences was reduced to a monolithic archetype that justified continued Western dominance. Interestingly, cultural studies scholars have asserted that the reliance upon stereotypes increases with challenges to racial hegemony.[92] The Eisenhower administration wrestled with African policy near the zenith of African and African American agitation against Western [White] hegemony over the Third [non-White] World. Unable to escape their cultural setting and having only limited mental maps of Africa, Eisenhower and his men relied upon that which was familiar.[93] Thus, they easily relied on negative stereotypes of Africans as a basis for shaping policy and silencing or ignoring dissent and as a means of absolving Western imperialism from the bitter fruits of its labor.

Washington's decision-makers rested their analysis of dynamic events on static notions of African primitivism as a way of simplifying a very complex confluence of political, social, and economic elements which they could not, or chose not to, decipher.[94] If American government officials could reduce Africans to the geopolitical equivalent of ungrateful children, they could ignore the various factors—spiritual millenarianism, trade unionism, the Negritude Movement, resistance to European assimilation, asymmetrical educational systems, agricultural exploitation and forced labor, international experiences and exposures, to name a few—which led to African nationalism.[95] The benefit of such a reductionist approach was that African subordination to European necessities was a fait accompli; through this construction, maintaining the essential ties between Africa and Europe was both prudent and honorable. The reciprocal burden placed on African nationalists was to prove their authenticity and maturity, as part of a popular movement loyal to the West and/or as a non-Communist political force. Given the United States' restrictive notions of neutrality, African nationalists could achieve formal self-determination only by submitting their countries to informal Western domination.

In the midst of the conflagration between competing economic systems and political philosophies, that is, the American Civil War, the enslavement of Africans was ushered toward a slow death. The formal fetters of slavery were replaced by a system of legal, economic, political, and social barriers that condemned the freedmen to informal subservience to White power. The central tenet of this compromise between North and South was the imperative to "[keep] the nigger down."[96] Less than a century later, the United States supported decolonization in the midst of a phenomenon characterized as a global conflict between competing economic and political systems. Its support for the ending of European imperialism meant the exchange of the formal fetters of colonialism for a system of economic, political, and military barriers that condemned the formal colonial subjects to informal subservience to Western hegemony. As such, it was simply a refinement of policy that would lead to a familiar result: African subordination to White Supremacist needs.

# CHAPTER THREE

# THE NEGUS AND I:
# AMERICAN FOREIGN POLICY
# TOWARD ETHIOPIA

## Ethiopia: An Introduction

American foreign policy toward Ethiopia cracks the door to the hidden racial aspects of Western diplomacy. Ethiopia was a sovereign nation long before the United States or the advent of European colonization of Africa. Ethiopia was a well-known African state that had factored in global and political social developments for centuries. The United States understood the strategic importance of having this nation, led by an international statesman, as a partner. Because Ethiopia committed itself to the West prior to the Cold War, the central aim of this chapter is to examine how Whiteness influenced American diplomacy toward a demonstrated ally.

American interests in Ethiopia reached a peak in the aftermath of World War II. The French and Italians had influenced this unique sovereign nation during the nineteenth century. Although the Ethiopians routed Italian forces at the turn of the century, Italy maintained its presence in Eritrea, and Mussolini's fascist government led a full-scale invasion in 1935. Italian dominance was thwarted in 1941 by combined British and Ethiopian troops. A little more than ten years later, Ethiopia fell under the shadow of the United States.

American foreign policy toward Ethiopia during the early Cold War era was shaped by Ethiopia's complicity in America's Cold War project and by Ethiopia's potential as a drag on independence movements and general radicalism in Africa and the Middle East. Generally, Ethiopia's location in the strategically important horn of Africa served as an additional impetus for American overtures. American bases in Ethiopia provided the American military a new set of eyes and ears with which to monitor developments in the Arab world. Ethiopia's conservative monarchy routinely sided with the United States on various international issues. Playing upon Emperor Haile Selassie's fears of Egyptian expansion and Somali independence, the United States was able to extract important military base rights near the Suez Canal and the oil-rich nations of the Persian Gulf. In exchange, the Ethiopian government received very limited American technical and military assistance earmarked only to ensure the survival of the monarchy.

Additionally, despite Ethiopia's long and storied history, American diplomats considered that nation nearly as primitive as any other African polity. They underrated Ethiopia's security concerns and, in spite of Ethiopia's clearly pro-West posture, refused to provide significant aid for economic, educational, or even military development. Not surprisingly, the Ethiopian government was incredibly disappointed in American aid. Haile Selassie's advisers consistently questioned America's commitment to Ethiopia and criticized the quantity and quality of U.S. support. Given the domestic turmoil facing the Haile Selassie regime, U.S. policy effectively, though unintentionally, helped to destabilize a staunch compatriot.

Although American officials understood the value of Ethiopia as a buttress against African and Arab militancy, they still had some reservations about this Amharic state. Because Washington believed that the Ethiopians were only slightly more sophisticated than colonized Africans, their rhetoric regarding Ethiopia differed little from other discussions about Blacks, whether continental or diasporan. In this regard, we witness the U.S. demand for Black self-abnegation projected onto the international scene. Additionally, the politics of Black insatiability ripples through American-Ethiopian relations as well. Since the dominant gaze of White males defined African behavior, we can discern the influence of masculinity on the ongoing negotiations for U.S. military and economic assistance.[1] Implicit in this critique of American diplomacy is the idea that Washington's actions did not mesh with its espoused ideas. Indeed, the Eisenhower administration's investment in African inferiority meant that U.S. policies subverted freedom, democracy, and autonomy. Therefore, this chapter concludes with an analysis of both the effects of White entitlement on the actions of the Eisenhower administration and, briefly, the effects of Eisenhower-era policy on Ethiopia's people.

## A Brief History of Ethiopia

Ethiopia is unique among African nation-states. Like Egypt, it has a history that spans millennia. Given the prevailing scientific consensus, Ethiopia is likely the birthplace of human beings.[2] Interestingly, the development of the modern nation-state of Ethiopia coincided with the zenith of European hegemony on the continent. As African peoples and their land were divided at the Berlin Conference of 1895, Ethiopia was expanding to its current size, an expansion checked only by British and French avarice.[3]

The various peoples of Ethiopia had diverse experiences governing themselves. The creation and expansion of a centralized government under rulers like Tewodros II, Yohannes IV, and Menelik II undid the tradition of parceled sovereignties or

*Zamana Masafent.* Firepower purchased from Britain helped the Amharic Christian rulers defeat their non-Christian rivals and pummel the Italians at the Battle of Adwa in 1896. Although that battle crippled Italian plans to overtake Abyssinia, it had greater symbolic importance as a historic victory of Blacks over the seemingly invincible White conquerors from Europe.[4] "By using diplomacy and/or war, and by exploiting the inter-European rivalry, Menelik presided over the formation of the modern Ethiopian state."[5] Two generations later, the born-again modern state consolidated its power and survived Italian occupation under the Grand Negus, Emperor Haile Selassie.[6]

The process of state consolidation also meant the ascendancy of the Amhara people. The price of Amharic hegemony was the marginalization of the Tigray, the Oromo, and others. The struggles between the Oromo and the Amhara, the great historical antagonists, were waged between the sixteenth and nineteenth centuries. In fact, the struggle between the two groups was so acrimonious that some Oromo were disappointed in the 1941 defeat of the Italians and the resultant return of Amharic hegemony.[7]

Interestingly, the Italian invasion of 1935 hastened the centralization of power in the hands of the emperor. Militarily, the Italian invasion provided for the creation of a modern Ethiopian Army much more loyal to Haile Selassie than its predecessors. Traditionally, Ethiopian warriors were loyal to regional leaders known as *Ras.* In times of conflict, the emperor called upon these nobles to supply soldiers and weapons to defend the crown. These aristocrats had their own rivalries and were notoriously fickle in their support of the emperor. Indeed, a major factor in the victory at Adwa in 1896 was the ability of nobles and peasants to overcome their feuding to collectively repel the Italian Army.[8] Yet, this camaraderie disappeared during the Italian invasion of the twentieth century.

When Mussolini's troops pounced onto the horn of Africa, Haile Selassie struggled to organize an effective resistance force. In addition, Ethiopian martial tradition—which compelled combatants to stand and fight, rather than lie on the ground—led to massive slaughter of those forces loyal to the emperor. The Ethiopian guerilla movement which, along with the British, defeated the fascists, was compiled from social elements ordinarily aloof to, or excluded from, military service—peasants and women. Although Black women would find little benefit from their wartime service, nonaristocrats and those Ras who remained loyal to Haile Selassie formed the vanguard of a new Ethiopian Army much more deferential to the Grand Negus.

In addition to having an army over which he could exert greater control, Haile Selassie also benefitted from the infrastructure improvements made by the Italians prior to their defeat. With improved roads, bridges, and modes of communications, Addis Ababa could more effectively control internal dissent in the hinterlands without having to negotiate for the cooperation of local or regional leaders and nobles.[9] The consolidation of the means of violence in the hands of a central government was mirrored by similar processes in the legal and bureaucratic arenas.

Haile Selassie revised the Ethiopian legal system to approximate more closely the juridical traditions of the West. The Grand Negus dismantled a legal system based upon indigenous traditions, entitlements, and beliefs in favor of a formalized structure of positivistic rules that inherently favored the powerful and the wealthy irrespective of lineage. For example, land ownership under the new system became increasingly concentrated in the hands of wealthy investors, many of whom had been locked out of the system because of their ethnicity or religious beliefs. Under the old system and in regions where landownership was often based on heredity, craftworkers, Muslims, and other Galla found themselves tenants on lands owned by privileged Amhara. Under the new system came the commodification of property, which allowed anyone with monetary wealth to purchase land; "in less than three decades after the end of Italian occupation, a good many of the big land and real estate owners in the towns of the *rist* region were Muslims and former craftsworkers."[10] Further, under the new legal regime, peasants found themselves bankrupted in their attempts to sue for their land rights, and Amharic nobles found that their heritage counted for little in protecting once untouchable property interests.[11]

Increasingly, Haile Selassie sought to develop a civil service system that relied more heavily on education and experience than on ancestry. Pre-1935 Ethiopia had been divided into more than thirty administrative units. By 1942, Haile Selassie had reduced the number of provinces to twelve, a number which increased to fourteen by 1962. This was no simple redrawing of province lines. It meant the complete subversion of the traditional power base of the nobility. Although Haile Selassie used high state offices as a means of satisfying privileged members of the aristocracy, this new system gave him greater control over their political power. Again, the result was that different types of people who traditionally had been locked out of government service careers found a slightly opened door.[12]

For example, the State Department's protocol expert described the first Ethiopian ambassador appointed during the Eisenhower administration, Ato Yalima Deressa, as Galla, a derogatory Amharic term for an Oromo.[13] Furthermore, numbers of Ethiopians sought training in Western or Western-style schools. A group of Ethiopian students wrote to President Eisenhower in 1954 to show their gratitude for their successful matriculation through the American University in Beirut, an education that was "supported substantially through U.S. training grants under [the U.S.] Technical Assistance Program in Ethiopia."[14]

In these and other ways, modernizing Ethiopia existed in a flux that the emperor hoped to control. Although many Amharic nobles found themselves in uncharted territory, the new empire favored Amhara over other ethnic groups. Consequently, the development of an Ethiopian national identity meant the constant undermining of separate indigenous identities.[15] What is immediately striking about the development of modern Ethiopia is that the post-World War II state resembled the American ideal for a Third World nation: a tightly controlled society with inordinate power centralized in the hands of a repressive leader. While managing the process of political homogenization, Emperor Haile Selassie (like his predecessors) also had to navigate the tricky waters of great power politics in a postwar world.

## Ethiopia-United States Relations to 1955

Prior to World War II, most Americans knew comparatively little about Ethiopia. This changed with the fascist invasion in 1935. African Americans, especially, rallied to support the Haile Selassie regime from its Italian invaders. African troops from Britain's West African possessions joined the battle and helped drive out the interlopers.[16]

Despite African American support for the beleaguered nation, official policy in Washington bolstered the invasion: "While the Roosevelt administration registered protests with the Italian government, refusing to recognize Italian authority in Ethiopia and briefly limiting American commerce with Italy, United States policy continued officially as neutrality. Within a year, American trade with Italy, including arms sales, resumed."[17] Nevertheless, Ethiopia cooperated with the United States and other Allied powers from the inception of the United Nations.

Ethiopian cooperation with America was, in large part, Haile Selassie's strategy of playing the United States against Britain in order to maintain Ethiopian sovereignty. Britain had played the leading role in defeating the fascists, but it engaged in heavy-handed negotiations of an economic assistance agreement with Addis Ababa in 1942. It could be argued that British sternness was a result of Menelik's victory over the Italians half a century earlier. In the late 1890s, Menelik expanded the national boundaries of Ethiopia into the British protectorate of Somalia. Although Washington's official stance in the 1940s was not to take sides in the negotiations, some policymakers perceived Britain's treatment of Ethiopia as essentially colonial.[18]

While American officials, sensing an opportunity, moved in quickly to help Ethiopia, Haile Selassie lobbied for further territorial expansion.[19] He demanded all of Eritrea as a completion of the unification of historical Ethiopia and as a much-needed access point to the sea. However, he had to prove his nation's value to the West. Just such an opportunity arose near the end of World War II.

As the nations of the world gathered in San Francisco in April 1945 for the United Nations Conference on International Organization, African Americans, among others, sought to raise the issue of racial equality at home and abroad. They met immediate resistance from Washington: "At the first meeting of delegates and consultants, Secretary of State [Edward] Stettinius announced that the American delegation would not introduce or support a human rights declaration for the proposed charter and that questions relating to colonies should be taken up sometime in the future after San Francisco."[20] Especially disconcerting to American human rights advocates was the coolness of the Ethiopian delegation.

Members of the press doubted the Black nation's commitment to the principle of racial equality:

P. L. Prattis reported that it was easier to meet with European delegations than with Ethiopian, Liberian, and Haitian diplomats, who would not grant interviews or return phone calls. He considered this behavior contemptible, especially since Afro-Americans had strongly protested the Italian invasion of Ethiopia and had volunteered to defend that nation's sovereignty. Afro-Americans, moreover, had always demanded that Liberia be treated as an independent nation and had criticized American occupation of Haiti in the early twentieth century.

Unbeknownst to the press was Ethiopia's concern regarding proper credentials for the conference. Thus, even if they had wished to satisfy the concerns of human rights activists, they did not want to alienate Washington. Although Haiti reversed its prior position and "ma[d]e racial discrimination a major issue," Ethiopia and Liberia were largely silent throughout the conference.[21]

The quiescence of the Ethiopian delegation makes sense on two levels. First, to raise the issue of racial discrimination would portend doom for a nation in the process of silencing its diverse voices.[22] Secondly, Ethiopia had to show that it could play the game of Western diplomacy in order to reach its larger goals. Ethiopia believed that its comportment at international gatherings was critical in this regard, and, in fact, its support of American military objectives drew praise from the West, as will be discussed more fully later in this chapter.

Although Ethiopia offered no public criticism of racial discrimination at the initial U.N. meeting, Ethiopians did not ignore this problem. According to some American officials, Ethiopia did not indicate any concern for American race relations during the first Eisenhower administration. At the end of 1958, however, officials in Washington noticed a shift in Ethiopian interests. In response to concerns emanating from the president's Civil Rights Commission, the State Department prepared a document entitled *Treatment of Minorities in the United States: Impact On Our Foreign Relations*. In the Area Review section of the document, the authors discussed the response of specific nations to American race relations. In the section pertaining to Ethiopia, the drafters remarked that "racial relations have not had major effect upon relations between Ethiopia and the United States. In the past, Ethiopians have shown relatively little interest in United States racial difficulties." Yet, from their perspective, the Little Rock crisis changed this apparent aloofness:

> [Recently,] however, the Ethiopian press kept close watch on United States racial issues such as the incidents in Little Rock and the Jimmy Wilson case. The Ethiopian delegation to the Accra Conference of Independent African States in April 1958 joined the seven other participating countries in condemning racial discrimination and segregation, calling upon the United Nations to intensify its efforts to combat racial injustice.[23]

Furthermore, it should be noted that Ethiopia consistently criticized South Africa's apartheid regimes.[24]

Haile Selassie's expansionist bid was aided not only by Eritrean nationalists (who detested the thought of being Italian subjects) but also by a Truman administration which did not want "any potentially hostile power" to have a trusteeship in such a vital area. The primary concern was "the maintenance of essential U.S. military rights, particularly in the Asmara-Massawa area." Because the Eritreans seemed too primitive to administer (and protect) an independent state responsibly, American elites considered an Ethiopian-Eritrean federation to be the best option.[25]

From that point, Ethiopia consistently supported American positions at the United Nations. In addition, Ethiopia provided soldiers for the American campaign in Korea. Because of Ethiopia's status as a long-standing independent Black nation, and its perceived influence on other African peoples, the United States valued its cooperation.[26]

As the Cold War continued, so did Ethiopia's backing of American diplomacy. Even observers in Washington acknowledged Ethiopia's endorsement of the Truman Doctrine and support of the U.N. position on Hungary. The Haile Selassie regime continued to play a role in support of the Free World. Ethiopia "retain[ed] a military liaison group in Korea and . . . voted for . . . postponing consideration of the Chinese representation issue."[27]

From 1945 and throughout much of the Eisenhower administration, Ethiopia proved to be a consistently loyal American ally. In the spring of 1953, Haile Selassie, through departing Ethiopian Ambassador Ras Imru, expressed a strong interest in visiting the United States. Undoubtedly, the emperor wished to pay his respects to the newly elected Eisenhower, who as a soldier had received the highest award granted by Ethiopia to a foreign citizen. In a memo prepared for the president, Under Secretary of State W. B. Smith noted that:

> His Imperial Majesty has wanted to come to this country for a long time and in January his Foreign Minister requested that the Emperor's desire be brought to the attention of the new administration. We have heard confidentially that the Emperor and Empress have accepted an invitation to visit England as guests of Queen Elizabeth early in 1954. It is suggested that you show sympathetic interest in a visit by the Emperor but a commitment at this time is not necessary.[28]

The emperor's trip to the United States in 1954 seemed to be a success. As Haile Selassie and his queen departed, they left President Eisenhower a large quantity of Ethiopian coffee as a gift.[29] Upon hearing that the vice president planned to travel to Ghana for that nation's independence ceremonies, Addis Ababa extended an invitation to Nixon to visit Ethiopia thereafter.[30] When Zaude Gabre Heywot left his ambassadorial duties in the U.S.S.R. to take the place of Ambassador Deressa in Washington, his remarks to the president reflected the general warmth between the two nations: "I need not review the history of cooperation and friendly relations which have so long existed between Ethiopia and the United States of America."[31] However, Ethiopia learned as early as the Truman years that its loyalty would not be reciprocated in kind.

Around the time of the summer 1951 anniversary of the Korean War, American military representative Lieutenant General Charles L. Bolte visited Addis Ababa. Brigadier General Abiye Abebe—the new Ethiopian minister of war—welcomed Gen. Bolte, who remarked that Ethiopia's contribution to the U.N. police action testified to Addis Ababa's commitment to the West. When Gen. Abebe asked for assistance in the establishment of a small mobile army and air force, Gen. Bolte responded that Korea was Washington's current preoccupation, but that "Ethiopia's needs would not be lost to sight." When the Ethiopian soldier asked directly about a military training mission, the American was generally agreeable, but his recitation of U.S. global priorities placed Africa last. Nevertheless, Gen. Bolte admitted that Asmara's Radio Marina was an area of mutual interest and testified that Washington would "always take with great concern any danger to Ethiopia."[32] Thus, Ethiopia's significance to America was dictated by its usefulness in advancing American diplomatic and military goals generally unrelated to Ethiopia's interests.

## Ethiopia: The Cold War and Black-Brown Radicalism

### Ethiopia and U.S. Cold War Objectives

Ethiopia consistently sided with the United States with regard to international issues. During his meeting with Vice President Nixon in March 1957, Ethiopian Foreign Minister Ato Aklilou Abte Wolde revisited Ethiopian support for the Free World. Ethiopia was "the only non-NATO state in the Middle East which gave active support to the UN action in Korea. It had, moreover, given valuable support to the United States and the free world on many matters within and without the UN."[33] In addition to its support of the American position on the Suez crisis, Ethiopia participated in the subsequent Five Power Commission, much to chagrin of its neighbors and a large and vocal contingent of its own citizens.[34]

Prior to the adoption of NSC 5615/1, Operations Coordinating Board staffers prepared a draft policy analysis focusing on security conditions in Ethiopia. OCB Staff Representative James Gustin considered the report a prototype for future policy papers on other portions of Africa. Despite its brevity—which Gustin applauded—the paper sketched in broad strokes the major pressures facing the United States as it attempted to maintain the "continued orientation of Ethiopia toward the West."[35]

The major fear expressed in the policy paper was that Ethiopia would abandon its pro-Western posture in favor of a position of nonalignment. Although the drafters acknowledged that American actions might exacerbate certain Ethiopian anxieties, their real concern was the pressure on the Haile Selassie regime from external and domestic forces:

> In view of the rising Soviet Bloc interest in and attention to Ethiopia and evidence of mounting internal pressure towards [a] middle ground in the world conflict, it is

evident that the present period contains serious challenge to the Western bloc . . . In order to ensure Ethiopia's continued place within the Free World, the U.S. has an unquestioned interest in devoting the necessary effort and resources to offset the immediate Soviet Bloc inroads and to assist this country to develop along Western standards. The problem is primarily one of internal security conceived in the broadest sense.[36]

Accordingly, if Ethiopia adopted a position of neutrality in the Cold War, it would mean not only a loss for the West but also a potential gain for global Communism.

Although Ethiopia felt for years that the United States took its support for granted, the Haile Selassie government continued to try to satisfy the requests of the West. However, Americans felt that Ethiopian dissatisfaction with U.S. aid had caused it to adopt a position of neutrality because it "declined to accept membership in the Suez Canal User's Association," despite Ethiopia's support for the United States with respect to the Suez crisis.[37] Nonetheless, Ethiopia warily stood by the United States when it sent troops into Lebanon in 1958 under the dubious pretext of staving off Communist aggression. In return for his understanding and constructive statement during the Lebanon crisis, Haile Selassie received a personal message of thanks from Eisenhower.[38] Yet, by the end of the Eisenhower administration, the strain of constant disappointment forced the Haile Selassie regime to reconsider its priorities.

Early in 1960, the nations of the world gathered at the Law of the Seas Conference at Geneva in an effort to revise international maritime law. One of the key questions was the acceptable width of territorial waters. Given the size of their nation and their fears of attack from the north and east, Ethiopia, like many small nations, sought the broadest possible size of its territorial waters. Yet, the twelve-mile territorial waters proposal supported by the Ethiopian delegation failed to achieve a majority.

When the American delegation requested that Ethiopia support an American-Canadian compromise proposal, the Ethiopians initially refused to comply. Fearful that the conference would end in disaster, President Eisenhower telegrammed Emperor Haile Selassie asking that he change Ethiopia's vote in order to support the United States-Canada plan: "I am addressing Your Majesty personally . . . because I believe that success of the conference would constitute an important milestone for the principle of amicable adjustment of different national views on a basis of compromise." After noting the broader, yet still insufficient, support for the United States-Canada compromise, the president asked for Ethiopia's positive vote by placing the matter in the starkest terms possible: "It is my belief that . . . the question before the conference is whether this compromise proposal will obtain the two-thirds majority in a vote in the plenary session, or whether the conference will end in failure."[39] On April 19, 1960, Haile Selassie sent a letter to Eisenhower indicating that Ethiopia would change its vote, as well as alluding to the important sacrifice of its national interest as a result:

As you well know, the defence interests of the smaller nations dictate the adoption of a wider belt of territorial water, and hence Ethiopia's preference has been for a twelve-mile territorial sea. Nonetheless, We have, in order that the U.S.-Canadian proposal receive the requisite two-thirds majority and that the Law of the Sea Conference end in success, in full confidence that the Government of the United States has and will take full cognisance of Ethiopia's vital interests in this matter, decided to support the U.S.-Canadian proposal.[40]

Based on its own disappointments with U.S. support, as well as the internal and external pressures on Ethiopia to stand apart from the East-West tug-of-war, Haile Selassie's previously unflagging support could not last indefinitely. Despite American concerns that Ethiopians did not appreciate the dangers of the global Communist quest, Ethiopia's move away from unquestioned obedience to the West had more to do with a desire for independence of action than a submission to Moscow's intrigues. The Ethiopians stood by the United Nations during the Congo crisis, going so far as to volunteer troops for the peacekeeping force. During a meeting with President Eisenhower, Ethiopian Prime Minister Ato Aklilou "said that the Ethiopian position is the same as that of the U.S. respecting much." Aklilou added that sending their troops to the Congo was a gesture in support of collective security, noting that "strengthening . . . the UN [was] the best guarantee of the security of smaller nations."[41] However, by the winter of 1960, American officials were surprised when, at the United Nations, Ethiopia voted against a moratorium on the question of Chinese recognition.[42] Although Ethiopia's record of support was significant in its own right, Washington had hoped that Ethiopia could serve another valuable purpose as a moderating influence among African and Arabic nations during the Cold War.

## A Speed Bump for Afro-Arab Militancy

Throughout the Eisenhower administration, American foreign policy toward Ethiopia was dictated by NSC 5615, 5615/1, and, later, NSC 5903, the former two documents comprising a specific statement on policy toward that nation and the latter being a policy statement regarding the entire horn of Africa.[43] Although members of the Eisenhower administration acknowledged Ethiopia's symbolic importance on the global stage, they regarded its people as semiprimitive.[44] As a result, the United States needed to cultivate among the Ethiopians both an understanding of the hazards of contact with global Communism and a sense of responsibility to serve as a positive influence on the rest of Africa:[45] "Recognizing Ethiopia's position as a pro-Western independent country in Africa, the U.S. must strive to develop a sense of responsibility and initiative on the part of the Ethiopians toward repelling communism and the expansionist tendencies of Egypt, thereby encouraging other African countries to follow their lead."[46]

Despite their belief in the backwardness of Ethiopia, Eisenhower administration officials sought to retain Ethiopia within a pro-West orbit.[47] Ethiopia's significance, in large part, grew from American concerns regarding the Suez Canal and Pan-

Arabism, not to mention the lack of development they perceived throughout the rest of Africa. Thus it is no surprise that nearly all of President Eisenhower's references to Ethiopia in his memoirs are within the larger context of Middle Eastern affairs.[48] Although the policy papers focused on Ethiopia's strategic importance, officials in Washington also understood the propaganda significance of an alliance with this East African nation. In fact, NSC 5615 stated that "it is of value to maintain close relations with an African state which has become a symbol of resistance to aggression and a champion of collective security."[49]

Interestingly, American officials admitted to themselves that the sum of Ethiopia's value was greater than its economic or military parts: "Ethiopia's importance to the United States transcends the country's limited power and somewhat isolated position. Current developments in the Near East increase the value to the United States of a friendly, stable government in this region of Africa."[50] By the mid-1950s Israeli independence, a radicalized Egypt, and Soviet pressure in the Mediterranean increased the White House's sensitivity for a pro-West, non-White political anchor near the Suez Canal. As a result, Ethiopia's strategic and diplomatic importance only increased following the joint British-French assault on Egypt as a result of Nasser's July 1956 takeover of the Suez Canal.[51] Vice President Nixon, who traveled to Africa in 1957, perhaps best summed up U.S. concerns about this Nile River power and the need for a politically viable Ethiopia.

In his trip report to the president, Nixon wrote that "Nasser's influence on the masses of the people in North Africa, the Sudan and the Moslem portions of Ethiopia remains high although probably less so than before his defeat by the Israelis. On the other hand, the Governments of these countries see in Nasser a threat to their independence and are therefore cautious in their attitudes toward him." Although he acknowledged that nations like Libya, Tunisia, and Morocco, along with Ethiopia and Sudan, were looking "toward close cooperation among themselves to enhance their combined capability to resist *Nasserism*," Nixon worried that this effort might prove to be insufficient:

> Egyptian propaganda, particularly radio broadcasts, is highly effective among the Moslem populations of the countries we visited. This contrasts with the ineffectiveness of our own propaganda efforts. I believe that Egyptian efforts can be combatted [sic] effectively only by building up the indigenous broadcasting capabilities of the states of the area. Thus a Radio Morocco, Radio Tunisia, etc. would be much more effective than an expansion of [Voice of America] facilities in this area.

In conclusion, Nixon recommended "that while avoiding any appearance of isolating Egypt, we quietly encourage and assist these states, both individually and collectively, to resist the efforts of Egypt to dominate them."[52] It is worth noting that Nixon's view of enhancing indigenous pro-West propaganda ran counter to the view of State Department and NSC planners who favored the use of the United States Information System to deal with Communist subversion efforts.[53]

Other reports emphasized Ethiopia's military cooperation with the United States:

> In 1953, Ethiopia concluded a base agreement with the United States under which we maintain a U.S. Army radio station at Asmara, which is now being expanded and which forms a major link in the Army's world-wide communication system. The U.S. Navy maintains a petroleum storage and a communication unit in Ethiopia and has established requirements for post-D-Day facilities. The U.S. Air Force has a requirement for a signal communications base in Eritrea in lieu of Aden. Ethiopia could also serve as a base of operations to protect the shipping lanes to the Far East, Europe and the Middle East.[54]

American staffers also remarked about Ethiopia's disappointment with Western reciprocation following Ethiopian political cooperation with the United States: "Even though Ethiopia remains oriented toward the West, it feels that the benefits of cooperation with the West have been small. Some Ethiopian leaders contend that the United States considers Ethiopia's cooperation less valuable than that of less friendly governments."[55] This frustration had grown from the time of Gen. Bolte's arrival in Addis Ababa in 1951 through November 1955, when Gen. Orval Cook arrived to survey Ethiopian martial needs. Ethiopia's irritation grew as the United States handed Egypt's Gamal Nasser $40 million while Ethiopia remained starved for developmental aid.[56]

Policy papers mentioned a small but growing Communist interest in Ethiopia, as well as tensions between the governments of Ethiopia and Egypt.[57] Although the tensions between Ethiopia and Egypt were quite real—and long-standing—the internal Communist presence seemed limited to a left-wing youth group. The major concern among officials in Washington was the Ethiopians' "exaggerated confidence . . . in their ability to cope with the political consequences of Soviet Bloc economic entanglements."[58]

The Soviet Union, China, Czechoslovakia, and Yugoslavia had enlarged economic, social, and political relations with Ethiopia since the end of 1955. In addition to the Soviet cultural center in Ethiopia's capital, the Soviets had built a popular seventy-two-bed hospital that was also used to train nurses. The Czechs were planning to construct a similar hospital, and Marshall Tito had provided Ethiopia with the lone boat in its navy. Adding fuel to the fire was the "greatly improved caliber of Soviet personnel now assigned to Ethiopia."[59] Thus, American officials lamented that "[a] major difficulty in achieving a reduction of communist influence is the lack of real appreciation by the Ethiopians of the communist subversive threat."[60]

Even if the domestic Communist threat was exaggerated by observers like U.S. Ambassador Joseph Simonson, the repression in Eritrea and "exclusivity of the dominant Amhara" were a match that could ignite popular dissent.[61] OCB staffers identified three potential security threats to the Haile Selassie regime, placing the potential Communist threat last on the list only because of their concern that it could exploit the other two. "The first threat is a latent one and concerns the autocratic and traditional nature of the Ethiopian Government." This threat had three elements: (1) the prestige and prominence of the Coptic Christian Church, its relationship to the emperor, and its control of wealth and resources in the nation; (2) Ethiopia's imperialistic desires toward Somalia; and (3) the potential struggle for succession upon the death of the emperor. According to OCB staffers, "the second threat is one that is usually found in backward countries where a government has been dominated by a strong personality." This threat was posed by dispossessed Amharic nobles or leaders, young intellectuals, and civil servants pessimistic about political and economic change under a monarchy; progressive army officers weary of perceived corruption by their superiors; or the large Muslim population. The concern in Washington was that increased pressures from radicals—ethnic nationalists, proponents of Muslim solidarity, and, least of all, Marxists—might foment internal militancy and destabilize the country.[62] Fearing that an end to the Haile Selassie government would jeopardize the nation's pro-West posture, as well as U.S. interests in Ethiopia and the entire region, U.S. strategy was determined to "provide the Ethiopian Armed Forces with limited military equipment and training of a kind suitable for maintaining internal security and offering resistance to local aggression."[63]

In addition to the internal stability provided by the Negus, the United States valued Ethiopia's ability to check radicalism throughout Africa. During the first Eisenhower administration, OCB staffers suggested that "the U.S. must strive to develop a sense of responsibility and initiative on the part of the Ethiopians toward influencing other African peoples to repel communism and the expansionist tendencies of Egypt."[64] In a summer 1958 report, Roy Melbourne informed the OCB and the National Security Council that Ethiopia "offered to take the lead in establishing close collaboration with Sudan and Somalia to deter the southward expansion of UAR influence."[65] Another OCB progress report on NSC 5615/1 noted that "Ethiopia played a constructive and moderating role in the Accra Conference [of Independent African States]." During a discussion on the Horn of Africa in the following year, Eisenhower and Herter discussed Ethiopia's importance to American geopolitical interests in the area. The president stated that he did not want the Red Sea "bottled up at both ends by people who might not necessarily be or remain our friends."[67] Accordingly, American officials deemed it necessary to provide only enough aid to Haile Selassie to maintain his government.

## The Richards Mission and the Politics of Black Insatiability

As alluded to earlier, one of the great sore points in the relationship between the United States and Ethiopia was the low level of military support the United States provided to its loyal and useful ally. In October 1956, Haile Selassie gave an "aide-memoire" to U.S. Senator Theodore Francis Green; the emperor intended it for the president. Secretary of State Dulles warned the president that the Haile Selassie letter complained of paltry U.S. aid and was written before the emperor was made aware of the magnitude of the U.S. aid program for fiscal year 1957. Without admitting that the emperor's complaint was justified, Foster Dulles outlined the substantial increase in U.S. technical, military, and economic assistance to Ethiopia. Dulles concluded his memo to Eisenhower with this declaration:

> We expect that aid to Ethiopia in subsequent years will depend upon legislative authority, the availability of funds and Ethiopia's own capacity to support the resulting programs. You may wish to assure Senator Green that we are fully aware of the importance to the United States of Ethiopia's friendship and that we are making every effort within reason to meet the Emperor's requirements.[68]

In policy papers, American officials repeatedly stated that the only tension in U.S.-Ethiopia relations came with U.S. efforts "to discourage or moderate over-ambitious Ethiopian proposals involving U.S. economic and military aid." The drafters mentioned the Ethiopian assertion that the United States should provide more assistance to the Haile Selassie regime because it already gave more money to countries less friendly and loyal than Ethiopia.[69] Although this problem was not new, the Haile Selassie regime traced its frustrations with the Republican-run White House to perceived violations of the 1953 military base rights agreement. The State Department assured the White House that it would take steps to correct the emperor's mistaken impression.[70] Yet, this impression persisted.

In January 1957, President Eisenhower asked James P. Richards, the former chairman of the House Committee on Foreign Affairs, to "devise effective methods of cooperating with interested nations for the improvement of their security and for their economic progress." Acting under the auspices of Eisenhower's Middle East Doctrine, the Democrat from South Carolina was authorized to determine what countries wished to cooperate in this Free World collective security effort, and to make commitments for assistance within the limitation of funds appropriated by Congress. "When Ambassador Richards left the United States in March 1957, he was scheduled to visit only Lebanon, Libya and Turkey. By the time he completed his mission, he had visited fifteen countries, including Ethiopia."[71] Ambassador Richards's arrival in Addis Ababa portended a favorable reaction by the United States to the candid statements of Ethiopian officials during Vice President Nixon's sojourn there.

When Nixon arrived at the American Embassy in Addis Ababa on March 12, 1957, he was greeted by a large Ethiopian contingent, which included the Grand Negus. After a brief session with Prime Minister Bitwodded Makonnen Endalkatchew, Nixon then met with Haile Selassie himself. After expressing his gratitude that the vice president found time during his Africa trip to visit his nation, Haile Selassie indicated "that he would like to talk in a spirit of great frankness about the current state of U.S. Ethiopian relations." The emperor then launched into a long speech that outlined Ethiopia's frustrations with its relationship with America and the "Free World." After addressing the political capital expended by Ethiopia when siding with the West in various disputes of global concern, Haile Selassie focused the bulk of his remarks on the disappointing U.S. provision of arms. Selassie placed the American promises of military equipment and training in the simple context of a friendly barter:

> In the military field, His Imperial Majesty personally gave orders to grant U.S. requests for military facilities in Ethiopia although they far exceeded the original demands, have since been greatly augmented when it came to implementing the agreement, and have now been increased by yet further demands.

After outlining Ethiopia's domestic and foreign security needs, Haile Selassie summed up by saying that "notwithstanding the extreme urgency of these needs for military equipment, the response from the United States has been rather discouraging." In addition to what clearly appeared to be a paltry level of military aid, the emperor added the fact that the U.S. grant of military aid to Ethiopia was handled on a year-to-year basis, while U.S. privileges had been and were being sought on a long-term basis. Thus, the United States expected a long-term commitment from its ally while extending only imprecise, short-term subsidies in exchange. Selassie's remarks were augmented by a lengthy, detailed report on the "Defense Problems of Ethiopia," which Nixon included in his trip dossier to the president.[72]

This fifteen-page document, likely prepared by Minister of Defense Ras Abebe Arogay, provided exacting detail of the American provision of arms and the substandard quality of those munitions. The author indicated that the total amount of U.S. military support to Ethiopia from 1953 to 1956 pursuant to the Mutual Defense Assistance Agreement equaled $12,568,000. Of this amount, $9.6 million was dedicated to Army material. However, the author states that the actual amount of material received by Ethiopia was less than $8 million, and that a precise value was difficult to determine because of the unwillingness of American officials to provide, after repeated requests by the Ethiopian Chief of Staff, accurate prices for equipment actually delivered. Based upon the expectation of receiving only another $5 million for arms and officer training for the fiscal year 1956-1957, Ethiopian officials clearly expressed their dismay:

> In consequence Ethiopia has been allocated only 17,168,000 U.S.$ during the period following the agreement and of this, equipment of a value of but 7,925,000 U.S.$ has, actually, been received in Ethiopia. Had the original figure been kept to, Ethiopia would have been allocated a total of 25,000,000 U.S.$ in arms assistance. Hence the Imperial Government is not satisfied with the way in which the Mutual Defense Agreement has developed as far as allocation of money for armament is concerned.[73]

Yet, the Ethiopians did not feel cheated only because of the inadequate supply of promised weaponry.

The author of the report continued by citing numerous examples of the poor quality of the material and munitions proffered by the U.S.: "Most of this equipment has been previously used and, upon arrival, has been determined to be serviceable, only after extensive repairs. Spare parts have been forthcoming, but, in many instances, have proved to be unutilizable [sic] for rendering serviceable the equipment received." After mentioning balky American transport vehicles, the author turned to handheld weapons: "On the occasion of the Jubilee Celebrations of his Imperial Majesty a quantity sufficient to equip not even one division had been delivered, unfortunately the rifles were incomplete. The troops were, therefore, compelled to parade with old Czechoslovak rifles." In addition to this embarrassment, American ammunition supplied to Addis Ababa "had been previously used and recharged . . . or was outdated." Consequently, the Ethiopian Armed Forces had to rely more heavily upon their own munitions factory in the capital to build up stocks of ammunition. Unfortunately, even this effort was hamstrung because Washington had not answered their request for U.S. help in retooling and upgrading this facility.[74]

Aware that American officials had suggested that U.S. aid was limited to what the Ethiopian Army could effectively operate, the author noted "that the programs of supplies [had] been carefully limited, for the most part, to the simple and light equipment well within the capacity of the troops." This statement served as a segue, of sorts, to the issue of training. Although the author waited until later in the report to address specifically the inappropriate training of Ethiopian officers—"training . . . based on the facilities during peace and war of a great power of almost unlimited resources"—he did raise the effect of race on the training of Black officers in a White environment:

> However, the principal objection, as revealed by past experience, is that the frequent and unfortunate experiences of the Ethiopian Officers with segregation in the United States, have been such that the program is far from serving its designed purpose of fostering closer and more friendly relations as well as improving the technical standards of the Ethiopian Army.[75]

Again, this recounting of the shortcomings of U.S. military aid was placed within the context of Ethiopian security needs, as well as within the familiar Cold War paradigm.

Ethiopian anxiety was based upon historical conflicts and regional rivalries that predated the Cold War. The nation had "five thousand miles of border to defend, bordering five different territories, and a seacoast of seven hundred miles on one of the most important and strategic bodies of water on the globe." First, the Ethiopians were concerned with possible dismemberment of their nation in order to create Greater Somaliland, a project attributed largely to the British. Second, they were disturbed by Egyptian propaganda directed at the majority Muslim population of the Ogaden province. Such propaganda suggested not only that Muslims in Ethiopia were being poorly treated and needed to make common cause with Muslims worldwide but also that Ethiopia was simply a pawn of the West. Of course, this propaganda seemed even more credible because of Haile Selassie's cooperation with the West during the Suez crisis. As Nixon's report stated, "if Ethiopia is to give privileges to the U.S. fleet at Massawa, serious political repercussions may be expected at this time, both as regards other countries in the Middle East and public opinion in Ethiopia itself." Third, Ethiopia was aware of other American allies gaining greater aid from the United States, while other countries in the region were lavished with weapons provided by the Soviet Union.[76]

In addition to the fact that tiny Transjordan received $25 million in military assistance annually, the Ethiopians asserted that Syria and Yemen received armaments from the U.S.S.R. in the amounts of $60 million and $7.5 million, respectively. Egypt, Ethiopia's chief rival, had received in the past year alone $450 million in military supplies. Adding insult to injury, "it should also be stressed that the arms deliveries as mentioned above, have as far as is known by the Imperial Government, been done without any demands for separate equivalent returns in the form of bases, etc." For the Ethiopians, the problem was threefold: (1) American military support was insufficient in exchange for U.S. military privileges; (2) the inadequacy of American support left Ethiopia vulnerable to attack by surrounding nations; (3) Ethiopia's weakness in the region was also an American weakness in the battle with the Soviet Union. This was particularly troubling to the Ethiopians because they believed that, of all the countries of the Middle East, theirs was the one "having the longest military traditions . . . the other regions having been, until recently, all colonial territories." In addition to concerns about American assistance for the development of infrastructure, education, and health, these shortcomings caused the imperial government to consider a complete reassessment of its relationship with the West.[77] Thus, the Ethiopians likely interpreted Ambassador Richards's visit as a positive response to their candor.

By 1956, American officials knew of Ethiopia's concerns about American indifference.[78] Yet, according to Eisenhower's recollection, the Richards Mission as originally conceived did not plan a stop in Addis Ababa. Ambassador Richards arrived in Addis Ababa roughly a month after Nixon's departure.[79] The fact that the Richards Mission visit to Ethiopia followed so closely on the heels of Nixon's visit was likely intended to encourage the Ethiopians to think that America was being responsive to their concerns. Because Ethiopian officials had indicated to their American counterparts their disappointment with U.S. military aid, Washington had hoped that the Richards Mission would abate concerns in Addis Ababa:

> The Richards Mission offered supplementary military assistance totaling [sic] $3 million and assistance in the establishment of broadcasting facilities costing $1 million, $200,000 for police equipment, police training up to $200,000, two helicopters and possibly cereals for famine relief under PL 480.

As Ambassador Richards concluded his assignment, the OCB acknowledged that the promises of the Richards Mission were intended to assuage Haile Selassie's frustration regarding low levels of U.S. aid and to strengthen Ethiopia's alignment with the West: "The Emperor had made strong pleas to Vice President Nixon and others before him for a substantially larger U.S. military assistance program. He also expressed dissatisfaction at the quality of equipment being provided and the slowness of deliveries."[80] Additionally, administration officials hoped that deliveries of material would be expedited "under a new higher priority designation for Ethiopia."[81] Based upon prior aid levels, the new commitment to aid may have seemed significant.

The July 1958 OCB report implied that the United States had not honored its promises. In direct reference to the Richards Mission, the Ethiopians claimed that Ambassador Richards promised a short-wave international-type facility while the United States was now saying that it would provide a medium-wave system geared for domestic use.[82] More importantly, the American requirement for counterpart funding, "a standard American technique to retain control over the monies and to test the sincerity of a recipient country," made American aid seem more like an anchor than a life preserver.[83]

American funding to Ethiopia was limited by Washington's conviction in African inferiority. As OCB staffers noted, "the U.S. must ensure that its actions are within the capacity of semi-primitive people to absorb them, and are directed toward an orderly development of that country." Given that the American aim was to direct aid toward internal security, Americans were concerned about the quality of Ethiopian security forces. Although admittedly loyal to the emperor, these units had "few capabilities for the investigation and surveillance of subversive activity and espionage. Salaries are low [and] the average enforcement officer is uneducated."[84] Even after the completion of the Richards Mission, OCB staffers concluded that one of the factors explaining Ethiopia's increasing demands for U.S. assistance was that the Haile Selassie regime had "little, if any, disposition to consider their ability to absorb and make effective use of increased military assistance."[85]

This conclusion seems surprising given the widely respected performance of Ethiopian troops in Korea and the uniformly high quality of the Ethiopian students who trained in the United States. Apparently, American officials did reserve some respect for the imperial bodyguard. The attribution of positive qualities to this elite squad alone—as if they were an aberration—bears a striking resemblance to the idea of the Good Black in the White imagination.

Undoubtedly, American military assistance to Ethiopia supported Washington's global objectives. Two geopolitical pillars established the boundaries for American aid to Ethiopia: (1) doing enough to maintain Ethiopia in a pro-West posture for America's global credibility; and (2) doing enough to maintain American base rights in the region. Admittedly, the Eisenhower administration followed this tack, in part, because of its concerns over Ethiopia's rivalries with Egypt and a potential Somali state. Although American officials disliked the Nasser government, they did not want this to be known, thereby giving fuel both to critics of the West and to leaders of the nonaligned movement. The fear was that if Ethiopia acted directly against Egypt, Ethiopia's posture as a pro-Western nation naturally would lead foreign observers to see U.S. complicity—or at least approval—of those actions.

The United States also did not want to become too closely identified with Ethiopian propaganda and expansionism for fear of antagonizing both Egypt and the potentially independent Somalia.[86] Additionally, Washington's emphasis on Ethiopia's internal security was geared toward entrenching its prototypical African strongman. American officials were aware of Haile Selassie's modernization project. They hoped to protect this centralization of power in the emperor's hands, thereby securing Ethiopia's allegiance to the Free World. However, Washington's attitude toward Ethiopia also grew from concerns about the supposedly insatiable desires of Blacks.

In addition to the aforementioned justifications for limited military aid to Ethiopia, the White House used the excuse of Ethiopia's inconsistent appreciation of the significance of a Communist threat, especially as Washington became aware of increasing Communist activities in Ethiopia, to justify low levels of aid.[87] As addressed in the preceding chapter, the United States was unwilling to support economic development for an African country that would not remain loyal to the West. Since Ethiopia had remained unquestioningly pro-West throughout the 1950s, perhaps Washington was peeved that Haile Selassie insisted on an independence of action.

Frustrated by what he perceived as American insincerity, Haile Selassie visited Moscow in 1959 and signed two major loan agreements: (1) a one hundred million ruble loan from Soviet Union and (2) a twenty million dollar line of credit from the Czechoslovakian government.[88] Haile Selassie's hand was forced by a confluence of events: the Ethiopian economy had been staggered by low global coffee prices; in the meantime, drought and famine in Tigre and Wello provinces tore at the nation's social and economic fabric. American demands for matching funds from Addis Ababa further strained a buckling infrastructure.[89] Although American officials were alarmed at Ethiopian overtures toward the Soviet bloc, the irony was that their behavior toward Ethiopia had actually fostered Communist influence at the highest level of Ethiopian government, as well as with the restive populations controlled by Haile Selassie's U.S.-funded internal security program.

Any consternation about Ethiopia leaving its Western orbit was allayed a year later. The Ethiopians supported America's position at the Law of the Seas Conference. Perhaps more importantly, Ethiopia supported the United States/United Nations position in the Congo.[90] At around the same time, August 1960, the Ethiopians requested an American to assist in the operation of their banking system.[91]

The discussions in NSC meetings and OCB reports regarding Ethiopia and the Richards Mission focused on Ethiopia's irritation with America's broken promises. Although the tone of official, internal discourse was dismissive, almost none of the comments denied Ethiopia's version of the commitments nor suggested that Richards had exceeded his authorization. More importantly, American officials were convinced that the Ethiopians tended to overreach. "A continuing problem facing the U.S.," wrote an analyst, "is Ethiopia's penchant for seeking special treatment in connection with various matters."[92] This sentiment was echoed a few years later by then-Secretary of State Herter.

When Secretary Herter sent a telegram to Prime Minister Aklilou via the U.S. Embassy in Ethiopia regarding issues raised during the Aklilou-Eisenhower conversation of September 1960, he added a confidential note to embassy personnel that indicated his concern for Ethiopian ingratitude:

> When you deliver above message you should tell Prime Minister we were very pleased meet with him in New York and were greatly impressed by his statement that it is Ethiopian policy to support the Secretary General on all broad questions concerning the United Nations. It is view of U.S. that all those of us who wish work through United Nations should maintain solid front against those who wish destroy it or who defy it. We cannot fail mention at this time therefore our disappointment that this year Ethiopia for first time voted against resolution that question of Chinese representation not be considered. American Congress and people who have so far given their support to special consideration accorded Ethiopia will find it difficult to understand Ethiopia's position on question to which U.S. attaches such great importance.[93]

Consequently, the strain on Ethiopian-American relations resulted, in large part, from the American belief that the Ethiopians asked for more assistance than they deserved and that those requests were based on insignificant rivalries and jealousies. In this light, any Ethiopian deviation from unquestioned support for the United States looked like ingratitude or a betrayal.

## At the Crossroads

Near the end of the Eisenhower administration, the cracks in the relationship between Ethiopia and the United States widened slightly. In November 1960, rumors that Emperor Haile Selassie had died briefly circulated through Western media. In particular, Haile Selassie was disturbed that the rumor had emerged from members in the Eisenhower administration. According to a State Department memorandum, the emperor's main "concern [was] based on a fear that the United States received the story from a source involved in or aware of a plot against his life." Secretary of State Herter explained to the president his fear that a true recounting of the actual missteps by American officials might heighten Haile Selassie's concerns and cause him to lose faith in the American Embassy contingent in Addis Ababa. Herter attached a proposed message of assurance to Haile Selassie, which Eisenhower signed with minor revisions:

> Ambassador Richards has communicated to me your understandable concern over the recent false report of Your Imperial Majesty's death . . . Because some news sources seemed to point to the State Department as the origin of the rumor, I have had a thorough investigation made. No additional specific information has been

uncovered in this connection, but as a result of my investigation, I can assure Your Imperial Majesty that I am satisfied there was no political motivation of any kind whatever involved. There is no doubt, however, but that newsmen, by their questioning, unintentionally propagated the story to the point where it became necessary for the department to determine its validity . . . If it was Your Imperial Majesty's concern that unfriendly sources in Addis Ababa might for ulterior motives have planted such false information with our Embassy there, I am happy to assure you that such was not the case. Nor is there any indication whatever that this report is related in any way to possible designs against Your Imperial Majesty.

Haile Selassie's reply suggested that he accepted the White House's explanation.[94] However, a few weeks later, the emperor's fears seemed to manifest themselves.

On December 13, 1960, a group of rebels composed of students and members of the Imperial Guard seized control of the government while the emperor was in Brazil. Although Emperor Haile Selassie regained power four days later, the threat to the stability of the emperor's regime shook the nation.[95] In response, Haile Selassie abandoned his efforts at economic development and concentrated more effort on the police and military.[96] President Eisenhower, apprised of the situation by the State Department, wrote the emperor and expressed his delight that Haile Selassie had returned home safely from South America with his power intact.[97]

The preceding analysis of American foreign policy toward Ethiopia reveals the numerous ways that race and racism influenced diplomacy. As with the racial interest convergences within the United States, an examination from a critical race theory perspective illuminates the limits of similar global intersections of interests. The Eisenhower administration supported decolonization in Africa in the hope of securing Africa's place at the bottom of the Free World hierarchy. With a properly subordinated Africa, the United States hoped to defeat the Soviet Union in the contest known as the Cold War. To effect this subordination, American officials dealt harshly with one of their staunchest allies.

American support for African political independence required that Africans subordinate their interests and concerns to those of the West. Washington's concerns about premature independence and the alleged need to teach Africans about responsible government were not reserved for Africans living under imperialism. The semiprimitive Ethiopians were seen as nearly as untrustworthy as the Cameroonians or the Congolese. As a result of policies colored by Whiteness, the United States effectively undermined the ideas of freedom and democracy which it preached.

Yet another way of understanding the stultifying effects of American diplomacy toward Ethiopia is to proceed from the perspective of gender. Therefore, at the first cut, it is necessary to examine masculinity and its manifestations in the relationship between American and Ethiopian men. Less conspicuous but equally compelling is a gendered assessment of Eisenhower administration policy toward Ethiopia and Ghana. An analysis of America's diplomacy toward this independent African state supports the hypothesis that interest convergences offer little benefit to Black women.[98] In addition, a critique of the discourse regarding American aid to Africa reveals the projection of American (i.e., White) masculinity onto the international scene, along with the challenge from Black masculinity.

## Whiteness and the Right to Define and Shape the World

Following his trip to Africa, Vice President Nixon penned a report to the president that offered a factual overview of his conversations with African dignitaries, as well as analysis of the current diplomatic posture of the United States and suggestions for future policy. Unlike OCB and NSC staffers who conceived of limiting American military aid to Ethiopia strictly for internal security purposes, Nixon thought that Ethiopia's positive military and diplomatic support for collective security warranted a reassessment of Defense Department attitudes toward Addis Ababa. Thus, his report entertained the possibility that it might be in America's military interest to build "an efficient fighting force in Ethiopia."[99] In contrast to his concern for how the Ethiopians might best satisfy American needs, Nixon seemed to dismiss Ethiopian concerns.

To his credit, Nixon mentioned Ethiopian fears regarding the influence of Egyptian propaganda on its Muslim population. Further, he gave his view that upcoming elections were merely window dressing for a regime more interested in maintaining the political status quo. In addition, Nixon asserted that the emperor's government was more interested in building its armed forces than in political, economic, or social reform. Yet, despite his perceptiveness in some regards, he described the tension between Washington and Addis Ababa as if it were simply the result of confusion—or deceit—on the part of the Ethiopians:

> There have been in recent years a series of misunderstandings between the United States and Ethiopia. The Ethiopians maintain, *for whatever motives*, that we are not living up to the impressions they received regarding our plans and intentions at the time of the base agreement in 1953 and the Emperor's visit to Washington . . . The Emperor made this case very forcibly to me and emphasized the need for a re-examination of relations between our two countries. I am assured that there has been no failure on our part to live up to our promises and I believe that many of the difficulties which have arisen are the result of misunderstandings which must be set straight as rapidly as possible.[100]

Granted, Nixon's comments on Ethiopia are only about a page in length, but there is no mention of Ethiopia's concerns about Great Britain and Somalia, Haile Selassie's explicitly expressed interest in development loans, or the domestic and international criticism Ethiopia had sustained for its pro-Western position.

At the very least, Nixon could have mentioned in general terms Ethiopian dissatisfaction with the provision of arms by the United States. Given both Haile Selassie's lengthy speech and the fifteen-page report appended to Nixon's report, Nixon had ample evidence of Ethiopians' impressions of the U.S. aid effort. Even with the assurances that the United States had abided by the terms of its agreements with Ethiopia, Nixon could have acknowledged the seriousness of Ethiopian concerns for receiving war material that was obsolete or barely maintainable and delivered slowly. However, from his perspective, the Ethiopians had no valid reasons for concern.

In contrast to the Ethiopian view of themselves as partly African and partly Middle Eastern, American policymakers generally considered Ethiopia an African nation. Americans attributed to Ethiopians all of the supposed defects inherent in Blackness. Accordingly, Ethiopians were simply an asset over which the United States exercised control, a pawn in this contest with the Soviet bloc. This White entitlement to define the world as one saw fit, exempt from alternative viewpoints, was so powerful that the construction of hospitals and showing of films by the Soviet Union and other members of the Eastern bloc was akin to "probing for weaknesses."[101] The Ethiopians not only had to accept Washington's perceptions of international affairs; they also had to sacrifice their interests in order to follow Washington's lead.

## Ethiopian Self-Abnegation

The demand for Black self-abnegation is evident in the tensions between Ethiopia's conception of its security needs and the U.S. definition of Ethiopia's real problems. The Ethiopians viewed their problems as largely external, while the Americans saw exactly the opposite. Unlike the spirit of compromise which Eisenhower invoked when corresponding with Haile Selassie about the critical vote at the Law of the Seas Conference, American planners insisted that joint relations would have proceeded much more smoothly if Ethiopians had adopted the American view of the situation:

> In order to improve the political feasibility of directing U.S. aid under this program toward first civil police needs, and second, regular military needs, an effort must be made to bring the Ethiopian Government *to recognize and accept* internal security as the primary mission of its armed forces.[102]

Although American officials paid lip service to the notion that democracy might flower in Ethiopia, the major concern was protecting the regime of the Grand Negus.[103] Thus, the bulk of American assistance to Ethiopia was military assistance aimed at controlling a potentially restive population: "The suppression of organized insurrection requires in addition to police-type action military type-action, which can be effectively conducted only by regular military forces." Thus, OCB staffers worried that the Ethiopian military could not protect the emperor's throne. Given the American disregard for "the general capability of the security force to cope with subversion, whether subtle penetration or widespread insurrection," they advised an emphasis on counterinsurgency training. "Preparation for guerrilla-type warfare should be the guiding criterion for the Ethiopian Armed Forces. These forces are presently in need of modern type arms and equipment as well as special training in order to be able to conduct effective counter-guerrilla campaigns or engage in guerrilla warfare if attacked externally."[104]

Thus, there was no concern in Washington for Haile Selassie's priorities or for the people who were enduring the emperor's modernization project. There seemed to be little concern even for those Ethiopian elites whom the Eisenhower administration had come to know and who seemed dissatisfied with political developments under Haile Selassie. The most important thing in the minds of American officials was that Ethiopia remain pro-West. To their minds, the best way to ensure that result was by firming the iron hand of the emperor, even if it seemed to be a short-term solution.

## The Irrelevance of Women in Ethiopia

Women played a significant economic role in Ethiopia. Yet, prior to European imperialism Africa was not, in the words of Bernard Magubane, "an eldorado of egalitarianism."[105] American diplomacy continued the marginalization of African women and exacerbated existing gender hierarchies within these countries. American foreign economic policy worsened the social position of women by hardening the asymmetrical system of obligations and reciprocities.[106]

Throughout Africa, "the great majority of . . . women are farmers."[107] In Ethiopia, women workers played the critical role of farmers of both cash and food crops. They played significant roles in "construction of housing, land cultivation, harvesting, food storage, and marketing."[108] Equally important, Ethiopian women—especially Amharic and Oromo—participated as soldiers in times of conflict. Despite a 1930 provision prohibiting women from engaging in combat, thousands of women fought during the Italian invasion and the subsequent guerilla wars. Case studies by Tsehai Berhane-Selassie prove that Ethiopian women's status declined steadily throughout the Cold War, a time marked by governmental insecurity and repeated challenges to social and political authority. Not surprisingly, the emperor's regime routinely excluded Ethiopian women from access to political power.[109] As workers, they bore the brunt of the nation's economic and natural catastrophes.

The famine, drop in world coffee prices, and civil disturbances of the 1950s wrought havoc with their lives. The financial reward for women's labor greatly declined. The famine meant less food for everyone in a household but certainly less for mothers and daughters. Drought also led to soil depletion and deforestation. Since women farmers typically worked less fertile land than men, they were the most adversely effected by natural disasters and the lack of governmental or international assistance.[110] In addition, deforestation forced women workers to expend greater time and resources procuring fuel sources and transporting them to market or home.[111] Insurrections and protests against the government of Haile Selassie brought increased duties and dangers: with men no longer in the home, women had to assume male tasks in addition to the heavy responsibilities they already bore; they also were vulnerable, alone or as part of a group, to physical and sexual abuse.[112]

Interestingly, the dislocation of Amhara under the emperor's modernization project resulted in the explosion of prostitution among all women, but especially Amharic women. Further, the oppression of the Oromo—exacerbated by U.S. aid which focused on the suppression of rebellion, rather than the expansion of democracy—hampered the ability of Oromo women to gain full political expression.

## Masculinity and American Foreign Aid

Taking a cue from Emily Rosenberg, one sees that the discourse of American aid to African nations contained competing and conflicting narratives of masculinity. In her presidential address before the Society for Historians of American Foreign Relations (SHAFR), Rosenberg stated, among other things, that the discourse on "dollar diplomacy" during the late nineteenth and early twentieth centuries contained a masculine narrative that identified the notions of American lending and supervision of borrowing nations with manliness. Although the exigencies of the Cold War prevented the Eisenhower administration from engaging in precisely the same practices as the Taft, Roosevelt, and Wilson administrations, the provision of American aid in the 1950s was no less masculine.

Ethiopia's criticisms of U.S. aid packages focused on several issues. To the Haile Selassie government, America provided poor-quality material in low quantities and did all of this in a seemingly haphazard fashion. A second level of criticism focused on the Ethiopian impression that their country received a pittance when compared to international aid to other nations less committed to the Free World. In addition, Ethiopian diplomats communicated their disappointment that the United States had not fulfilled the promises of the Richards Mission. In each of these arguments regarding the type, quality, and amount of American aid, Ethiopia challenged the American ideal of objectivity and impartiality. Moreover, Haile Selassie countered the American discourse by seeking funds from the Soviet bloc. As such, Haile Selassie refuted any American fantasies of African impotence and dependency by revealing his willingness to seek alternative sources of aid.

## Conclusion

The sad postscript suggests that Ethiopian projections of masculinity—tolerable to Washington when done internally—on behalf of its nationalist undertakings strained relations with the United States. The ossification of gender stratification in the Horn of Africa was, in part, the result of the increasing impositions of global capitalism.[113] Interestingly, Ethiopia's allegiance to the West garnered surprisingly few benefits. The upshot was that American officials demanded unquestioning obedience from their African counterparts. In return, Ethiopia received support that actually caused further dissension within the nation. Addis Ababa's fragile control over its multiethnic state slid as central government repression increased. Notably, the embitterment of Ethiopian women aided the growing resistance to the Haile Selassie government in the early 1960s.[114] Thus, American diplomacy toward Ethiopia helped destabilize a friendly government.

# CHAPTER FOUR

# LESS THAN STRANGERS: GHANA AND THE UNITED STATES

## Ghana: An Introduction

Like Ethiopia, Ghana had a strong leader with his own strategy for the nation's advancement. As delineated in chapter 2, official American policy toward decolonization in Africa did not allow for Black self-determination. As a result, this conformist U.S. strategy—girded by White Supremacist notions—made Ghanaian nonalignment untenable for Washington.

American relations with Ghana, though officially friendly, were decidedly cool. In fact, in the years following the Eisenhower administration, the relationship turned hostile as Ghana continued to challenge the East-West dialectic of U.S. diplomacy.[1] American diplomats and planners in the Eisenhower administration, though unfamiliar with West Africa, worried about the politics of Kwame Nkrumah and the Pan-Africanist model which was Ghana. As a result, the United States was reluctant to aid Ghana in any way that might suggest a break from the pattern of African subordination to the West.

## A Brief History of Ghana

The peoples of modern-day Ghana come from nearly one hundred different ethnic groups. They emerged from political entities like the Gonja, Dagomba, and Nanumba kingdoms or the city-states of the Ewe and the Nzima.[2] By the early nineteenth century, the competing empires of the Asante confederation of the north and the southern Fante states dominated the political environment. In fact, the Fante states were so sophisticated that they changed forms and aligned with other states like the Wassa and Akyem in order to meet the challenge to the north.[3]

Europeans entered the picture in the fifteenth century as the Portuguese noble Prince Henry the Navigator made contact along Africa's shores as a way of circumventing Moorish control of the Iberian peninsula and the Islamic trading routes of North Africa and Southwest Asia. European encroachment resulted in wars between the Portuguese, Dutch, and British, as well as among the indigenous nations in the area. The accumulation of wealth and weaponry by entities like the Asante empire temporarily balanced the struggles between indigenous peoples and foreigners.[4]

European conquest of modern-day Ghana hardly was inevitable. In fact, the uncertainty meant that British control came as a result of centuries of contacts, treaties, and bloody skirmishes.[5] British hegemony was secured only over a period of time, starting with a succession of nineteenth-century military campaigns known as the Ashanti Wars and ending with peace negotiations following victories in 1896 and 1900. The wars between the Asante and the Fante also served to increase British influence in the area. The British expansion of the colony crossed further ethnic and geographical lines, adding even more diversity to the subject population. British administration of the colony meant a continued policy of using ethnicity to undermine collective action. For instance, the British encouraged and recognized the reformation of the Asante Confederacy in 1935. In contrast, professionals and students gained political power as part of an anticolonial, multiethnic vanguard. Given Britain's historical reliance upon the divide-and-conquer strategy amongst the peoples of the region, British governmental support for ethnic loyalty is best understood as a means of preventing political integration and unification of diverse groups around the idea of collective independence.[6]

Nationalist fervor in the interwar years surfaced throughout the Gold Coast as urban dwellers and rural peasants alike protested living conditions as well as the absence of power to change them. As with much of West Africa, popular grievances centered around "land, taxation, education, indirect rule, limited economic growth and foreign economic domination, [and] racism," as well as self-rule.[7] In addition to British intransigence, the most difficult obstacles facing Ghanaian nationalists were the political cleavages between their diverse peoples.[8]

Radicals like Wallace Johnson tried to bridge these gaps by organizing workers and youth and emphasizing local as well as international issues like the trial of the Scottsboro Boys and the Italian invasion of Ethiopia. Reformists groups like the Gold Coast Youth Conference, though elitist, explicated a critique of alien economic domination that was understood by Ghanaians of all stripes.[9] By the 1940s, people in the Gold Coast were preparing for independence. The only question was whether Britain was equally ready.

## Nkrumah and Pan-Africanism

Kwame Nkrumah was born in 1903, well after the close of the tremendous military activity by his people. Nevertheless, he grew up in a tumultuous atmosphere. Historian John Henrik Clarke describes the British colony of the Gold Coast as "a colony whose people never acknowledged their colonial status. In the Ashanti Wars and the subsequent revolts, the people let it be known that they would never live peacefully under foreign domination." Thus, Nkrumah "grew to manhood while the agitation against the restrictions of colonial rule was being converted into agitation for eventual independence."[10]

Nkrumah left Ghana in 1935 and ventured to the United States, where he enrolled in Pennsylvania's Lincoln University, a historically Black university. He also earned an M.A. from the University of Pennsylvania. His sojourn out of Africa led him to Europe as well.[11] It was during this period, as Italy invaded Ethiopia, that the kernels of a philosophy began to develop. His formal training was supplemented by the informal education he received in Harlem and London as he met and talked with other Africans, African Americans, and Black British about the conditions of the global Black community. As Clarke noted, during the "depression years Nkrumah began to learn how hard it was for black people in [the United States] just to stay alive and support their families."[12]

Nkrumah returned to Ghana in 1947 and—following a split from the nationalist but moderate United Gold Coast Convention (the UGCC)—founded the Convention People's Party (the CPP). Just a year before his return, Britain began a campaign of Africanization with regard to colonial political control. British concessions were cold comfort to a population growing increasingly restive as the mother country bled Ghana for its own economic rebuilding. The violence of the colonial administration during the 1948 economic riots—which led to Nkrumah's arrest—and the "resentment against the British government for using the Cocoa Marketing Board to skim off much of the profit from African cocoa farmers" proved a lightning rod for radical nationalists like Nkrumah. Although he was arrested for his political activities and the UGCC disassociated itself from him, Nkrumah's popularity skyrocketed.[13]

Nkrumah skillfully maneuvered through the class and ethnic divisions within the colony to insist upon self-rule. This dramatic stand exposed the snail-paced reforms of the British government, and the CPP program of Positive Action galvanized those both inside and outside of the elite or political class. Nkrumah also carefully read British domestic politics. Knowing that the Labour Party still held a majority in Parliament, and that the Gold Coast colonial administration was accountable to Parliament, Nkrumah implemented his radical, nonviolent approach both to inspire the indigenous populations and to gain sympathy in London. Nkrumah and the CPP won the 1951 elections in a landslide, defeating the more conservative indigenous elements and forcing Britain to recognize their mass appeal. A year later, Nkrumah became the first African prime minister in the British Commonwealth.[14]

With the aid of able organizers like Kojo Botsio and Komlo Gbedemah, Nkrumah continued to build the CPP, whose object was to fight for self-government for the Gold Coast and lift the colonial mountain of British, French, and Portuguese rule off the collective backs of Africans.[15] Nkrumah's Pan-Africanism was not simply a vacuous ploy but an ideology conceived from theory and cross-border human suffering. This vision was born from his experiences abroad, as well as his political apprenticeship back home, bridging the political rifts in indigenous societies that had thwarted so many others. Even his marriage to an Egyptian woman symbolized his belief in trans-Saharan, continental solidarity.[16]

What was it about Nkrumah and Ghana that made one American official describe him as terrifying?[17] First, Nkrumah's Pan-Africanist philosophy contained a withering critique of both imperialism and capitalism:

> We have demonstrated that the imperial powers will never give up their political and economic dominance over their colonies until they are compelled to do so. The growth of the national liberation movement in the colonies reveals: (1) The contradiction among the various foreign powers and the colonial imperialist powers in their struggle for sources of raw materials and for territories. In this sense imperialism and colonialism become the export of capital to sources of raw materials, the frenzied and heartless struggle for monopolist possession of these sources [and] the struggle for a redivision of the already divided world . . . (2) The contradictions between the handful of ruling "civilized" nations and the millions of colonial peoples of the world. In this sense imperialism is the most degrading exploitation and the most inhuman oppression of the millions of peoples living in the colonies. The purpose of this exploitation and oppression is to squeeze out superprofits. The inevitable results of imperialism thus are: (a) the emergence of a colonial intelligentsia, (b) the awakening of national consciousness among colonial peoples, (c) the emergence of a working class movement, and (d) the growth of a national liberation movement.[18]

Second, Nkrumah envisioned Ghana as a template for revolutionary struggle throughout Africa. The prime minister "made his country the rallying point and the inspiration for African [peoples] who had to win their freedom."[19] Yet, Nkrumah was not content as a symbolic champion. Because Ghana was the first country in tropical Africa to attain independence through its own exertions, Nkrumah came to regard this priority in time as giving Ghana the status of prototype, a road which all African territories must travel, a vanguard of the African revolution. There can be little doubt that Nkrumahism, which he propagated as the ideology of the African revolution, was an attempt to distill his own experiences within diasporic Black communities and the Gold Coast/Ghana into a coherent doctrine for the liberation and development of dependent African territories. Because all along he saw Africa as a single society or a nation, he was emboldened to regard methods and tactics that had proved viable in his own corner of the continent as applicable to the rest of Africa.[20]

Third, Nkrumah acted affirmatively and decisively to bridge the differences between the diverse peoples of Ghana and the continent. Nkrumah's broad appeal within the Gold Coast forced the British to negotiate with him despite their qualms:

> The British would greatly have preferred to negotiate with the "good boys" of the UGCC, but these were powerless. Like it or not, they would negotiate with Nkrumah. The whole question was: could they negotiate with him? Would he prove "sensible," this man of fiery reputation and "communist" associations?[21]

In short, Nkrumah embodied the most significant threat from Africa of the 1950s to Washington's global sanctuary. His rhetoric was a rejection of bilateralism, an indictment of global capitalism, and a philippic against global White oppression of non-White peoples. By his actions, Nkrumah worked toward a collective liberation of Africans from the supposedly beneficial ties with its former colonizers. The synergy from Pan-Africanism's discursive, intellectual, and practical support for African decolonization is exemplified by Ghana's foreign relations on the continent.

Ghana's financial and moral support amplified the stirrings of independence throughout West Africa. Nkrumah envisioned a political union of West African states as a nucleus for continental unity.[22] The prime minister labored with Arab leaders to such an extent that, through his efforts in the Casablanca Group, he "was able to bridge the gap between the Africans and the Arabs in the continental politics of the early 1960s."[23] He was especially effective in assisting the fledgling movements in central Africa, by helping to dismantle the Central African Federation and aiding Zaire's rise from colonial bondage. If nothing else, Nkrumah's belief that he could do so much to aid his fellow Africans was a dramatic boost to African self-respect.[24] Nkrumah also had a special concern for the colonial situation in East Africa. Ghana's foreign policy within Africa is best highlighted by his diplomacy towards the peoples to Ghana's east and south.

Nkrumah grounded his role as a continental bridge builder in his philosophy as well as in the practical desire to protect all of Africa's emerging nations from Western retribution. "The literature on the structural characteristics of African international relations invariably points to the influence of Nkrumah's Ghana in East Africa as a prototypical case of the creation of bridges between regions." Nkrumah worried about the strong possibilities of neocolonialist manipulations in East and Central Africa, given the existence of powerful European settlers, Asian capitalists, and a body of expatriate civil servants. "In particular, he was convinced that the architects of the disbanded Central African Federation . . . were determined to help create a new federal structure in East Africa from which they could stage a comeback and recoup the losses sustained from the mangled, racist, exploitive system in Central Africa."[25]

In April 1958, Nkrumah convened the initial Conference of Independent African States in Ghana's capital, Accra. The conference brought together the eight independent nations on the continent, with the exclusion of the Union of South Africa. The conference grappled with the issues of continental unity, imperialism and colonialism, African economic development, and apartheid in South Africa; combating global Communism was not a priority. A sign of the warm relations between East African nationalists and Nkrumaism was the presence of Julius Nyerere, Joseph Murumbi, and Sheikh Mushin as observers. A further indication of Nkruma's influence is the fact that only after this and other gatherings did East African nationalists become Pan-Africanists.[26]

Nkrumahism, however, was not universally welcomed in Africa. Some nationalists, like those in Nigeria, opposed Pan-Africanism on functionalist grounds: "Nigeria's position was that economic integration must precede political union and that economic integration itself must begin at the sub-regional level and proceed in stages beginning with functional co-operation and co-ordination and leading towards, perhaps, a common market." Although Nigeria cooperated with

Ghana on some levels, most conservative governments were scared by Nkrumah's so-called socialism, while others were reluctant to support a United States of Africa.[27] Further, since many were just beginning to taste self-government anew, they were unwilling to cede power to a federal authority. American officials relied on Black criticisms of Pan-Africanism to delegitimize Nkrumah's liberatory project.[28]

Nevertheless, Nkrumah posed a serious danger to American objectives throughout the continent. What distinguished Nkrumah from other African leaders was that he was the first head of state to articulate and execute a holistic approach for continent-wide revival: "Despite all the divisions between the various African blocs, the cause of African unity had made considerable progress since the [1945 Pan-African] Manchester Congress." The fact that the Pan-Africanist ideology "derived from an elaborate criticism of what was wrong with the African situation universally, as well as from an elucidation of the tragic gap separating the vast opportunities and possibilities that exist for the advancement and dignification of the African people," meant that Nkrumah's message of collective self-determination had great appeal throughout the continent. Even Emperor Haile Selassie echoed the Pan-Africanist tenor of the Accra Conference when he convened the May 1963 Addis Ababa Summit which resulted in the creation of the Organization of African Unity:

> What we still lack despite the efforts of the past years, is the mechanism which will enable us to speak with one voice when we wish to do so and to make important decisions on African problems when we are so minded.

To the Eisenhower administration and others, Nkrumah represented the symbolic and substantive blade, which could sever the essential ties between Africa and Europe. For the West, undermining Nkrumah's credibility and Ghana's potential became a critical objective.[29]

## Accra and Washington

The papers and notes from Department of State personnel and National Security Council meetings indicate a real concern in official circles about both Nkrumah/Pan-Africanism and the imagined susceptibility of the Ghanaians to Soviet influence. In the minds of those in Washington, the supposed malleability of Nkrumah and other radicals masked the legitimacy of the Ghanaian struggle and the authenticity of indigenous solutions for nation-building. Their dominant gaze affirmed their stereotypes of Nkrumah and his people as truths.[30] As previously noted, Washington identified most non-White autonomy-seeking movements as Marxist-controlled.[31] This American construction of African self-determination applied to Ghana as well.

Beneath a welcoming facade, Americans were distrustful of Nkrumah's Ghana. Superficially, Americans extended open arms to the Nkrumah government. In turn,

Ghana cooperated with the United States on certain issues and kept Washington abreast of its internal political achievements.[32] However, diplomatic pleasantries masked Washington's disrespect and fear of Nkrumah.

## The Politics of Self-Abnegation and the Dominant Gaze

Politically, Washington was as unprepared to accept unconditional African independence as it was to accept Black equality at home. Again, the men who drafted, discussed, and implemented NSC 5719/1 conceived of Africans south of the Sahara as generally unable to rule themselves. Although NSC 5719/1 gives only passing mention to Ghana, later planning papers provide a more detailed assessment.

Initially, American analysts were cautiously optimistic that the United States could maneuver Ghana into a Free World orbit. A 1958 OCB Progress Report on NSC 5719/1 stated that Ghana had "shown the expected growing pains presumably associated with newly independent states and that there had been signs of authoritarianism and neutralism." Although the growing pains were interpreted by Americans as a struggle of Blacks to grasp the concepts of governance and representative democracy, Nkrumah's biographer indicates that the real struggle was the destitution of the Ghanaian people as a result of colonialism.[33] American belief in African inferiority, coupled with the misconception that the British had paved the way for African self-rule, convinced White Americans that Black independence was problematic. Increased trade between Ghana and the Soviet Union also worried American officials. Additionally, the OCB's favorable assessment of Washington's influence on Accra buttressed the American notion that Nkrumah's policy of nonalignment could be manipulated by non-Africans.[34]

These overestimates of American power and Soviet intent, along with underestimates of African competence, justified America's desire to maintain the bonds between former colonial master and servant.[35] Moreover, they blinded the United States to the things Ghana needed. British historian Basil Davidson remarked that:

> It would be said that Africans had been given the great good fortune of receiving self-rule and independence on a golden dish, polished, shining, and fit for many years use. The truth was different. The dish they were handed in 1951, and again in 1957, was old, cracked and little fit for any further use. Worse than that, it was not an empty dish. For it carried the junk and jumble of a century of colonial muddle and "make do," and this the CPP ministers had to accept along with the dish itself. What shone upon its golden surface was not the reflection of new ideas and liberation, but the shadow of old ideas of servitude.[36]

By late 1959, warning bells began ringing in official circles regarding Communist influence on Ghana. Although Americans in Accra acknowledged that Ghana would probably maintain its policy of nonalignment, they were concerned over the trend in Ghana-Soviet relations: "Embassy Accra . . . feels that Ghana may get so involved with the Bloc that the situation will get out of hand." Again, the notion that developments in Ghana might get out of hand is plausible if one believes, as American officials did, that the Nkrumah administration was childlike and impressionable.[37]

Even after Nkrumah and the CPP had nearly ten years of administrative experience under their belts, the Eisenhower administration still conceived of the Nkrumah government as pliant. Prior to his meeting in the fall of 1960 with Nkrumah in New York—and as global delegations were preparing to discuss the Congo situation in the United Nations—Eisenhower was briefed by a State Department memo with talking points for the meeting. The memo prepared the president to discuss several issues with Nkrumah, notably efforts by the Soviet Union to influence the trajectory of Ghanaian politics and the alleged Communist plan to destabilize the country. The discourse of the memo not only characterized the Soviet Union as nearly omnipotent subversives but also cast Ghana as politically naive. After mentioning Ghana-Soviet agreements on trade, technical support, and education, along with the opening of the Chinese Embassy in Accra, Assistant Secretary of State Douglas Dillon charted for the president what he considered a predictable path of Soviet penetration:

> Following standard communist practice the Soviet Bloc is now working at an increasing rate toward expulsion of Western influence by: (1) goading anti-Western trends; (2) highlighting affinities between Ghana and the Communist world; and (3) offering economic opportunities and cultural exchanges with no ostensible strings attached. When the groundwork has been laid the USSR will: (1) foment internal disorder; (2) stimulate outside pressures to weaken the Government's position throughout Africa; and (3) complicate economic problems. The use of individual Ghanaians and groups favorable to the Communist cause would become vigorous and more overt. You may wish to cite the dangers of further involvement with the Soviet Bloc and urge President Nkrumah to minimize relations with the Soviet Bloc in the self-interest of Ghana.[38]

Although there appears to be no evidence to support Dillon's contentions, his fears of Nkrumah being hoodwinked by the Soviets may have come from his limited knowledge of Nkrumah. For example, the biographical sketch of the Pan-Africanist leader that was attached to Dillon's memo offers a reductionist explanation for Nkrumah's ascent to the pinnacle of Ghanaian politics: "Nkrumah has used his immense popularity and personal magnetism to attain the great political power he has today."[39] Thus, American officials were woefully ignorant of Nkrumah's intelligence and political savvy. Nevertheless, State Department preparations for the president's September 1960 meeting with Nkrumah foreshadowed a looming crisis in the relationship between the two countries. The political tensions between Accra and Washington were crystallized during the Congo crisis.

Although apparently uncertain about many of Nkrumah's strengths as a leader, the United States was well aware of Nkrumah's analysis of colonialism. However, their ire with the Pan-Africanist was not based upon rhetorical flourishes alone. Indeed, Eisenhower and his advisers despised Nkrumah because his analysis was correct, because he was publicly unveiling American duplicity, and because he often refused to comply with American dictates.[40] In the realm of White Supremacy, non-Whites are not allowed to observe and evaluate the actions of Whites, to gaze upon White behavior, or name it. Black self-abnegation includes turning one's eyes from Whites and silencing any criticism of them as well.[41]

As noted above, Nkrumah was especially critical of Western attempts to reinforce the political, social, and economic subjugation of Africa following the attainment of independence. His theory on neocolonialism, though scoffed at by contemporary critics, held that "any oblique attempt of a foreign power to thwart, balk, corrupt, or otherwise pervert the true independence of a sovereign people is neo-colonialist. It is neo-colonialist because it seeks, notwithstanding the acknowledged sovereignty of a people, to subordinate their interests to those of a foreign power."[42] To Nkrumah, neocolonialism was more dangerous than colonialism because it concealed the machinations and motivations of power and left the oppressed with little recourse to ease their suffering:

> Neo-colonialism is also the worst form of imperialism. For those who practise [sic] it, it means power without responsibility and for those who suffer from it, it means exploitation without redress. In the days of old-fashioned colonialism, the imperial power had at least to explain and justify at home the actions it was taking abroad. In the colony those who served the ruling imperial power could at least look to its protection against any violent move by their opponents. With neo-colonialism neither is the case.[43]

Nkrumah hypothesized that the pattern of balkanization taking place in central Africa was an effort by Western powers to retain economic spheres of influence on the continent.[44] Although official American policy denied this idea, Nkrumah correctly gauged American interest and intent with regard to the Congo.[45]

## The Crucible of the Congo

As will be demonstrated more fully in chapter 6, American official policy was to support Belgian interests in the Congo. As the Congo crisis unfolded, American officials acknowledged the legitimacy of Patrice Lumumba but worried about his political alignment. The fact that Lumumba was a leftist, presumably anti-Western, and allegedly obedient to Moscow, meant that the United States needed to find some way of undermining his power. Aware of the secession in the Katanga province and the Belgian military presence there, American officials saw another opportunity to implement their policy of maintaining the ties between Africans and their former colonizers. As a result, the United States hoped to use delay and, later, a United Nations-sponsored peacekeeping force as methods of strengthening Belgium's position in the Congo, especially in Katanga province. Of course, this approach was complicated by the need to conceal it from global scrutiny. Intensifying matters further was the Eisenhower administration's awareness that Nkrumah was acting as Lumumba's mentor.[46]

Initially, American officials hoped to use Nkrumah, surreptitiously, to achieve their aims.[47] Upon meeting with Nkrumah in late April 1960, William Flake, U.S. ambassador to Ghana, assured other administration officials that the Pan-Africanist leader was committed to preventing the Congo from sliding into the Soviet bloc.[48] A few months later, Eisenhower sent a message to Nkrumah through diplomatic channels indicating that he considered the Congo crisis a "grave [danger] to world peace." The message also assured Nkrumah that the United States believed "that the immediate problem [was] the speedy resolution of the Belgian troop and Katanga questions" and that the Americans were "supporting [United Nations Secretary-General Dag Hammarsjkold] to the hilt" in that regard. However, the bulk of the message focused on postcrisis management of the Congo. To that end, Eisenhower sought Nkrumah's support for the American proposal to create an exclusive contract between the Congo and the United Nations for the provision of much-needed administrative, technical, and financial support.[49]

Three days later, on August 5, 1960, Nkrumah replied to Eisenhower's communiqué and emphasized the need for the hasty withdrawal of Belgian troops from Katanga. Noting the lack of popular support for the secessionists because Katanga was a creation of Belgian maneuvers, Nkrumah worried about the failure to initiate promptly the relevant U.N. resolution. In a thinly veiled warning, Nkrumah wrote that "if any Power was not clearly to oppose Belgium in her present conduct, the position of that Power on the African continent would be fatally compromised." A few lines later, Nkrumah was less oblique:

> There is a suspicion, which I would like to believe is quite unfounded, that the United States of America, France and the United Kingdom are not giving their full support to the United Nations decision that all Belgian troops should be withdrawn from the whole of the Congo. The view which is being taken by some African States is that these powers are deliberately delaying on this issue in the hope that a Katanga state can be created and that the Belgian military occupation can continue and be ultimately justified on a *de facto* basis. I am glad indeed to note your proposal that the Congo should be protected against conflicting power politics and other pressures. However, the first task before any other issue can be considered is the withdrawal of all Belgian troops.

Nkrumah then left the matter of technical assistance to the Congo for lower-level officials. Nkrumah openly rejected the fundamental White House proposition that undermining potential Communist influence in central Africa was the priority, saying that "any other issue is of little importance so long as Belgian troops remain in the Congo."[50]

During the aforementioned September 1960 meeting between Eisenhower and Nkrumah in New York, the two leaders discussed the Congo crisis. Initially, Nkrumah had a hard time getting the American contingent to talk specifically about the Congo; Eisenhower, for instance, spent a substantial portion of the meeting reminiscing about his World War II exploits. Finally, when Eisenhower asked Nkrumah for his views on the situation, the latter responded optimistically by saying that the problems were not insoluble but needed to be worked out through the United Nations Eisenhower agreed, referred to his speech before the United Nations earlier that morning, in which "he had been careful not to place the problem on what he described as a bi-polar basis," and said that "our policy is to solve problems through the UN even when we ourselves would prefer them worked out in another way."[51] Nkrumah left the meeting heartily dissatisfied because the Americans did not seem to share his anxieties and sense of urgency regarding the worsening situation in central Africa.[52] Although the encounter left Eisenhower pleased, he felt deceived by Nkrumah's speech later that day. In his memoirs, Eisenhower claimed that Nkrumah "cut loose with a speech following the [Soviet premier, Nikita] Khrushchev line in strong criticism of Secretary-General [Dag] Hammarskjold."[53] Yet, the American president's sense of betrayal seems inexplicable.

In his speech on September 23, 1960, Nkrumah outlined the history of the Congo prior to independence and then suggested that the Lumumba-Kasavubu government was the only legitimate government in the entire country, including Katanga. After articulating a legal argument regarding the validity of the Lumumba government and the indivisibility of the Congo, Nkrumah offered six recommendations for U.N. action: (1) that the U.N. Command in the Congo support the legitimate government and that the peacekeeping force be composed of military personnel from the independent African states and placed under African command; (2) that the United Nations should recognize the Lumumba government as the only legitimate one in the Congo; (3) that all private armies, including the Belgians, be disarmed; (4) that the new U.N. Command support the legitimate government in accordance to the first Resolution of the Security Council, upon which the independent African states relied; (5) that the United Nations should recognize the territorial integrity of the Congo; and, (6) that all financial and technical aid be arranged solely with the legitimate government of the Congo, channeled through the United Nations, and supervised by the independent African states.[54] Additionally, Nkrumah's speech touched on other global dilemmas and proposed solutions to them—for example, the admission of the People's Republic of China to the United Nations, permanent seats on the U.N. Security Council for Africa, Asia, and the Middle East; and NATO pressure on Portugal to surrender its African colonies—all of which were antithetical to American policy.[55] Not only had Nkrumah suggested that the Congo was representative of worldwide struggle of non-White people for independence, he had also boldly asserted that the Congo crisis was an African problem that was best solved by Africans.

American officials should not have been surprised by Nkrumah's speech because it offered nothing they had not heard previously from the Pan-Africanist.[56] Contrary to Eisenhower's claim, Nkrumah's presentation and diplomacy differed markedly from Khrushchev's. Nkrumah never sought the dismissal of the U.N. Secretary-General Dag Hammarskjold. In fact, unlike Khrushchev, Nkrumah explicitly stated that "it would be entirely wrong to blame either the Security Council or any senior officials of the United Nations for what has taken place."[57] In contrast, Khrushchev had stated "that the colonialists had been doing their dirty work in the Congo through the Secretary-General of the UN and his staff."[58] In comparison to Khrushchev's remarks and alternative plan for a three-member group to act as the U.N. Secretariat, a speech which Herter called a "declaration of war," Nkrumah's speech seemed tepid.[59] The Eisenhower administration reduced Nkrumah's clear call for support of both the democratic will of the Congolese and African self-determination in cooperation with the United Nations to a naked attempt at personal aggrandizement. In other words, as Herter told the media, Nkrumah's speech "sounded to me as though he were very definitely making a bid for the leadership of what you would call a left-wing group of African states. He . . . went out of his way from the point of view of showing a very close relationship to what Mr. Khrushchev said."[60] Therefore, the political discord between Accra and Washington was not simply a result of Nkrumah's diplomacy. Rather, the problem rested, in large part, with White officials who demanded unconditional, uncritical obedience from non-White leaders.

## Severing the Economic Umbilical Cord

With regard to economic development, the United States acted as an impediment to, rather than a supporter of, Ghanaian economic plans. Nkrumah hoped to transform the cash crop economy of Ghana into a more diversified one that would include mining and light manufacturing.[61] Ghana, like many other African nations, hoped for favorable terms during negotiations on international commodities agreements. Unfortunately, they could not count on the United States to support their position since the United States was unwilling to enter the debate as anything other than an interested observer.[62]

National Security Council Action Memorandum number 1926 reveals the NSC's concordance with the position adopted by the Council on Foreign Economic Policy as to avoiding any involvement in an international agreement on commodity prices. NSC Action memo 1926 adds that "the United States is prepared to discuss and explore . . . approaches to problems arising from commodity price and market instability . . . [but] will not participate in any discussion or meeting with respect to an international commodity agreement and will make no commitment as to U.S. participation in such an agreement."[63] It was believed that serious American involvement or commitment to an international commodity agreement would have compromised the veiled objective of working with the imperialist countries at the expense of their colonial subjects by forcing the United States to support its European allies explicitly.

An instructive example of a foreign economic policy guided by White Supremacy is the Volta River Project. Shortly before Nkrumah became prime minister of the Gold Coast in 1951, he and his advisers supported the British-conceived plan of creating a hydroelectric dam on the Volta River. The immediate gain from such an endeavor would have been the provision of power for the processing of bauxite, one of the country's most important mineral resources, into aluminum. In the long run, it was their hope to use the facility to modernize the entire nation by (1) creating business opportunities for Ghanaians outside the agricultural sector, (2) providing Ghanaians with access to advanced technology in the hopes of spurring scientific and economic innovation, and (3) providing a new source of energy to Ghana's consumers, institutions, and businesses.[64] Ghana was unsuccessful in its initial attempts to interest private British, Canadian, or American investors in the venture.[65] Ultimately, the Eisenhower administration was shamed into discussing the project when American racism assaulted a Ghanaian official:

> A glass of orange juice changed the entire situation. In October 1957, a waitress at a Howard Johnson's restaurant in Dover, Delaware, refused to serve a glass of orange juice to Ghanan [sic] Finance Minister K. A. Gbedemah. Still smarting from the international effects of the confrontation over the integration of Central High School in Little Rock a month earlier, the Eisenhower administration was greatly embarrassed by the latest example of segregation. Eisenhower and Vice-President Richard Nixon invited Gbedemah to the White House for a highly publicized meeting. Gbedemah used the opportunity to plead for U.S. assistance in the Volta dam project.[66]

Within two weeks, Ghana forwarded to the United States a copy of the project report published jointly by the governments of the United Kingdom and Gold Coast.[67] From this point, Nkrumah and Eisenhower engaged in a two-and-a-half-year courtship regarding a tangible American commitment to the project.

A month after the Howard Johnson's incident, Nkrumah wrote to Eisenhower explaining the serious nature of the planned undertaking, with a brief history pertaining to negotiations and financial considerations, and an engineering analysis. Conceding that "by any standards this is a great project," Nkrumah urged his American counterpart to endorse a venture which was wanting only for monetary support. For various reasons, British and Canadian governments and private investors hesitated. Thus, Nkrumah noted that "it is apparent . . . that the scheme cannot be brought to life unless it receives a new and powerful stimulus." Although firmly convinced of the potential success of the project, the Nkrumah government could not go it alone. Nkrumah's request was for American public investment, ideally through the recently established development loan fund. "We are not asking for any gifts," he emphasized and, as a show of good faith, invited Eisenhower to send a team of federal officials to examine the proposed project.[68]

Despite this overture and the fanfare surrounding Nkrumah's visit to the United States to discuss the project with representatives of Kaiser Industries, the federal government remained lukewarm.[69] In the OCB Progress Report on NSC 5719/1, the authors discussed the venture and America's role therein: "The Government of Ghana has linked the country's economic development largely to the elaborate Volta River Project which would provide hydroelectric power for refining aluminum from large bauxite deposits." Perhaps because the OCB cost estimates for the project were startling—seven years for completion at a cost of $900 million—it was reasoned that the United States would only "serve as a catalyst in encouraging private enterprise participation." For emphasis, the last sentence of this section of the report stated that "care is being taken to make sure that it is understood that the present interest of the United States does not involve any financial commitment."[70]

Three months later, in the summer of 1958, Nkrumah traveled to the United States to meet with Chad Calhoun of Kaiser Industries. When he stopped in Washington, he was greeted with a nineteen-gun salute and lunch at the White House. Following the meal, Nkrumah and Eisenhower issued a joint statement regarding their discussion on both direct government aid and private investment in the project. Yet, the president refused to commit federal government funds for the project.[71]

When the Kaiser engineers issued their report in February 1959, the price tag for the project dropped to $300 million. Kaiser's *Reassessment Report* reduced the expense of the project by eliminating from consideration costs for population relocation from the dam site, health and sanitation infrastructures, transportation and logistical infrastructure improvements, and new towns for the dispossessed. Based on the assumption that Ghana would bear these ancillary costs, the difference between the OCB estimate and Kaiser's approximation was not as stark as it might appear. Equally important was the fact that Kaiser's reassessment of costs gave a false impression of a more cost-effective project while obscuring the true nature of Ghana's financial burden. This financial sleight of hand paid great dividends for Kaiser in Washington.

In September 1959, Nkrumah updated the president on the project. As he had in the first letter, Nkrumah highlighted the importance of the Volta River Project as a path toward a new economic and political future for Ghana. He also mentioned his discussions with Kaiser Industries:

> At the beginning of this week in Accra, Mr. Edgar Kaiser and I reviewed the entire project in detail. I informed Mr. Kaiser of my firm intention of proceeding with the construction of the dam and power installation, and invited him to take the initiative in forming a consortium of aluminum producers which would be willing to establish in Ghana a smelter of sufficient size to justify the financial investment in the power project. Mr. Kaiser agreed to do this. He appreciates the need for quick action, and I hope to receive firm proposals from him before the end of this year.[72]

Kaiser, along with Reynolds Metals Company and ALCOA, among others, formed a consortium to invest in the project. On December 16, 1959, the consortium, named the Volta Aluminum Company (VALCO), then reached an agreement in principle with Ghana to begin the project.[73]

The American president's responses were vague, noncommittal missives that simply let the Ghanaian know that his letters were received. However, official policy toward the Volta River Project began to shift as the end of the decade drew near. Gradually, the White House came around to the position that it should provide some financial aid to Ghana.

By the end of 1959, it was clear that American firms were going to get involved with the project, despite the fact that less than eighteen months earlier there had been serious doubt as to American business interest.[74] Thus, a dovetailing of events and official concerns spurred Washington into action. Domestically, the Eisenhower administration began to believe that support for the project would greatly enhance the Republican Party's reputation on matters of concern to Africa: "Democratic presidential candidate Kennedy had been particularly outspoken in attacking Eisenhower's inattention to Africa. Therefore, Eisenhower's pledge to aid Ghana was in part a political move to illustrate increased concern with Africa."[75] This was especially important since Nixon, the father of the administration's policy toward Africa, was Kennedy's Republican opponent.

In the international arena, however, the administration was wary of a repeat of the Aswan Dam fiasco: "The offer and withdrawal of U.S. aid to Gamal Nasser not only led to the Suez crisis of late 1956 but also greatly damaged American prestige in the underdeveloped nations. African and Asian leaders charged that Washington offered aid only with political strings attached."[76] Secretary of State Dulles's withdrawal of aid was doubly disastrous because the decision had been based, in part, on the assumption that the Soviet Union either was unable or unwilling to provide alternative funding to Egypt, a neutralist country.[77] Therefore, federal government financial backing for the Volta River Project could be used as a means of repairing America's damaged credibility in the Third World. Nevertheless, all of these considerations were complicated by official misapprehensions regarding the Nkrumah administration.

As noted above, the Pan-Africanist emerged as a strident critic of U.S. policy toward the Congo.[78] Additionally, Eisenhower believed that Nkrumah's Pan-Africanism was similar to Nasser's Pan-Arabism: political ideologies that masked the power-hungry designs of demagogues. Eisenhower noted in his memoirs that Nkrumahism was an ambitious plan "to expand the borders of Ghana by means other than voluntary federation."[79] Some American observers pointed to the number of Marxists or leftists in the administration, yet these individuals encouraged American investment in Ghana. George Padmore, Nkrumah's adviser on African Affairs and a longtime Marxist, declared "that if the U.S. was 'really worried about Communism taking root in Africa,' it should undertake 'a Marshall Aid programme for Africa' and, more specifically, 'construct the Volta River project in the Gold Coast.'"[80] In spite of Nkrumah's assurances that he would not nationalize foreign holdings, Eisenhower and his aides were concerned about providing economic leverage and political prestige to a Black version of Nasser. To further compound matters, American officials felt that Nkrumah would not hesitate to seek aid from the Soviet Union. These men either were unaware of or unconcerned with Nkrumah's deliberate and measured response to an unconditional Soviet economic aid offer of $14.7 million.[81]

Despite these qualms, the State Department announced in August 1960 that Washington would loan Ghana $20 million, contingent upon its ability to secure additional financing. Shortly thereafter, Ghana proclaimed that the World Bank and Great Britain had committed to loaning $40 million and $14 million, respectively.[82] American officials noted that Ghana's contribution to the project would total $84 million.[83] Such an underestimate of the true nature of Ghana's contribution to the Volta River Project was made possible by Kaiser's revised cost estimate.

The impetus for even this conditional aid was White self-interest. At the time of the announcement of American support for the Volta River Project, attendees at a National Security Council meeting were discussing the viability of the venture, among other things. Beginning with a discussion of the bauxite deposits in Guinea, Secretary of Commerce Frederick H. Mueller "pointed out that the cost of aluminum is the cost of power and the US government might have to provide some sort of guarantee to the private group interested in aluminum development in Africa on the matter of the cost of power." In his pitch for support of private enterprise, Mueller added that the cost of power in Africa was higher than the cost to Kaiser Aluminum for power obtained at Bonneville Dam. Under Secretary of State C. Douglas Dillon pointed out that Ghana was paying 6 percent interest on its loan from the World Bank, "while Bonneville had no similar interest cost." Mueller responded by saying that "we would have *to give these businessmen an even shake* if we wanted to keep this great resource for the Free World."[84]

Dillon then described the negotiations between the United States, Ghana, and VALCO. He indicated that financing arrangements would dictate the cost of power. Treasury Secretary Robert B. Anderson raised the issue of Ghana's desire to control most, if not all, of the power. Dillon suggested that Ghana would not control all of the power at the inception of the project but that the Ghanaians would probably want to do so at some point in the future. Anderson responded by saying, "If we are going to put up much of the money for the project, we ought to have a lot to say about how the power is distributed."[85]

Once the deal was cemented, Ghana sought additional funds in order to transmit electrical power beyond the immediate vicinity of the dam. Nkrumah repeatedly pressed the United States for this additional assistance.[86] The larger transmission net that Nkrumah and VALCO supported would mean additional power to sell to nearby mining concerns—which would directly ease the financial burden on Ghana—and, ultimately, resources to improve the quality of life throughout Ghana.[87] Washington replied that the additional transmission facility was unnecessary.

In advising the president, Secretary of State Herter ignored Kaiser's support for the full-scale transmission system when he asserted that such a project was superfluous: "The Ghanaians contend the additional transmission facilities would result in a better project from an economic viewpoint since the extra power could be used by private consumers and mining companies. We are not convinced that sufficient facts have been provided to support this position. The World Bank agrees with us."[88] The Eisenhower administration refused to take on this additional cost, perhaps, because the wider transmission facility might not have aided the growth of an American business monopoly in Ghana. Additionally, since construction of the additional power plant did not have to coincide with construction of the dam, the United States had achieved its objective with regard to international credibility; no more follow-through was required. Equally likely, the Eisenhower administration also rationalized this refusal as a means of punishing Nkrumah for his ingratitude. Eisenhower's negative response to Nkrumah's appeal came after Nkrumah's supposedly jarring criticism of the West in relation to Lumumba and the Congo.[89] In contrast to the wide dissemination of the State Department's announcement of financial support for the project, the instructions to embassy officials at the bottom of the rejection telegram read "White House would prefer text not be released."[90]

Although the Eisenhower administration was conservative fiscally, this alone does not explain Washington's response to the Volta River Project. Because Ghana was extremely important to the continued prosperity of the West, Washington's resistance to the project arguably was an attempt by the Eisenhower administration to facilitate the continued reliance of Ghana on Great Britain and the United States. Moreover, American reluctance to back the project financially was also based upon the Eisenhower administration's implicit rationale for decolonization to protect Western hegemony from any radical challenge.[91] The American desire to strengthen the essential ties between Ghana and the West meant that the British could give Ghana political independence while protecting the other institutions of colonial dominance.[92] Additionally, it bears noting that the United States and Britain were prepared to give Nasser a combined $70 million for the construction of the Aswan Dam, more than twice the amount these countries loaned to Ghana for the Volta River Project.[93]

More importantly, the Eisenhower administration's fiscal conservatism actually underscores the influence of race on these deliberations. It is important to understand what the Eisenhower administration was willing to fund, and what these decisions concealed, in order to observe the impact of White Supremacy. Economic or fiscal conservatives generally are reluctant to spend public funds in areas that they consider incidental to the operation of the government. Spending public funds in nonessential areas is tantamount to market intervention, another phenomenon that fiscal conservatives seek to avoid unless such intervention aids corporate interests.

An important starting point is American domestic policy during this same time period. The White House's silence in response to the lynching of Emmet Till was both a discouraging signal to African Americans and an indication of the administration's narrow vision regarding racial justice. Eisenhower's top lawyer, Attorney General Herbert Brownell, justified official acquiescence by saying that the White House's hands were tied: "[Since] there was no evidence that the perpetrators had crossed state lines . . . we had to turn down requests for federal prosecution of the Till case because we lacked jurisdiction."[94] A federal investigation at the time might have unearthed the murderers' accomplices or discerned that local officials aided and abetted the perpetrators by moving slowly in their investigation and not returning an indictment against Roy Bryant and J. W. Milam, in spite of confessions of kidnapping by the two. If found, such evidence would have demonstrated clear constitutional violations. Tellingly, just such an investigation had been initiated by Medgar Evers, Ruby Hurley, and other members of the NAACP, who went undercover to gain evidence in the matter.[95] Despite pressure from citizens and activists from home and abroad, the administration did little when the murder trial of the two White men accused of killing Till ended in an acquittal.[96] One international reaction was typical of many. A Swiss newspaper editorial cried, "This cannot be! Surely an official denial will be issued. If not, that is the end of any belief in American democracy!"[97]

With regard to voting and employment discrimination, the Eisenhower administration indicated its dedication to the principle of gradual change and concern for White interests. Like its largely superficial efforts at desegregating the military, the 1957 Civil Rights Act did little to stop Black disfranchisement. As late as 1955, the Justice Department refused to send a representative to the House Judiciary Committee hearings on voting rights protections.[98] Although the Justice Department did intervene in an effort by White Tennessee landlords to remove from their fields any Black sharecroppers who had registered to vote, members of the administration expressed doubts about the seriousness of the matter.[99] Their support for fair employment was little better.

The administration's antidiscrimination program aimed at government contractors, the President's Committee on Government Contracts (PCGC), lacked legal enforcement authority and the political will to aid seriously Black workers, belying the Committee members' claims of being exponents of aggressive action on behalf of fair employment. PCGC inquiries, based on an informal process of conciliation with accused corporations and labor unions, placed "primary reliance . . . upon education, persuasion, mediation, and conciliation, rather than upon enforcement by the imposition of penalties."[100]

PCGC efforts at educating employers and unions included the publication of a newsletter, public speeches that encouraged the hiring of women and non-Whites, seminars for procurement personnel of government agencies, and even short films like *The New Girl*. Although committee members believed that they had the power to hold public hearings as part of a discrimination investigation and that they could issue cease-and-desist notices, or that they could recommend the revocation of a government contract with a recidivist violator, they felt that such steps were too extreme to be useful. Given that its principal mission was educational "planning and programming rather than administering the nondiscrimination policies . . . relating to federal contracts," the PCGC offered Black workers only the cold comfort of repeated admonitions to discriminatory contractors and unions.[101] The PCGC's unwillingness to confront corporations at home was mirrored by its inability to include antidiscrimination language in federal government contracts with foreign governments.[102] On the whole, the administration's fair employment crusade did little to arrest widespread occupational segregation, underemployment, and declining Black self-employment.[103] Despite the president's belief that states would accept responsibility for ensuring fair employment, "the Eisenhower administration handed over to its successors a perpetuating, and in some respects worsening, economic crisis for blacks."[104] A similar pattern emerged with respect to housing discrimination.

Throughout the 1950s, the Eisenhower administration supported the home financing programs spawned by the Home Owners Loan Corporation (HOLC) of the New Deal era. De facto and de jure housing segregation in the United States preceded Franklin D. Roosevelt's attempt to stimulate the construction industry, and the economy as a whole, through the HOLC. Nonetheless, several government practices served to reinforce and encourage patterns of segregated housing. One example is the HOLC's institutionalized racist evaluations of potential homeowners and their neighborhoods. HOLC administrators created four categories of neighborhoods, with the highest-risk neighborhoods coded *red*. Black neighborhoods were always depicted in red, and even those areas with small percentages of Black residents were characterized as hazardous. Private banks provided few, if any, loans to red-coded neighborhoods or even to those working-class White or ethnic communities that existed in close proximity to Blacks. HOLC's rating procedure systematically undervalued communities that were non-White or racially and ethnically diverse. Moreover, HOLC's evaluations influenced the underwriting practices of its successor institutions, the Federal Housing Administration (FHA) and the Veterans Administration (VA).[105]

FHA and VA loans encouraged the suburbanization of the United States and the concomitant immiseration of urban areas occupied increasingly by non-Whites. As with HOLC evaluations, FHA appraisals included the racial composition of a neighborhood as a factor in determining whether to lend money for the purchase or rehabilitation of housing. The racialized nature of FHA and VA appraisals and loan programs supported the continued racial segregation of the nation's housing stock. In fact, the FHA recommended the use of racially restrictive covenants until 1950, two years after the Supreme Court's decision in *Shelley v. Kramer* declared state enforcement of such clauses to be unconstitutional.[106]

Despite the incredible disparities in lending for White and non-White applicants, the Eisenhower administration refused to intervene in the domestic housing market to repair this damage. Indeed, Eisenhower appointees like Albert M. Cole eschewed government intervention to cure housing discrimination. Cole, serving as Director of the Housing and Home Finance Agency (HHFA), also relied on a program of cooperation and conciliation with the private housing industry.[107] In fact, Cole caused an uproar when he stated at a San Francisco press conference that "it was not incumbent upon the Federal Government to impose integration on any form of housing that received government aid."[108] Adding fuel to his claim that "where segregation is legally enforced by state or local laws, then the [federal housing] agency observed such laws," Cole gutted the HHFA Race Relations Service by transferring the remaining two staffers to unrelated positions.[109] Although Cole claimed that he had been "both misquoted and misinterpreted," his response to heavy criticism was to outline and defend the federal government's role in the field of housing: "It is a role of assisting, stimulating, leading, and sometimes prodding; but never dictating or coercing, and never acting in a way that would stifle the proper exercise of private and local responsibility."[110] Not surprisingly, Cole's retort to alarmed activists reflected the administration's attitude toward other forms of racial oppression.[111] Compounded by disparities in housing appreciation and mortgage rates, the Eisenhower administration's refusal to regulate the housing market helped Whites ultimately to gain an $82 billion wealth advantage over the current generation of Blacks, not to mention the transfer of vital businesses, jobs, and infrastructure to predominantly White suburbs. Civil rights groups consistently appealed to both the executive and legislative branches of the federal government in the 1950s for reforms to end housing discrimination. One such advocacy group chided both the president and his housing chief for their lapse in dedication to the idea of equal opportunity, especially because "the eyes of the world are upon us, and our future well being may depend on how the United States carries out its responsibility to all its citizens."[112]

The Eisenhower administration's unwillingness to regulate lending practices in order to ensure an equitable distribution of financing between Whites and Blacks effectively protected White privilege and ensured African American economic, social, and political subordination. Likewise, the White House's recalcitrance opened Black home buyers to White violence in housing developments in Chicago, Louisville, and Levittown, Pennsylvania. Providing evidence of the intersection of racial and economic subordination, one Levittown White "conceded that the black father [of a family new to the neighborhood] was 'probably a nice guy, but every time I look at him I see two thousand dollars drop off the value of my house.'"[113] The White House's failure to intervene and halt or change the racial status quo in the domestic sphere is indicative of its reluctance to alter the racial status quo in the international sphere.

From a world-systems perspective, with its core/semiperiphery/periphery economic hierarchy, American support for the Volta River Project might have undermined the carefully integrated global economy it had so painstakingly constructed after World War II. Political neutralism and import-substitution programs, of which Nkrumah was in favor, were efforts at national self-sufficiency that might have undermined the efficiency of a unitary Free World economy. Moreover, if the United States allowed or encouraged this type of economic autarky, it could have set a dangerous precedent for other African nations to follow. Ultimately, as Ghana's policy of import-substitution took shape, foreign firms like Britain's United Africa Company and Unilever dominated the process through the construction of breweries, as well as detergent and textiles processing facilities.[114] Dependency theorists like Walter Rodney suggest that the fact that nearly all core nations are White and all peripheral nations are non-White is not coincidental. From Rodney's standpoint, a long-range view of Western refusal to engage in technology transfers with African states foreshadowed the Eisenhower administration's indifference toward the project.

The circumstances of African trade with Europe were unfavorable to creating a consistent African demand for technology relevant to development, "and when that demand was raised it was ignored or rejected by the capitalists . . . Placing the whole question in historical perspective allows us to see that capitalism has always discouraged technological evolution in Africa, and blocks Africa's access to its own technology."[115]

Recall that Secretary Mueller argued that in order to save the Volta River Project for the Free World, the American concern must be helping American business interests, not Ghana's. Absent from the dialogue was any interest in how foreign aid might help Ghana or U.S.-Ghana relations. Add to this the aforementioned American discomfort with Nkrumah's rhetoric, and a more complete explanation for Eisenhower policy emerges. As the president noted, the United States was unwilling to provide any type of assistance for the orderly economic development and political progress of the emerging nations of Africa "if we are unable to achieve our objective of maintaining the Free World orientation of the area."[116]

The Eisenhower administration's support for the Volta River Project had nothing to do with enhancing indigenous economic development in Africa. The discourse of the NSC meetings revealed that official policy was intended to guide the emerging nations back to their former parent countries for economic aid, thereby maintaining the economic disparities created by colonialism. As it was often stated, the Europeans had to carry a fair share of the economic burden of Third World economic development because the United States could not do it alone.[117] Additionally, because Africa had become a "battleground of the first order,"[118] Western nations had to meet the difficult problems facing African nations as a way of responding to the aggressive Soviet bloc attack there.[119] Accordingly, administration backing for the Volta River Project was directed toward preemptive control of African resources in order to deny them to the Soviets, assisting American business penetration of African economies, and enhancing American prestige in the Third World.[120] To do otherwise would jeopardize the essential ties between Europe and Africa and sever the umbilical cord that nourished White, capitalist redevelopment.

## A Conclusion From A Different Vantage Point

The preceding analysis of American foreign policy toward Ghana reveals the numerous ways that race and racism influenced diplomacy. The Eisenhower administration supported decolonization in Africa in the hope of securing Africa's place at the bottom of the Free World hierarchy. Because the Cold War served as a site to repair the reputational value of Whiteness, Eisenhower's diplomacy toward newly independent Ghana posed the United States as a potentially supportive ally despite American efforts to constrain Ghana's national self-expression. The cost of American friendship was social dislocation within Ghana, further demonstrating the skewed nature of U.S. foreign policy.

American support for African political independence required that Africans subordinate their interests and concerns to those of the West. Washington's concerns about premature independence and the alleged need to teach Africans about responsible government harken to the Teddy Roosevelt-Woodrow Wilson Second Wave policy toward Africa.[121] Domestic strife in Ghana, a direct result of the limits of British decolonization, was compounded by Washington's choice to privilege Western needs above those of Africans. As an example, African businesswomen faced severe disadvantages because of European imperialism and, later, American support for Western reconstruction. Simultaneously, American officials chafed as the Nkrumah administration projected its masculine identity into relations with the United States. Ironically, America's Cold War diplomacy sought to teach these primitive children to undo their long-standing traditions of man- and womanhood.

## The Struggle for Female Autonomy in Ghana

In Ghana, asymmetrical patterns of economic development, similar to those found in Ethiopia, hardened during the Cold War with regard to women's work. Women in precolonial Ghana retained a good deal of autonomy vis-à-vis their men. Their power changed during the early colonial period, only to erode significantly throughout the late nineteenth century and into the Cold War era. The early success of the Volta River Project might have had positive economic and educational benefits for Ghanaian women. Increased economic diversity would have lessened the national burden on cocoa producers to provide the lion's share of government revenues. Economic diversification would also have led to fewer encroachments by men into women's economic spheres and reduced tension between postcolonial governments and the market women. Faced with a stagnant economy, the Nkrumah government and its successors used scarce resources to refurbish only that infrastructure which supported industrial concerns, creating a transportation barrier for women workers.[122]

Undoubtedly, increased production of electricity would have spurred school construction. As it was, the education of women in Ghana experienced an upward trend during the Nkrumah administration. However, it did not equalize with the rate for men until the late 1970s. Greater access to educational opportunity for women has consistently translated into greater job access, resource development, lower birth rates, and the expansion of career options for women.

Western insistence on the maintenance of Ghana's peripheral economic position led to country-wide suffering, especially among women farmers and food traders. Therefore, the international interest convergence—U.S. support for decolonization in exchange for Ghanaian integration into the global capitalist economy—accelerated the deterioration of women's power. Not surprisingly, the embitterment of these women manifested itself in many ways, the least of which was joining the domestic anti-Nkrumah forces in the early 1960s, just as their Ethiopian sisters aided the growing resistance to the Haile Selassie government.[123]

## Foreign Economic Policy and That "Man Thing" Again

As addressed in the previous chapter, foreign economic policy is informed by a masculine discourse and ritual. Rosenberg suggests that one of the chief characteristics of international lending was the "performance" of giving economic assistance.[124] Coupled with that performance were demonstrations of self-restraint and rationality, human qualities generally attributed to White men. Likewise, objectivity and impartiality were masculine behaviors that informed the aid process. Americans assumed this masculine, superior posture vis-à-vis African nations in many respects aside from the donor-recipient relationship. For instance, the note taker at the September 1960 U.N. meeting between Eisenhower and Nkrumah referred to the American representatives by their official titles, President and Secretary of State. In contrast, the scribe referred to the Ghanaian head of state simply as Mr. Nkrumah.[125] Both Ethiopia and Ghana challenged America's role as the masculine provider or tutor and offered a competing narrative of African masculinity. Yet, Nkrumah's challenge took a form altogether different from Haile Selassie's.

In a period of dramatic geopolitical change, it is not surprising that Eisenhower administration officials found comfort in simplistic racialized binary explanations of Black behavior. Most Americans believed that Blacks, from the continent or throughout the diaspora, were antithetical to Whites. As such, Blacks were passive objects to be acted upon by active White (male) subjects.[126] Thus, the world of diplomacy and foreign economic aid was dominated by Whites, their concerns and perceptions. Nkrumah's actions questioned the cherished ideals of American objectivity and rationality. Furthermore, Nkrumah usurped much of the masculine role the United States had become accustomed to playing.

Recall that Nkrumah sent to Eisenhower a completed proposal for the dam. In his first letter, Nkrumah told his American counterpart that everything was in place except the financing. Although the prospectus was a joint undertaking between Britain and preindependence Ghana, it revealed that Nkrumah did not need American technical advisers to validate the project. Second, Nkrumah bypassed the federal government and found potential investors in the American private sector.[127] Third, Nkrumah pressed the United States for additional funds once the Eisenhower administration committed itself.

Although the Eisenhower administration might have interpreted this behavior as more evidence of Black insatiability, they were probably disturbed at another, unconscious level. Nkrumah demonstrated his willingness to change the terms of the agreement, typically the exclusive domain of a dominant power. Like Haile Selassie, Nkrumah offered a countervailing narrative of an ambitious, hard-working, intelligent, risk-taking African (male) leader. Nkrumah's sense of self is perhaps best captured in the title *Osagyefo*, meaning teacher. Therefore, Nkrumah's insistence on behaving and being treated as a peer, as a (White) man, and on offering historical lessons about the West further destabilized Washington's parent-child style of diplomacy toward Africa, let alone the racial sanctuary that Washington constructed.

## Conclusion

Relations between Ghana and the United States were shaped by factors other than the supposedly corrosive influence of global Communism. Although American officials interpreted various episodes in the relationship primarily in Cold War terms, their language and behavior reveal a deeper operational imperative. To a large extent, the Eisenhower administration worried about developments in Ghana because the Nkrumah government refused to engage in the self-censorship generally expected of Blacks. By returning a critical gaze upon U.S. foreign policy, Nkrumah disrupted the comfortable space the Cold War provided for Whiteness. Moreover, his program for Pan-African unity threatened the objectives of America's Cold War diplomacy.

With respect to U.S. economic diplomacy, Ghana refused to abandon its dream of the Volta River Project when faced with the White House's refusal to provide aid. Nkrumah seized a seat at the Western development table, refined a development plan, and secured American corporate interest. Had Nkrumah been a White head of state, his assertiveness and perseverance would have earned him respect in Washington's power circles.

Politically, Ghana's negative assessment of Western behavior during the Congo crisis nearly pierced the veil of American support for African democracy and revealed that U.S. interests were truly in line with Belgian interests. Moreover, Nkrumah rejected the politics of Black self-abnegation, openly supporting Patrice Lumumba and effectively standing squarely between this "bad nigger" and the Free World's lynch mob. Finally, Nkrumah's Pan-African vision charted a clear path for political, social, and economic development independent from European and American dictates.

Nkrumah's insurgent politics subverted Washington's conception of a Free World. To Nkrumah and most of his African contemporaries, Europe represented bondage, racial warfare, political subjugation, and genocide, while America was the home of a large population of descendants of African slaves who dwelled in a new form of servitude. His critique of imperialism implied that European dependence on and addiction to African exploitation made the metropoles unwilling to succumb to non-White demands for liberty without force. Indeed, there was no Free World other than the new one Nkrumah and his non-White peers across the world were seeking to create. Given the foregoing assessment, an obvious question remains: if this is how America treated its friends, how did it treat its enemies? Chapters 5 and 6 provide an answer.

# CHAPTER FIVE

# DIPLOMACY WITH THE NOT-SO-DISTANT COUSIN: THE UNITED STATES OF AMERICA AND THE UNION OF SOUTH AFRICA

## The Talking Mirror

When H. E. Wentzel Christoffel du Plessis—the newly appointed ambassador to the United States from the Union of South Africa—arrived in Washington in the summer of 1956, he brought with him the typical diplomatic salutation. Yet, because he sojourned to America in the midst of growing global criticism of the South African regime, his words were especially poignant.

> Mr. President, the peoples of the Union of South Africa and of the United States of America are nurtured in the traditions and ideals of the Western world, and their systems of Government are founded on a deep sense of the importance of freedom in promoting the welfare and happiness of mankind . . . It is the firm desire of the Government of the Union of South Africa that the ties of friendly understanding which so happily exist between the United States of America and the Union shall be maintained and strengthened to the mutual benefit of our countries and peoples.[1]

This statement underscored the similarities of the experiences of Whites in their respective countries and their shared notions of freedom. Of equal import is the fact that the statement also underscored the shadow experiences of Blacks.

Like the United States, the Union of South Africa was a colonial-settler society. It was a country dominated by outsiders who had usurped the land from the indigenous population and isolated them in restricted areas. Like those in the United States, South Africa's settlers came from different European nations but lived under British hegemony. Thus, one cohort of the settler population chafed under the dominance of another and its supposedly liberal attitudes toward Blacks. South Africa also was a country that nurtured a well-defined system of racial segregation and oppression, in part the result of a compromise between competing, sometimes belligerent, White factions.[2]

South Africa, like the United States, was a product of European imperialism and, as Marx would say, the stage of capitalism known as primitive accumulation. Similarly, the White South Africans' claims to the land rested on the legal theory of *terra nullus*, or empty lands. With the ascendancy of legal positivism, scholars of international law believed that non-Christian (i.e., non-White) peoples had no real control over their land and, thus, were not nations. The positivists argued that no sovereignty existed "where [Europeans] find no native government capable of controlling [W]hite men under which [W]hite civilization can exist."[3]

According to this logic, the savages of the African coast and hinterland were no different than the savages of the Appalachian range, New England, or the Mississippi Valley. The land upon which they resided was not theirs because they (1) roamed over it and failed to enclose and cultivate it or (2) lacked sovereignty, institutionalized political authority, and a collective cultural identity.[4] Central to the mythology of White South Africans, especially the Afrikaners, was the idea of settling the wilderness, of bringing civilization and progress to the southern subcontinent. South African Ambassador to the United States J. E. Holloway said as much in a conversation with then-Under Secretary of State Christian Herter:

> South Africa believes in freedom, the Ambassador said, and it is therefore often asked why the Union does not give its natives the right to vote. The great bulk of the native population is still on the fringe of barbarism, he said, and the South African Government would not be so stupid as to give these people the right to vote. Rather, the Union is trying to raise the educational level of the natives and this is a long process.[5]

Yet, twentieth-century South Africa was as much a product of tensions between Whites as it was a result of tensions between Whites and non-Whites.

The bitter struggle of the Dutch and their progeny against African peoples and the British resulted in an Afrikaner population—the majority of the White population—suspicious of non-Afrikaners: "The efforts to reach a unity among [W]hites carried the high price of institutionalizing racial domination."[6] Despite this racial reconciliation, the Afrikaner population remained isolationist, brooding, and paranoid. British Prime Minister Harold Macmillan, meeting with President Eisenhower following the Sharpeville Massacre in March 1960, described them in this way: "They were intense Calvinists who felt themselves God's anointed . . .

There was even a certain nobility in the tenacity and sense of righteousness with which they held to their views."[7]

Historically, relations between South Africa and the United States were sympathetic, if not collaborative. In the Yankee mind, Africa was similar to colonial America, replete with bestial human inhabitants and boundless lands waiting for White cultivation. Notably, American support increased during World War II: "South Africa's gold production played an important role in Allied wartime economic strategy and South African troops contributed significantly to Allied campaigns against Axis forces in North Africa."[8] Although many American observers were shocked by the Nationalist Party's triumph in South Africa's 1948 elections, they were troubled not so much by the formalization of White Supremacy in the policy of apartheid, but more so by (1) the international reaction to a fellow White country enforcing overt racial restraints and (2) the potential which apartheid created for internal unrest and, perhaps, non-White, Communist-inspired revolution. As such, the issue for American officials never was the impact of White Supremacy on non-Whites but, rather, the potential impact of untrained, radical non-Whites on the stability of the Free World.

## Whiteness as Property and American Faith in the United States

Because the Afrikaners who controlled the Union of South Africa were considered White, their country was considered White. As such, South Africa was exempt from the interventionist foreign policies of the United States toward other African nations. There was no need for the United States to maintain the essential ties with the West, and there was no need for the United States to insist upon the development of responsible governance.[9] The designation of South Africa as White meant more than a racial characteristic. It implied the enjoyment of a property right privileged above all others—the property interest in being White. In South Africa, as in the United States, race, rights, racial privileges, and national identity were inextricably linked.[10]

Descendants of the English and the Dutch were the principal groups of Whites who controlled Southern Africa. The Dutch were particularly hostile to the Africans they encountered not merely because they had been slave owners but because their psychic value rested primarily on the complete denigration of Blacks. For the Dutch pioneers, the creation of a White country meant the social, political, and economic obliteration of the indigenous population.[11]

As mentioned above, the Afrikaners resented and resisted British hegemony in the early colony. The Union of South Africa, created in 1910, was forged from a compromise between British and Afrikaner colonists. At the time of union, there were differences with regard to explicit racial restrictions in the British and Afrikaner provinces. Significantly, the right to vote in the British-controlled Cape Colony and Natal Province was restricted to those who met certain property qualifications. Because of this, elite Blacks actually enjoyed the franchise for a number of years. By comparison, the constitution of the South African Republic (also known as Transvaal) proclaimed that "the people are not prepared to allow any equality of the non-[W]hite with the [W]hite inhabitants, either in Church or State."[12] As the provinces unified under one government controlled by a local parliament, certain reform-minded elements in the British government hoped that the liberal views of the British colonies would slowly permeate the thinking of the Afrikaners.[13] In fact, the reverse occurred.

With union came a pronounced upsurge in Afrikaner political power. Because they outnumbered the British colonists, they began to dictate the style and scope of legislation aimed at the Black population. The dizzying array of codes that controlled Black access to land, employment, residence, and unfettered mobility—mirroring the developments in American politics throughout the nineteenth century—imperiled the African quest for freedom. The crowning blow to South Africa's Black elites was the complete disfranchisement of Blacks as part of the notorious Hertzog Bills of 1936.[14]

As workers, Afrikaners flexed their muscles in response to the demands of Black labor and the profit motive of White industrialists. In February 1920, 71,000 Black miners, supported by the African National Congress (ANC), began a strike that paralyzed the industry. The strikers sought a wage increase, as well as an end to "their dislocation from the expanded economy by unionized, skilled, and semi-skilled White workers."[15] The violent force of police and White vigilantes broke the strike.

Two years later, White workers went on strike in response to what they perceived as the treachery of the mine owners: "In the postwar decline, the mine owners had considered modifying the color bar to compensate for declining profits and rising costs. This would allow them to weaken the militant White unions and train Blacks for skilled jobs, while continuing to invoke race as justification for maintaining lower Black wages."[16] Afrikaner unions and English-speaking socialists joined forces under a banner of "Workers of the World, Fight and Unite for a White South Africa."[17] When negotiations between the workers and the government broke down, the strike was broken through an intimidating military operation, massive arrests, and the executions of four workers.[18] The lesson of South African class conflict was that White workers would collaborate with the interests of the ruling class as long as they maintained their privileges of higher wages, job status, and work conditions in relation to Black workers.

Socially, Afrikaners resisted the growing numbers of Blacks moving into South Africa's urban centers. Equally disconcerting to Whites was the project of African education that produced a small, but growing, number of Black professionals. Even though their career choices were highly constricted, their academic attainment and presence challenged notions of White superiority. Accordingly, the political turn to the extreme right in 1948 can be viewed, in large part, as an Afrikaner response to increasing African demands for political, legal, economic, and social spaces equivalent to those of Whites. As would be expected, "Whites feared that any accommodation of Blacks would precipitate a slippery slope of gradual integration—just what educated Blacks hoped would happen."[19]

This is not to argue that the British were egalitarian with regard to Africans. On the contrary, the English-speaking population in South Africa proved just as racist as the Afrikaners. The difference in their behavior perhaps is attributable to the fact that the identity of the British descendants was based on strong beliefs in Anglo-Saxon superiority and a heritage of empire, which also included a domination of the Dutch.

The British settlers in the Cape and Natal were imbued with a sense of manifest destiny quite similar to their North American counterparts. Additionally, the large influx of British settlers in the nineteenth century had a worldview shaped by both a belief that they were spreading the civilizing effects of Great Britain and by class snobbery. These immigrants included barristers, merchants, and engineers, as well as skilled and semiskilled craftsmen. It also can be said that their sense of wealth accumulation was much more keen than the Afrikaners' because they came from the England of the Industrial Revolution. This sense of superiority over the Afrikaners led to the development of laws and a political structure that privileged English speakers. For the British, comparing themselves to the Dutch frontiersmen and dirt farmers was akin to comparing a feudal landlord to a monopoly capitalist.[20]

The British settlers' animosity toward the indigenous communities of South Africa was mitigated only by their need for labor. There was no question in the British mind that the Africans had to be subdued. Nonetheless, the "importance of the African's labor power would ensure that his exploitation and oppression did not lead to his negation—to his physical annihilation—since such an eventuality would also imply the negation of the colonizer himself."[21] The need for labor was so great that eventually the British shipped indentured servants from India to the sub-continent. The British also recognized the political usefulness of the African. The theoretically color-blind constitution of the Cape Colony, which allowed for a merit-based franchise, effectively excluded non-Whites and workers of all races from parliament while maintaining the veneer of democracy. Arguably, because the Whites of English descent controlled both the Dutch and the non-Whites in the area, their sense of racial privilege did not demand a thorough system of legalized segregation.[22] In turn, the Afrikaners were obsessed with formal dominion over non-Whites because their White skin privilege had been challenged from both the top and the bottom of the racial hierarchy.

When the Cold War began, South Africa reinforced its strategic importance to the United States. Economically, America supplanted Britain as the major supplier of goods to South Africa. Consequently, South Africa became the United States' fourth-largest foreign market. American war and industrial power depended heavily upon minerals like uranium, copper, cobalt, manganese, chromium, platinum, vanadium, and industrial diamonds, which were mined primarily in South Africa and the Belgian Congo. Paul Nitze dramatized this reliance when he wrote that "in the case of those minerals where we lack self-sufficiency continuing access to the minerals of the rest of the world is an absolute requirement of the very life of the nation." A U.S.-South African agreement in November 1950 greatly aided the American cause in Korea.[23] This reliance did not change with the presidential election of Dwight Eisenhower.

NSC 5719/1 outlined the economic and strategic importance of South Africa: "Total American investment in Africa South of the Sahara is now about $500 million, the majority in the Union of South Africa." South Africa held more gold, dollars, and convertible currencies than the rest of sub-Saharan Africa combined. Furthermore, South Africa was critical as much for its geographic location as for its supply of minerals: "From bases in certain areas of Africa South of the Sahara, the Communists could pose a serious threat to communications in the Atlantic, the Indian Ocean, and the Red Sea . . . Denial of the area to Communist control is also important in order to prevent both economic dislocations to western Europe and Communist access to strategic materials."[24]

For the officials of the Eisenhower administration, the South Africans were a reliable, if stubborn, ally. They consistently voted with the United States on the vast majority of positions taken by the American delegation to the United Nations.[25] Eisenhower and his advisers considered the South Africans to be Westerners. They had a common background and common interests; in June 1955, the president hosted a contingent of international golfers, which contained two South Africans.[26] Technologically, the South African regime had access to modern weapons. Their agreements with the United States and other Western nations ensured either direct shipments of arms and machinery or the money with which to purchase them. As such, the Americans had great faith in South African loyalty to the Free World and their ability to control the country's non-White majority.

More to the point, Americans supported this racist regime principally because it was White. Minority rule in South Africa was neither inevitable nor irreversible. Yet, the Eisenhower administration treated it as such. Recalling the administration's comments about the general unpreparedness of Africans for self-rule, one need have no doubt that they believed that the Africans denigrated in South Africa also were unfit to rule. American officials made both deliberate and unconscious choices to support apartheid regimes even as they worried that they were an international incident waiting to happen. The South African ruling class's property interest in Whiteness protected them from the same fate as Lumumba—or, later, Nkrumah— even though they seemed determined to provoke a non-White, and potentially Communist, insurrection.

## U.S. Concerns about Apartheid
## and Black Nationalism

The Afrikaners' Nationalist Party victory in 1948 was the result of a mix of domestic and international factors.[27] Reduced to its core, however, it can be said that this shift in South African politics emerged from increasing Afrikaner political, social, and economic insecurity. In essence, the majority of the White population reacted with trademark insecurity to increasing gains by non-Whites, both at home and abroad.

Apartheid, "an intensification of racial segregation, a doctrinaire commitment to [racial] separation in all spheres,"[28] was the logical extension of well-established customary and legalized segregation in South African society. Although some controversy exists as to the continuities and contrasts between pre- and post-apartheid society, White Supremacy was an accepted theoretical basis for White minority control.[29] Yet, this racial theocracy could not function without supplicants. By the 1940s, White South Africans were dismayed by the decline of the British Empire and the incremental liberation of non-White countries. India's independence was particularly troubling because its admission to the United Nations resulted in greater global criticism of the impact of South African racism on its Indian population.[30] Moreover, the constant struggles for non-White access to political and social power repeated themselves during the interwar years and thereafter shook the prevailing racial ideology to its core.[31]

Dr. Daniel Malan's triumph signaled the ascendancy of Afrikaner political might. The Nationalist victory of 1948 ushered in the debilitating apartheid system but also invigorated the multiracial forces of resistance. The ANC of this period was a mass-based, nationalist group that eschewed the militant Africa-for-Africans approach for a militant integrationist stance. The differences between African nationalist groups in South Africa were similar to those between the NAACP, the Student Nonviolent Coordinating Committee, and the Republic of New Afrika.[32] This diversity was conveniently glossed over by White men on both sides of the Atlantic who could not conceive of Black self-rule. Both South Africans and American policymakers equated Black independence with treachery or, worse yet, Communist manipulation. Years before the drafting of NSC 5719/1, President Eisenhower confided to Senator Ralph Flanders that, in his opinion, most nationalist sentiment really was camouflaged Communist agitation. He applied this view to South Africans as well.[33] NSC 5719/1 gave short shrift to racism on the African continent:

> Racialism is, of course, closely allied to the colonial question but is most acute in the Union of South Africa and, to a lesser extent, in Central and East Africa . . . U.S. influence is restricted by the extremely distorted picture Africans have been given concerning the race problem in the United States.[34]

Thus, from the official perspective, racism was a problem of the Blacks and could be mitigated only if they matured and gained a realistic picture of race relations in America. Special Assistant to the Secretary of State Julius Holmes, writing to John Foster Dulles about South Africa, noted that "there is being built up on the basis of envy and resentment a burning hatred for the [W]hites; the atmosphere of sullen hostility was very apparent in Johannesburg."[35] State Department updates on developments in South Africa continued to be myopic.

American officials believed that "the illegal Communist Party of the Union of South Africa continue[d] to exercise potent influence on the African National Congress, the oldest and largest native organization in that country." This assessment differed little from that of the South African elites who lived in closer proximity to the ANC.[36]

The trial of Black activist leaders underscored the general White fear of Communist provocation of Africans. In 1956 the South African government opened prosecution against 156 ANC activists accused of treason. Charging that the ANC was interested in liberating the country's non-White population from White Supremacist oppression, government attorneys argued that the demand for racial equality was imbued with a hostile intent toward the government. Further, the demands of the group's Freedom Charter—to achieve equality within the lifetime of the leaders—necessarily envisioned the violent overthrow of the government.[37] Central to the prosecution's position was the theme of Africans enthralled by global Communism:

> "The essence of the case," in the view of the prosecution, was the fact that the liberatory movement was part of an international communist-inspired effort "pledged to overthrow by violence all governments in non-communist countries where sections of the population did not have equal political and economic rights."[38]

However, not every White South African was convinced of such a vast, global conspiracy.

The White South African judges who presided over this case rejected the prosecution's assertion that the ANC was a Communist group. Conceding that ANC demands were far-reaching, that some ANC activists occasionally used violent rhetoric, and that the group often revealed anti-West attitudes, the judges interrupted the defense's case to announce a unanimous not-guilty verdict. The judges held that the prosecution had failed to establish that the ANC had adopted a policy of violence and that the ANC was a Communist organization.[39] Their skepticism of Communist influence over the ANC was shared by foreign observers at the trial.[40] Unfortunately, such proof was insufficient to overcome the White Supremacist fantasies of the Eisenhower administration.

An OCB report elaborated on the supposed Marxist blind spot among African nationalists:

African desires for self-government as well as the racial policies of the Union of South Africa, make Soviet pretensions to be the champion of the oppressed colonies acceptable in some areas, so that Western attempts to picture Soviet Russia as a colonialist power itself have simply not been believed by African leaders. This continuing lack of appreciation on the part of African leaders regarding the real aims of the USSR makes difficult any United States efforts to create an understanding of these aims and to thwart indigenous movements, which play into the hands of the communists.[41]

As to the goals of the White South Africans, the OCB report was more sanguine:

The basic problem in the Union of South Africa remains the same as it has for years, namely the racialist policies of the Nationalist Government. There have been a few minor but significant indications that some Nationalists and thinking Afrikaaners [sic] are beginning to have qualms of conscience about their racial policies. The United States has attempted to exploit this nascent trend by avoiding provocative statements in the United Nations and elsewhere, which in the past have tended to increase South African intransigence, and by discreet, but nonetheless frank, conversations with South African leaders. It should also be recognized that world public opinion may be having some effect but it has been clearly demonstrated that public postures by the United States and other governments against South Africa's racial policies are not productive.[42]

These self-serving, and at times contradictory, statements from members of the Eisenhower administration echoed long-held positions and concealed American racial assumptions that actually endangered the Free World.[43]

American military and political support for the Nationalist regime enhanced the ability of White South Africans to narrow acceptable Black dissent into the stifling confines of debates regarding separate development. Further, American military support enabled the racist regime to augment its repressive tactics against non-White protest. With no recourse, Black nationalist groups remained highly radicalized, and some turned to the only other source of global power that might mitigate their suffering. Ironically, in trying to contain anti-West sentiments among Blacks, American policy was ensuring them.[44]

American decision-makers recognized that the intransigence of the Nationalist government was, in the words of Ambassador Byroade "driving [the nation] to catastrophe."[45] Unlike in the Congo, the Eisenhower administration could have easily identified educated Black elites with moderate-to-liberal inclinations who had participated in politics for generations.[46] For example, in declining an invitation from the NAACP's Walter White to attend a dinner in honor of Dr. Z. K. Matthews, Allen Dulles nevertheless asked White to brief him on Matthews's political views the next time Dulles and White met.[47] Cooperation between Eisenhower officials and Black South Africans could have warmed South Africa's non-White population to the Free World and could have offered a viable alternative to supposedly Marxist-influenced Black and Brown radicals. However, for the United States to have engaged in such a project would have meant that American officials believed in the viability of Black political leadership, among other things, which they did not.

First, they could not hear the argument of historical Black political competence because the evidence was not in proper form; in other words, no writings of Black political activities existed in societies which privileged oral traditions and which continued to be repressed by Whites.[48] Of course, in the modern era, the exclusion of Blacks from political power merely was proof of their unsuitability; they were incapable of running a government since they had no experience doing so. Second, Washington perceived as a potential threat the "core of relatively-sophisticated, politically-conscious, and articulate 'elite'—numbering possibly a hundred thousand—whose influence [was] capable of extending beyond the borders of South Africa."[49] American officials in South Africa warned that "the 'danger-spot' of the next decade lay among the urbanized masses" who lived in close proximity to Black elites. Arguing that these elites needed a safety valve to ease their anger toward the South African government, the embassy staff wrote:

> And in the urban areas are concentrated the "educated elite," with its veneer of European culture and ideas, capable of leadership, aggressive and ambitious, psychologically susceptible to the extremes of Black Nationalism or Communism, frustrated at the limited opportunities available, and increasingly resentful of restrictions imposed by the Whites.[50]

Although one of the rationales for America's psychological operations in Africa was to influence non-White elites, for the Eisenhower administration to assume that there were any Blacks who could run the country along with or better than the Whites was simply incomprehensible.[51] Most likely, members of the Eisenhower administration saw this group of Blacks as similar to the middle-class Blacks in America who were instrumental in the burgeoning domestic protest movement.[52] If so, they could easily dismiss them as self-serving troublemakers. Thus, the White House's only remaining fear was that the intractability of apartheid might lead to increased instability.

American elites were troubled by the consequences of the increasing racial stratification of South African society, but what they failed to acknowledge—or admit to themselves—was that American society had been just as exclusionary when European immigrants were the numerical minority. In Washington, White Supremacy was not problematic.[53] The primary concern in policy circles was three-fold: (1) the global psychological and political ramifications of apartheid and America's refusal to condemn it;[54] (2) White South African reactions to U.S. opinions, U.N. votes, and statements (official and journalistic);[55] and (3) increased non-White radicalism as a response to the lack of racial reforms.[56]

Eisenhower administration discourse never centered on the non-White population, except in vague references to Communist-inspired protests. If anything, American foreign policy discourse was analogous to the nineteenth-century moderate abolitionist critique of antebellum slave culture; the apartheid governments of South Africa were maintaining an anachronistic society in a world demanding change. The Eisenhower administration's gradualist approach toward racial reform on the continent of Africa was exemplified by Clarence Randall's gentle questioning of Firestone executives regarding "certain phases of [its] operation in Liberia" in response to African charges of racial segregation and forced labor.[57] Similarly, the administration tried to avoid involvement in the Asian and African protests of racially segregated movie theaters in Salisbury, Rhodesia.[58]

However, unlike the abolitionists of nineteenth-century America, the Eisenhower administration never conceived of intervening in South African affairs as a means of imposing a refined, though nevertheless stratified, racial order. In fact, the president indicated his compassion for the crisis facing the South African government. With respect to a British suggestion of jointly drafting an innocuous resolution in the United Nations critical of South Africa following the Sharpeville Massacre, Eisenhower said

> that he agreed with such a procedure. He had strong feelings that one could not sit in judgment on a difficult social and political problem six thousand miles away. He had to say that our own problem was in his mind in this connection, and that he had some sympathy with his friends in Atlanta on some of their difficulties.[59]

American liberalization of racism was not possible in the South Africa of the early Cold War. Equally important, the strength of the Free World failed when confronted with the White entitlement to exclusive power. If apartheid was wrong, in the American elite mind, it was wrong because it fed Soviet propaganda, further isolated a trusted ally from world opinion, and encouraged the non-White population to align themselves with either the Soviet bloc or untrustworthy Third World nationalists; all of these explanations could lead to a disastrous confrontation and perhaps lose to the Free World the abundant resources at the tip of the continent.[60] In this manner, the Sharpeville Massacre of March 1960 drew only a vague reference in NSC discussions. In fact, as will be discussed more fully below, the incident was not discussed in terms of the loss of African life but with regard to the potential loss of control in African affairs.

The problem was not simply that American elites viewed apartheid only within the context of Western security or that they failed to see the moral dimensions of apartheid. The fact is that they inverted observable fact to fit their worldview. The threat to the Free World was the supposedly emotional, Communist-inspired Black and Brown nationalists, when, in reality, the threat to global stability was White Supremacy itself. Moreover, for the Eisenhower administration to subvert White control of South Africa implied the falsity of the noble, pure, innocent White identity they so desperately sought to rehabilitate. Consequently, American recognition of, or intervention to remove, this threat was inconceivable. American policymakers considered the moral dimensions of subverting the normal operations of White Supremacy and found it abhorrent. To ask Whites to be ruled by Blacks was not simply immoral; it was tantamount to blasphemy!

## Blacks with Guns

From the dawning of European imperialism, the gun was the great equalizer that allowed the minority White collective to oppress the global majority of non-White peoples. Symbolically, the rape of South Africa was possible primarily by the imposition of European weaponry on the non-White people of the subcontinent.[61] The survival of White South Africa in its privileged position was possible only through this continued imposition, abetted in large part by the United States. The British experience in East Africa provided ample evidence for this proposition.

In the late 1940s Kikuyu dissent against the White settler regime in Kenya exploded. What began as labor unrest on Kenyan plantations evolved into full-scale guerilla warfare. The Mau Mau movement led to armed assaults against Whites and their Black accomplices. Although the insurrection was suppressed after four years of battle, the images of Blacks engaged in violent struggle against White authority forged a lasting image in the minds of people the world over.[62]

Based upon the experience of British expatriates in Kenya, South Africa was potentially the most volatile place on the continent. This alone may have justified stronger U.S. exertion to moderate the official manifestations of White Supremacy in Johannesburg. Instead, American officials felt comfortable foregoing any diplomatic arm-twisting, in part, because the oppressed majority lacked the weapons to unseat the Whites, who were well armed by their connections to Western powers. The authors of the 1960 National Intelligence Estimate regarding South Africa wrote: "Despite their number, the Africans are presently too weak and disorganized to mount a broad and sustained campaign of resistance in the face of the means of coercion available to the [W]hite community."[63]

There was little official concern regarding White violence against Africans. More importantly, despite their proclamations of their belief in freedom, members of the Eisenhower administration could not conceive of allowing for armed dissent in South Africa because Blacks had no right to be armed. This was especially so given that Americans had little knowledge about the masses of the indigenous population. What they did know was that the South Africans feared the implications of the Mau Mau.[64] Although Blacks in South Africa were not preparing for an all-out armed assault on the minority government, they did engage in massive non-violent protests like the Defiance Campaign. The South African government considered the Defiance Campaign to be a major threat, particularly since it coincided with the Mau Mau uprising: "Observers around the world drew differing lessons from the Mau Mau: in the Third World it was seen as further evidence that colonialism must end very soon, while in South Africa, [W]hites believed that its potential influence on the local Defiance Campaign must be countered by stronger measures of 'law and order.'"[65]

In 1948 Truman administration officials recognized the potential threat caused by apartheid and feared an eventual, though perhaps distant, non-White rebellion.[66] Truman administration confidence was bolstered not only because it believed that "there was little chance of an effective [B]lack challenge to [W]hite rule in the immediate future," but because they knew that American trade provided the apartheid regime with the financial backing to suppress dissent violently.[67] As in other areas, the Eisenhower administration followed the course set by its predecessor.

Scenes of nonviolent civil disobedience repeated themselves during the 1957 bus boycotts in Johannesburg and Pretoria. Although police and employers harassed walking Africans, the ten-week action won Black workers a reduction in a government-imposed bus-fare hike. This and other protest activities signaled the intensification of Black political struggle outside the prevailing political structure.[68] One easily could surmise that the intensification of Black struggle would lead to greater levels of government violence against Africans; however, the events following the Sharpeville Massacre show that this was not Washington's interest.

On March 21, 1960, a large crowd of demonstrators gathered in Sharpeville as part of a nationwide campaign against the humiliating pass laws. A crowd of several thousand initiated a nonviolent protest that was brutally halted as police wantonly fired into the assemblage. The police killed 67 Africans and wounded 186 others, including 40 women and 8 children. Journalists captured the carnage in photographs that ran in newspapers across the globe.[69]

In the aftermath of the Sharpeville Massacre and of the indigenous triumph against the pass system, NSC members discussed the political climate in Pretoria:

> Mr. [Allen] Dulles thought that the events in South Africa had been well described in the press. The principal questions now were: what is the shape of the future? And what political decisions are needed? He believed the South African Government would be able to hold the situation in check but noted that the [B]lacks in South Africa had gained a substantial victory for the first time in forcing the abandonment of the identity papers system. This first victory would probably spur the [B]lack population of South Africa on to attempt other victories. *However, very few arms were in the hands of the natives because of past restrictions and penalties against the possession of fire arms. This situation would provide an opportunity for exploitation by the Soviet Bloc. Especially after the Congo becomes independent, there would be great opportunities for smuggling arms to the natives of South Africa.*[70]

It should be noted that the Black victory Dulles described was a temporary moratorium on pass arrests offered by the Verwoerd government in the hopes of appeasing Black militancy. In the meantime, the apartheid regime relied upon other, more repressive measures to control the African population. Then, just a month

Despite this private anxiety, the administration openly accepted the good will generated among the Afro-Asian bloc in the United Nations and the non-White population in South Africa by Lincoln White's statement.[77] Behind closed doors, another critical issue surfaced.

As the Congo crisis raged north of the continent's White enclaves, Americans became aware of an ambitious South African security plan:

> Mr. Dulles reported that the government of the Union of South Africa was consulting the Portuguese and perhaps Southern Rhodesia in an effort to build up a buffer belt across the southern part of Africa. If the Union could build strong points in Angola, Rhodesia, and Mozambique, it could create a *cordon sanitaire* against events such as those taking place in the Congo. The Portuguese, however, are not particularly enthusiastic about this scheme because they are reluctant to cooperate with South Africa.[78]

It should be noted that the United States was willing to supply arms to Belgium and Portugal almost free of charge. Thus, the South African *cordon sanitaire* is best understood within the context of a joint State-Defense report "with respect to the provision of grant military assistance to nations which may be financially able to pay." The president had initiated an effort in late 1959 to have "the Secretaries of State and Defense . . . 'take steps that would achieve, at the earliest feasible time, the ultimate objective that new commitments for the provision of military equipment on a grant basis should not be offered to nations which are financially able to pay for such equipment.'"[79] An initial report was rendered to the NSC that recommended halting grant military assistance to Great Britain, Germany, France, Austria, and Luxembourg.[80] A second report focused on the Netherlands, Italy, Portugal, Belgium, and Japan:

> The conclusion of the report seems to be that, although each of the five countries may be expected to make some increase in the amount of resources it will commit to the defense effort, nevertheless none of the five countries will be able to achieve and maintain the force objectives which the JCS consider to be minimal without continuing military assistance from the U.S. for at least six years, FY 1961 and then FY 1962-66. In other words, the ultimate objective originally envisioned by NSC Action No. 2158—making no new commitments for the provision of military equipment on a grant basis to nations financially able to pay—does not appear, in the case of the five countries in question, early of accomplishment.[81]

If Portugal could work out its differences with the Afrikaners, they, along with the Belgians, could create the aforementioned buffer zone without undue strain to their economies. Of course, this also meant that the resources Belgium might devote to the orderly development of the Congo, or the viable secession of Katanga, would not impinge upon its NATO commitments.

Aware that the White colonies and settler-colonial state wanted to create a *cordon sanitaire* between themselves and the rest of Africa, the Eisenhower administration's push for an international arms agreement for Africa also meant a White settler monopoly on violence.[82] As a variant of America's experience, the insecurity and fear of the White minority in South Africa prohibited the Black majority from defending itself against tyranny. Because the Eisenhower administration knew that the southern African buffer zone foreshadowed the murderous repression of non-Whites inside and outside the Union's borders, its military grants aided and abetted the further subjugation of Black lives to White whims. Moreover, they added to the imbalance of power that created the potential for further links between authentic Black nationalist groups and their Communist sympathizers.[83]

This strategy is consistent with the general view that Black resistance to White minority rule was not bona fide. In other words, Blacks had few legitimate complaints and that festering unrest was merely the work of innate jealousy, outside agitators, or Communist dupes.[84] American officials seemed to accept South African government assertions that "the native population [was] contented except for external agitation," whether the tainted influence came from irresponsible U.N. delegates, foreign media, or Communist-influenced Black elites.[85] At least one American in South Africa was apparently convinced that the apartheid government was simply paternalistic: "[Prime Minister Verwoerd] spoke of the Black man in kindly and clearly sincere terms. He honestly believes his policies are best for all concerned."[86] This sentiment also was consistent with the White South African farce that outlawing the ANC and PAC was necessary, in part, to protect peace-loving Africans from intimidation by violence-minded agitators.[87] Furthermore, differences of opinion existed with regard to the supposed inability of South African Blacks to see through Communist blandishments.

Members of the Eisenhower administration at least acknowledged the legitimacy of some nonviolent, non-Communist Black protest. Yet, official American criticism of the South African government did not extend to the treason trial of ANC leadership, which included Nelson Mandela.[88] They also knew that the Union's strategy was to keep the non-White population disarmed and subdued. Thus, faced with these countervailing concerns, they chose to undermine democracy rather than sacrifice White privilege. Consequently, the only recourse was to ensure that a White minority regime—there and in the rest of Africa—effectively suppressed Black nationalism, maintained stability and order, and did so without much embarrassment. Such an approach missed a prime opportunity to end tyranny.

The Blacks in South Africa were forced into a situation that demanded that they radicalize their protest or suffer greater restrictions on their lives and liberties. American platitudes about democracy and freedom, if put into effect in South Africa, could have prevented further bloodshed in a country preparing for a one-sided race war. Unlike the Afrikaners, Blacks in South Africa had three options: (1) faith in the Free World's commitment to self-determination and the building of relations with the West; (2) cooperation with the Soviet Union and the Communist bloc; or (3) cooperation with Africa's independent nations. Furthermore, because

Black South Africans had few arms, the possibilities of a peaceful, brokered settlement were greater than between two antagonistic, well-armed foes.

On the other hand, South African Whites had only one option. Because they were both psuedofascist and anti-Communist, they would not turn to the Soviet Union for support if they were isolated from the Free World.[89] Thus, American arguments about their lack of diplomatic leverage and the need to foster a constructive discourse with the South Africans were laughable.[90] In this regard, perhaps the American fear was that a South Africa weary of American criticism would align with a European power, thereby diminishing U.S. hegemony over its Free World partners.[91] Ultimately, had the United States and the rest of the Free World turned their backs on the White minority government, the Afrikaners would have had no choice but to capitulate to non-White demands.

Official American policy was justified by the desire for stability. The Eisenhower administration, despite fearing the international outrage and potential revolution apartheid might spawn, reasoned that stability could not be guaranteed through a Black majority government. Their view of Blacks was consistent with those of their ally, the White South Africans.[92] Their blind faith in Black inferiority informed their analysis that order could be maintained only through the reinforcement of White minority rule, that the only feasible order was a racial hierarchy with Whites artificially imposed over non-Whites. The Eisenhower administration's stubborn commitment to an ideology of White Supremacy placed them inside a policy paradox.

American policymakers knew that, because of the intransigence of the apartheid regime, Communist penetration of the country could increase. Increased radicalization of non-White protest then meant further risks to stability and Western access to South Africa's strategic materials. As the risks of subversion increased, so did the repressive force which, in turn, heightened the potential for subversion. Although the United States claimed that it was unwilling to engage in an ever-spiraling struggle with the Soviet Union on the continent of Africa, the government was willing to do so in the struggle between a well-armed, psuedofascist White minority and a poorly armed, non-White majority. Although it may have appeared as if American foreign policy toward South Africa was frozen, it was driven by one of the hidden impulses of the Cold War: the impulse to maintain firm, White control over non-White people and their resources.

## Conclusion:
## Living in the Very House of Difference

American foreign policy toward South Africa during the early Cold War was based upon the American desire for the continued sustenance of the United States upon African wealth. The White House's interpretation of South African affairs heavily rested upon a persistent, pernicious racial iconography. In this iconography, the

Afrikaners were proud, engaging, and intellectual; Black South Africans were sullen, resentful, and prone to violence.[93] Consequently, the Eisenhower administration's twin concerns, placed within its racialized perspective, led to a singular focus on support for an antidemocratic White junta.

Because these agitators either were thought to be Communist-inspired or Communist pawns, American decision-makers dismissed the quest for non-White power as haphazard and a detriment to the security of the Free World. On the other hand, they recognized that the existence and maintenance of apartheid threatened their effort to repair the reputational value of Whiteness. However, because Afrikaners were White, Eisenhower officials refrained from forcing them to sacrifice their privileges and, instead, attempted to ignore or minimize the threat of overt White Supremacy to the racial sanctuary of the Cold War. The failure of this strategy is perhaps best observed by the continued subordination of African women.

In South Africa, African women were extremely active in trade union organizing and the political activism of groups like the ANC. As many African men later admitted, female leadership and motivational and organizational skills were essential to the survival of Black resistance to apartheid. Their militancy is evidenced by the fact that women like Lillian Ngoyi, Florence Matomela, and Elizabeth Mafekeng were banned, placed under house arrest, or imprisoned alongside their more famous male comrades.[94]

The Eisenhower administration put aside the idea of creating Western-style democracy in South Africa because, on its face, the nation was a representative democracy. Yet, for African women, the most significant issues centered around the destruction of families through forced migrant labor schemes; gender-segregated living arrangements; a lack of educational, economic, or housing options; and subjugation to male authority.[95] Female access to the ballot might have helped to some degree had men considered these women qualified to enjoy the franchise.

In particular, the American effort to persuade Afrikaners to moderate the more egregious effects of apartheid missed the systemic injustices that plagued Black women. In refuting the efforts by Afrikaner scholars to characterize as apolitical the autobiography of a Black South African woman, Anne McClintock argued that the protagonist's harrowing experiences were not universal:

> But being a perpetual minor in the eyes of the law and under permanent tutelage of a male relative, being endorsed out of one's home on marriage and forced to depart for a husband's bantustan often hundreds of miles away, being ineligible for residence rights without the signature of a male relative, pregnancy, birth, and child raising under the most perilous of circumstances: these are not problems that are faced by [W]hite men or [W]hite women. These are problems not even faced by [B]lack men.[96]

Of course, the moderation of apartheid could not protect Black women from sexual exploitation and social ostracism. One American official in South Africa recounted a sex scandal in the Johannes Strijdom government:

There was much talk in Pretoria still about the former private secretary to Strijdom who during the election campaign was brought into court for having an affair with a native girl. *He was fined £25; she was given six months of hard labor.* While he lost his job as Secretary, I understand he was elected on the Nationalist ticket over his United Party opponent to the House.[97]

The narrow boundaries that Washington set for South African stability confined Black women to lives wrought by interlocking racial, class, and gender subjugation. Further, the Eisenhower administration's efforts at gentle persuasion prolonged the marginalization of African women in South Africa. As in other parts of the continent—and within the United States—Black women remained irrelevant. Thus, the experiences of this group of Blacks most poignantly demonstrate the failed promise of U.S. Cold War diplomacy toward Africa. At the critical moment when it needed to determine the true villain in this tragedy, the Eisenhower administration shrugged its shoulders, embraced its White brethren, and closed a door on African democracy.

# CHAPTER SIX

# STABILIZING THE HAPPY COLONY: THE UNITED STATES AND THE BELGIAN CONGO

Africans in the Congo faced problems similar to those of Black South Africans. Despite Congolese agitation for freedom, Belgian overlords were reluctant to consider independence for their lone colony. As it did in South Africa, the United States relied heavily upon the natural resources in the Belgian Congo. Thus, as African nationalism swept across the belt of the continent, American officials worried about supporting White allies while continuing to tap the riches of these Black lands.

The U.S. response to this dilemma was consistent with its overall strategy in colonial Africa: to preserve the essential ties between Europe and Africa. As a result, American diplomacy in this period worked to maintain Belgian control of the largest colony on the continent while destroying the hopes for a democratic, multiracial, multiethnic central African state. Moreover, American fears of Communist subversion on the continent were the pretext under which White decision-makers treated Black protest as if it were illegitimate.

## U.S. Interests in the "Happy Colony"

NSC 5719/1 hinted at the nature of America's interests in the Congo:

> We wish to avoid in Africa a situation where thwarted nationalist and self-determinist aspirations are turned to the advantage of extremist elements, particularly Communists. We also wish to avoid the deprivation of African markets and sources of supply to Western Europe, and the economic dislocations that could result from the termination of the social and economic development programs of the metropolitan governments in the dependent areas.

More specifically, the drafters noted that "the Belgians appear in the best position to continue the economic development of their dependent area, the Congo, a rich area in its own right." After noting that the members of the European Common Market were prepared to invest more than $500,000,000 in their colonial holdings—with the Congo presumably due for a large portion of that infusion of capital—the drafters of NSC 5719/1 discussed the prospect of adequate economic development support for their African territories:

> One very important factor will necessarily be a metropolitan power's appraisal of the likelihood that it will be able to maintain close political and economic ties with a particular colonial territory, either through an extension of the colonial relationship itself or through the development of a mutually-satisfactory new relationship, which could include continuation of trade discrimination in favor of the metropolitan powers. *Should one or the other relationship fail to develop, the incentives of the metropolitan powers to provide financial or economic support, either through public or private investment, are likely to suffer rapid deterioration.* Thus our success in attaining the previously-stated U.S. objective of preserving the essential ties between Europe and Africa, will probably have an important impact upon the rate of Africa's economic progress, while lessening Africa's reliance on U.S. assistance.[1]

Thus, American diplomacy toward the Congo was intended to (1) maintain the hierarchical links between Belgium and its colony; (2) support decolonization without giving the impression that the U.S. was going to underwrite independence; and (3) "attempt, as appropriate[,] to have removed discriminatory laws which discourage private American investment."[2] These conclusions were based both on American needs and the Belgium veneer of benign paternalism.

The Belgian administration of the largest colony in Africa was brutal.[3] The genocide perpetrated upon the Congolese was masked by the allegedly altruistic nature of King Leopold's venture[4]: "It was necessary that the Congo be productive, not to enrich the sovereign, who did not care about that, but to feed the governmental machinery necessarily expensive in a new and unorganized country."[5] Even admirers of Leopold noted that the economy of the Belgian Congo was organized to provide maximum enrichment for Europeans, not for Africans. The colonial administration thrived under Belgium's full control during and between the world wars. Notably, productivity in the Congo meant an economy that provided the resources demanded by the West. By the end of World War II, the entire productive capacity of the colony was placed at the disposal of Britain and France and, later, the United States.[6]

Despite the inherent racial skew in the Congo's economy, the Belgian colonial administration "won particular praise from observers for its policy of training Africans in industrial and mechanical skills."[7] Such praise came from members of the Eisenhower administration as well:

With respect to the Belgian Congo, [Clarence] Randall said that in a conversation with the Governor General, the latter had made the point that a man must eat before he can enjoy freedom. The Belgians have therefore concentrated on providing some economic opportunity for the natives in the colony. Having done fairly well in this field, the Belgians are now beginning to move cautiously toward greater political freedom and development for the natives.[8]

The super-profits of colonialism and the facade of the happy colony masked a roiling dissatisfaction among the Congolese because of the consistent, violent subordination of their interests.[9]

As in other parts of the continent, the barbarity of colonial governance relied upon collaboration between the invading power and one or more indigenous groups. Belgian imperialism, first perpetrated by King Leopold's personal yoke and later controlled by the state, benefited from its savagery and a weakened Congolese resistance that resulted from significant population loss brought about by both the Atlantic and Islamic slave trades.[10] Yet, resistance to imperialism was consistent, if hardly successful.

Early twentieth-century unrest stirred by the Christian sect of Simon Kimbangu shook the complacency of colonial authorities. Workers' rebellions in the 1930s provoked punitive expeditions by labor agents and the military that shocked even Belgian officials. Like many of their Black counterparts in the United States, the soldiers of the *Force Publique*, the colonial army, chafed under menial roles and the expectations of their obedience. Yet, as the numerous indigenous groups cobbled together a nationalist coalition after World War II, independence seemed far away.[11] Such an eventuality did not disturb Americans, as long as the Belgians made some concessions to future political power for Blacks. Indeed, the tension between Belgians and Americans chiefly stemmed from Belgian fears of American economic objectives.

Americans from the public and private spheres were interested in developing American business in the Congo. During the 1950s, the Belgians encouraged small-scale American business investment in the Congo. However, Belgian enthusiasm waned as Belgians came to believe that the American thirst for the Congo's riches was unquenchable.[12] According to officials in Washington, the great fear in Belgium was the increasing American presence in Africa: "Belgian officials have been increasingly suspicious of all U.S. activities in the Belgian Congo, so much so that it has been necessary to approach the Belgians at a high level and tell them frankly the reasons for increased U.S. interest in Africa, and the need for U.S. diplomatic and consular representatives fulfilling their normal duties without let or hindrance."[13] Like the Portuguese, the Belgians abhorred the American discourse on decolonization. Equally disturbing to the Belgians was their impression that American businesses were seeking to supplant Belgian firms. To counter these impressions, "the Belgians were assured that the United States had no intention of replacing them in their colonial areas nor in promoting irresponsible and premature nationalist movements."[14]

In 1958, the Belgians grudgingly provided the indigenous populations in the Congo with a political concession: the Belgians held municipal elections in three major cities. Although conceding that this was a limited move, American officials averred that it was "a step in the right direction."[15] The Congolese were frustrated with this snail's pace of Africanizing the local political process and pushed for swifter change. As the Belgian government slowly began to cede power to the indigenous populations at the turn of the decade, protests erupted in major cities throughout the colony. Violent repression of the demonstrations by the *Force Publique* led to more riots. Many American officials seemed surprised at the violent reactions in Leopoldville and used this as evidence to support their belief that the Congolese were not ready for independence. Notably, historian Basil Davidson argued that the Belgians, having reached the same conclusion, accelerated the independence process in the hope of using Congolese inexperience and internal conflict to prolong "the underlying colonial structure."[16]

Immediately, the Eisenhower administration set to work on understanding and, then, muting the ramifications of the nationalist disturbances. In November 1959, Allen Dulles reported to the National Security Council on developments in the Belgian Congo following riots in Stanleyville and Leopoldville. Noting that the disturbances followed the arrests of nationalist leaders, as well as the announcement of a four-year plan for independence, Dulles turned the discussion over to Maurice Stans. Stans, who served as director of the Bureau of the Budget, had recently returned from the area. Along with Secretary of State Herter, he remarked on the strong tribal animosities in the colony. Stans was particularly disturbed by the fact that the Congolese listened to media from other parts of Africa, rather than the Voice of America. In addition, he was pessimistic about the Congolese version of nationalism: "While the natives of the area shout for independence, their concept of independence is very vague and generally can be reduced to the hope of getting a handout from the government. Mr. Stans said he was forced to conclude that the best thing for the area would be a plan which did not grant independence for twenty-five years."[17] Stans's attitude reflected the beliefs of the Belgians.[18]

By January 1960, the United States was prepared to make its stand against Congolese independence. The NSC Planning Board agreed upon three coequal objectives for Africa: (1) "maintenance of the Free World orientation of the area, denial of the area to Communist domination, and the minimization of Communist influence therein"; (2) "orderly economic development and political progress towards self-determination by the countries of the area in cooperation with the metropoles and other Free World countries"; and (3) "access to such military rights and facilities and strategic resources as may be required in our national security interests." The president agreed with this notion but believed that the latter two objectives were contingent upon achievement of the first.[19] To achieve the primary objective, it was imperative that the United States control the political process within the Congo to find an appropriate Congolese leader.

The White House felt compelled to do whatever was necessary to keep the strategic resources of the Belgian Congo firmly within the Free World's grip.

Conceding that independence was on the horizon, the NSC was distressed about the prospects for democracy in Africa. Their fears about the development of Western-style democracy were based upon their pessimistic views of the Africans:

> The Vice President said that the British had told him that Ghana, although the most viable nation in Africa, had only a 50 percent chance for an orderly economic development. The British anticipated that in many countries of Africa such as Nigeria, a South American pattern of dictatorship would develop. [Nixon added] that it was difficult to realize the problems faced in Africa without visiting the Continent. *Some of the peoples of Africa have been out of the trees for only about fifty years.*

The budget director agreed with the vice president: *"Mr. Stans, while disclaiming any expertness, said he had formed the impression that many Africans still belonged in the trees.* This was an area where agitators were able to prey on the superstitions of the people to an unbelievable extent." Because *"African leaders were incapable of exercising power when they obtained it,"* their need for advice made them easily impressionable.[20] Accordingly, the United States had to find a Congolese leader whom it could influence, thereby providing the proper guidance for these supposedly feral, feeble-minded people.[21]

Despite some uncertainties as to the implications of events there, the American tactic was to work closely with the Belgians to resolve the nascent crisis. Livingston Merchant, assistant secretary of state for European affairs, reported at a mid-January 1960 NSC meeting that the American ambassador in Belgium "was about to have discreet talks to see how we might cooperate with Belgium in achieving our aims, *which are identical with those of Belgium*, without suffering the stigma of supporting a colonial power."[22] In the summer of 1960, the United States, along with Britain and France, slowly acted to provide a small number of troops to support a U.N. peacekeeping force geared to stabilize the first tumultuous moments of postindependence Congo. Their support for the Belgian position meant that Katanga could secede, if necessary, and allow the Belgians to continue their exploitation of the Congo's resources. By October 1960, the Eisenhower administration was aware of Belgium's continued extraction of minerals in Katanga and was willing to collaborate in the facade of Katanga's independence by purchasing uranium ore before it could fall into "the wrong hands."[23] The logical extension of this policy suggested that if the future of the Congo lay with a dictatorship, the United States wanted to anoint the dictator.

## The Problem with Lumumba and the Search for the "African Strongman"

Related to America's concerns about continued, unfettered access to the Congo's resources was the American distrust of Patrice Lumumba. To those in Washington, Lumumba represented the worst kind of Black, an allegedly uneducated, ungrateful trickster and a demagogue frantically searching for international advice and support.[24] As such, he could, in the American mind, prey upon the superstitions of the Congolese while being a leftist dupe. Although they knew that he was the only political figure in the Congo with a national, rather than strictly ethnic, following, they could not stomach supporting an individual who they agreed represented Congolese autonomy and, potentially, a severance of the ties between the Congo and the West.[25] As mentioned previously, Lumumba's open association with his mentor, Kwame Nkrumah, confirmed the White House's worst fears.[26] This construction of Lumumba differed widely from the perceptions of the Congolese and many others.

Essentially, Patrice Lumumba was a political leader who focused on the political, economic, and social autonomy of the indigenous peoples of the Congo. As he evolved into a Pan-Africanist, Lumumba relied upon a non-Marxist critique of colonial problems. His nation-building project rested on the common experience of Congolese exploitation by Belgian colonial administrations, rather than an adherence to theoretical analysis of class formation.[27]

As an emerging nationalist politician with the MNC (the Congolese National Movement Party), Lumumba was highly critical of Western imperialism, in general, and Belgian colonialism, in particular. When the Belgians cracked down on the nationalists in 1959, Lumumba was the leading figure arrested. His arrest increased his popularity, and his subsequent release further stoked the flames of independence. His demands for a new Congo and his ability to transcend ethnic particularism in a quest for a national identity gained him significant support throughout the colony. Thus, it was no surprise, except to many Westerners, that Lumumba's party enjoyed a landslide victory in the May 1960 elections.[28]

Like other African nationalists, Patrice Lumumba articulated an African-centered political sentiment which had been building for decades among the colonized people of the Congo. "The objective of the MNC is to unite and organize the Congolese masses in the struggle to improve their lot and wipe out the colonialist regime and the exploitation of man by man," he once stated.[29] Significantly, Lumumba repeated his party's willingness to accept Western technical aid, even a willingness to work with the Belgians: "We want to free ourselves to collaborate with Belgium in freedom, equality, and dignity. Collaboration is not possible when the relationship is one of subjugation. The Congolese must enjoy the immediate and total exercise of fundamental freedoms and every sort of political, administrative, private, and public right."[30] Although his political thinking evolved greatly between 1956 and the time of his death in 1961, certain continuities are discernable: (1) the Congolese right to self-determination; (2) the territorial unity of the Congo through a strong, centralized government and a supra-ethnic political party; (3) the sequential implementation of economic and social reforms; and (4) the adoption of a foreign policy patterned along the lines of Pan-Africanism and nonalignment.[31]

Like Nkrumah, Lumumba was a Pan-Africanist. However, Lumumba never emphasized a strict class perspective when developing grassroots support for the

MNC and independence. Accordingly, the most important aspects of MNC organizing were its emphases on education—postsecondary and political education—for the masses of Congolese, a sense of national unity among the Congo's various ethnic groups, and an end to racial and economic discrimination against Blacks, irrespective of gender or class. Interestingly, Soviet officials did not consider Lumumba to be a Communist and were disappointed in the prospects of his leading a Marxist party in Africa.[32] In fact, his lack of doctrinaire Marxist perspective is best illustrated by his stance on the issue of nationalizing foreign industry:

> Given the present state of affairs, Congo cannot develop without capital . . . *And our political program does not call for nationalization.* But what the Congolese government will demand is that the national revenue be distributed equitably and that the industrialization of the Congo be based on the satisfaction of the needs of the people . . . *We are going to study the direction we want our government to move in without making violent changes in the beginning, because we would risk undergoing a certain period of crisis or encounter difficulties were we to do so.*[33]

Again, the Eisenhower administration had trouble comprehending an independent Black leader. To most American officials, such leaders were either opportunists—because they were unwilling to bow to Western dominance—or Communists' pawns because of their Marxist beliefs or their irresponsible critiques of the West.[34] Perhaps Lumumba's greatest sin in the eyes of the West was his direct, uncompromising style, guided by a practicality and forthrightness that cast a critical gaze upon Belgian elites and disrupted the racial sanctuary of the Cold War.

By June 1960, the United States admitted Lumumba's political might, while emphasizing his purported flaws:

> General [Charles] Cabell [Deputy Director of the CIA] said that in the Congo, which is obtaining its independence today, Patrice Lumumba is emerging as the strong man. His government, however, is weak and will have a Leftist tinge with five out of his ten cabinet ministers being inclined toward communism. Lumumba himself appears to be neutralist in attitude, with a Leftist and opportunistic bent. He is reported to have solicited communist funds to help him obtain his present political position.[35]

General Cabell finished his report by noting that, because of its dire economic condition, the Congo would be "susceptible to Sino-Soviet offers of economic assistance."[36] Exacerbating American fears, Lumumba's government broke relations with Belgium in July 1960 and demanded that Belgian troops promptly withdraw from all parts of the Congo. The Katanga secession, coupled with spotty but serious food shortages and other social problems, proved to Washington the ineptitude of the Lumumba government.[37] According to Allen Dulles, Lumumba's determination to have a united, independent Congo "placed the Belgians in a difficult position." Dulles reported to the NSC that the "Belgian Government had recognized the

Congo and was opposed to its fragmentation. However, it also wanted to protect its large investment in Katanga." Secretary of State Herter added "that it was understating the matter to say that Lumumba was anti-West." This uncertainty of the situation was only increased by the fact that the provisional governor of Katanga, Moise Tshombe, was pro-Belgian. Complicating matters further was the ambivalence of the populace of Katanga with respect to the Belgians, in contrast to the attitude of their supposed leader.[38]

The Belgians were disturbed by Lumumba's unrelenting critique, his boundless energy, and his historical memory, the greatest example of which came at the Congolese independence ceremonies on June 30, 1960.[39] After Belgium's King Baudoin delivered a paternalistic speech, newly appointed President Joseph Kasavubu provided a measured, conciliatory reply. Then Prime Minister Lumumba stepped toward the microphone and delivered a withering broadside which shattered the veneer of Belgian magnanimity and Congolese gratitude:

> For though this independence of the Congo is today being proclaimed in a spirit of accord with Belgium, a friendly country with which we are dealing as one equal with another, no Congolese worthy of the name can forget that we fought to win it . . . a passionate and idealistic fight, a fight in which there was no effort, not one privation, not one suffering, not one drop of blood we ever spared ourselves . . . The wounds that are the evidence of the fate we endured for eighty years under a colonialist regime are still too fresh and painful for us to be able to erase from our memory. Back-breaking work has been extracted from us, in return for wages that did not allow us to satisfy our hunger, or to decently clothe or house ourselves, or to raise our children . . . We have been victims of ironic taunts, of insults, of blows that we were forced to endure . . . because we were blacks. Who can forget that a black was addressed in the familiar form, not because he was a friend, certainly, but because the polite form of address was to be used only for whites? . . . We have known that there were magnificent mansions for whites in the cities and ramshackle straw hovels for blacks, that a black was never allowed into the so-called European movie theaters or restaurants or stores; that a black traveled in the hold of boats below the feet of the white in his deluxe cabin.[40]

Upon painting a scene of life eerily familiar to diasporic Africans, Lumumba briefly outlined the political, social, and economic justice objectives of the new government and asked that the Congolese continue to exalt national unity above ethnic differences. He began his summation by saying, "Thus the new Congo, our beloved republic . . . will be a rich, free, and prosperous country, with regard to both its domestic relations and its foreign relations." He concluded by asserting that "the independence of the Congo represents a decisive step toward the liberation of the entire African continent."[41] King Baudoin and his entourage were so outraged that they almost skipped the dinner reception.[42] In a master stroke, Lumumba rent asunder the veil of Western beneficence. His clarion call for Congolese and African independence revealed the farce of America's racial sanctuary and threatened American policy objectives. Not surprisingly, Eisenhower pointed to Lumumba's speech as the beginning of trouble in the Congo.[43]

By the time Lumumba trekked to the West, American officials had received ample notice from the Belgians and American diplomats abroad of Lumumba's statements and behavior. During July 1960 officials in Washington requested advice from foreign offices about "handling him."[44] When Lumumba met with Henry Cabot Lodge, he indicated that the Congolese had great faith in America:

> Lodge called on Lumumba . . . this morning at his hotel at latter's request. He [Lodge] began by outlining US attitude toward Congo as stated both in SC [UN Security Council] and in private talks with Belgians. Lumumba replied by describing pre-independence hopes for Belgian cooperation and assistance. Instead, he said Belgium had left Congolese . . . without treasury, gold having been taken to Brussels just prior to independence.[45]

Weeks later, he found that his faith had been misplaced. Despite being told of Belgium's thievery, American officials stubbornly continued to attribute all social and economic problems to the supposedly incompetent Lumumba government.[46] Not only did the United States actively support the Belgian position, but the Eisenhower administration also tried to use its diplomatic powers to undermine Lumumba.

When the Congolese prime minister arrived in New York in July 1960, Eisenhower officials were at a loss to explain his presence, the purpose of his trip, or how he was able to travel to New York. Nevertheless, Anderson and Herter asserted at an NSC meeting that "if it was to our advantage to keep Lumumba away from the Congo, then we ought to arrange for him to stay in the U.S. for awhile." Herter noted "if [Lumumba] stayed away from the Congo long enough, he would find that he had no government when he returned." To this the president added "that we might provide Lumumba with a three weeks tour of the U.S. on a modest basis."[47] Yet after Lumumba was the subject of Kasavubu's coup d'état, the administration was unwilling to grant him a visa to travel to New York in order to appeal to the United Nations and likely encouraged Mobutu to arrest him if he tried to leave the country.[48] These passport discussions had little to do with the legal aspects of visits to the United States by foreigners. Instead, Washington was willing to trap Lumumba in either the United States or the Congo in order to reach its objective of removing him from power.

American officials in various positions considered the Lumumba government to be a threat to U.S. interests which needed to be destroyed. Because they recognized Lumumba's immense popularity, American elites realized that confronting him was necessary, but that doing so openly would lead to disastrous results.[49] Eisenhower officials were aware that conspicuous Western support for any African opposition party could be a political "kiss of death."[50] Thus, as they had in other theaters, American officials turned to the tactic of covert operations. They justified the need to subvert the democratic processes of the Congo for two principal reasons: (1) democracy would serve only to entrench Lumumba; and (2) to restore order in the colony, they needed an authoritarian figure. Their belief in the infantile character of African peoples demanded no less.

Even before the outbreak of disturbances in the Congo, Allen Dulles noted a trend toward military autocracy in the emerging countries of Africa and Asia. Secretary of Defense Neil McElroy pointed out that, though at times troublesome, military leadership could stabilize backward societies. Thus, the United States needed to cultivate pro-Western African military leaders.[51] Dismissing advice he had gotten from the King of Morocco, who maintained "that U.S. policy should be to help the countries of Africa to become independent and then assist in their development," Eisenhower insisted that America first find a way to reach the proper authoritarian personnel.[52] This was critical because American officials were convinced that "Africans [did not] understand Western-style democracy and beyond their village, [looked] to their chief as the dictator."[53] Vice President Nixon had concluded that "although we cannot say it publicly . . . we need the strong men of Africa on our side."[54]

Other researchers have noted the high esteem in which the Eisenhower administration placed covert operations.[55] To that end, Allen Dulles "authorized a crash-programme fund of up to $100,000 to replace the [Lumumba] government . . . with a pro-western group."[56] Although NSC attendees believed that some of the members of Lumumba's cabinet were not as radical as he, none of the ministers or other officials seemed suited for the role of strongman. The White House was interested in steering Kasavubu, but mistook his inability to break the confines of ethnic politics for laziness. Thus, the choice for American covert support became Col. Joseph Mobutu, a young army officer who controlled the only functioning units of the *Force Publique* and was a member of Lumumba's MNC.[57]

Finding and supporting a strongman was especially important since, from the American perspective, the crux of the problem in the colony was that Belgian political stewardship was nonexistent and "no one, literally no one, in the Congo [knew] how to run a government department."[58] The issue would become even more critical because of the likelihood of further internal instability caused by high unemployment and the possibility that the World Bank might renege on a promised loan. Adding to these woes was the fact that the Belgians were continuing to mine in Katanga and none of the mining revenue was going to the rest of the fledgling nation.[59]

With Mobutu in pocket, the United States believed that it could sabotage Lumumba's movement without causing much suspicion. Mobutu was a trusted aid of Lumumba's and had been at his side during the Round Table Conference in Brussels between Congolese nationalists and the Belgian government.[60] This process would be aided by widening the rift between Lumumba and Kasavubu.[61]

From the summer of 1960, American officials worked to minimize or closely monitor Lumumba's movements across the Congo. In so doing, they undermined his support and boxed him in for either Mobutu or the pro-Belgian Moise Tshombe of Katanga.[62] In September 1960 Kasavubu dismissed Lumumba as prime minister, a move which Lumumba rejected. Mobutu then moved against Kasavubu in order to, in his words, neutralize all political parties and restore order in the Congo. However, the United States encouraged Mobutu to work with Kasavubu. With the new Kasavubu-Mobutu team moving to end Soviet and radical penetration of the Congo, U.N. troops were the only thing keeping Lumumba safe. On September 18, 1960, Mobutu announced to American officials in the Congo that he had ordered Lumumba's arrest, though that proved easier said than done; U.N. troops prevented Mobutu's men from serving the arrest warrant on Lumumba. Thus, the best the Americans could achieve was to trap Lumumba within the prime minister's mansion, encircled by nearly one thousand troops from the *Force Publique*, now reconstituted as the National Army of the Congo. Although Mobutu collaborated with Western wishes, there was some U.S. concern in 1960 about his long-term viability as a national leader. Nonetheless, he seemed to be the best "horse to back."[63]

American hatred for Lumumba was such that the CIA twice attempted to kill him during the fall of 1960.[64] The Eisenhower administration had better luck diplomatically when it engineered a U.N. vote to accept Kasavubu's credentials as Congolese head of state.[65] On November 27, Lumumba escaped confinement in the prime minister's mansion and headed for Stanleyville. Lumumba's escape caused a great deal of worry in Washington that his reemergence on the political scene might be imminent, thereby disrupting the administration's carefully orchestrated scheme. Within a week, Lumumba was arrested by the Army. Despite the United Nation's limited support for Lumumba as part of a political solution to the crisis—much to the United States' chagrin—Mobutu, Tshombe, and the CIA coordinated their efforts to assassinate the Congo's most powerful unifying force.[66] Simultaneously, the United States sought to protect Belgian interests in another manner.

## Outside Agitators and U.S. Salvation for the Congo

As with many Whites in Jim Crow-era America, U.S. officials were convinced that the nationalist activities in the Congo were engineered by outside agitators. The paternalistic stereotype of happy, childlike Blacks gratefully living under White tutelage and supervision was central to the fantasy of White superiority. Since Whites needed to believe that Blacks consented to subordination, any protest against the accepted racial hierarchy had to have its genesis outside of the Black collective.[67] As with Whites of previous generations, Eisenhower officials were determined to stop the supposed provocateurs.

Given the dire situation his country faced, Lumumba sought aid from Western, Communist, and nonaligned nations.[68] That he was not a Marxist mattered little in Washington because the American fear of Communist influence served as both a convenient rationale and an irrational determinant. In other words, the American anxiety regarding a Communist presence provided a reason to move forward against a perceived African opponent. When that opponent was not verified, as with Lumumba, the belief was that the threat was imminent and needed to be addressed preemptively. Their major concern allegedly was China and the Soviet Union. However, as events unfolded, the United States also worried about the defense of

Lumumba by other African leaders. Ultimately, the Eisenhower administration's paranoia resulted in a growing distrust of the United Nations as well.

Although policy papers noted a limited Communist presence in much of Africa, Nixon and others felt that NSC 5719/1 unduly downplayed the Communist threat on the continent:

> The Vice President . . . believed that he detected a tendency . . . to underestimate the seriousness of the Communist threat in Africa. After all, we do not have to count only card-bearing Communists as a measure of the Communist threat. In Africa, the Vice President predicted, the Communists will clothe themselves in Islamic, racist, anti-racist, or nationalist clothing. The potential danger of Communist penetration he believed to be very great, because the Communists were always in a position to support and take advantage of extremist elements, where the United States could not do so.

Secretary of State Herter concurred with Nixon's assessment that the language of NSC 5719 was too optimistic with respect to the Communist threat. Herter "therefore suggested the addition of language which would indicate that the potential Communist threat to Africa was greater than the actual threat at the present time."[69]

According to Allen Dulles, the signs of Soviet manipulation of Lumumba and the Congolese were everywhere. The only issue facing the United States was proving it. Because of the rapid pace of change, Africa had become a "battleground of the first order."[70] Washington's belief in the inherent incompetence of African leadership heightened the potential for Communist subversion and offered circumstantial evidence of non-African influence.[71] The Congo's rapid progression toward freedom was only comprehensible as a disguised Communist plot:

> Secretary Gates, referring to Mr. Dulles' comments on the orientation of Lumumba, said he understood there were indications—[REDACTED]—that recent developments in the Congo were Communist-inspired. For example, interviews [REDACTED] seemed to indicate that persons had been sent to the tribes in advance of independence with instructions. The revolt appeared to have been synchronized. It was important, Secretary Gates felt, to step up our efforts to prove that the revolt was Communist-inspired. Mr. Dulles agreed. He stated that we had interviewed [REDACTED] Lumumba may have sent out instructions and these instructions may have been under a Communist directive. *The insurrection had been simultaneous in many areas and it was therefore difficult to find any other explanation.*[72]

As the pages on the calendar of 1960 dwindled, the United States sought to defeat two groups of interlopers: radicals outside Africa and within the United Nations.

## Interloper One: The Communist Bloc

Under American-Belgian duress, the cross-ethnic coalition of the Lumumba government cracked. Even as the United Statese's frantic support of Mobutu, Tshombe, and Belgium began to take its toll on Congolese solidarity in the fall of 1960, Dulles cried that a "Soviet freighter, believed to be carrying equipment for Lumumba, is still off the African coast." Whether relying upon a story about supposed Telegraph Agency of Supreme Soviet (TASS) embellishment of a written interview with Lumumba or his surprising withdrawal of an earlier request for Soviet troops, American officials were convinced that Lumumba was a Communist pawn. What they refused to acknowledge was that Belgian violence and, later, American refusals of aid forced Lumumba to seek aid from the USSR in order to maintain the Congo's fragile union.[73] Even the Soviet premier was shocked that the United States rebuffed Lumumba: "Why? . . . Explain to me why . . . Really, are the Americans that stupid?"[74] Consequently, the United States prepared to take a more interventionist approach to the Congo.

Stung by the U-2 spy plane incident and the revolution in Cuba, the Eisenhower administration did not want to lose more ground to global Communism. Because American policymakers would not acquiesce to Soviet dominion in the Congo, the United States was willing to confront the Soviets militarily in Central Africa. In a personal letter to his brother Edgar, President Eisenhower noted that the Free World nearly lost 60 percent of its oil reserves with the January 1953 emergence of the Mossadegh government in Iran.[75] In the heat of the summer of 1960, the United States was unwilling to lose one of the Free World's largest caches of uranium, cobalt, and diamonds.

During the August 1 meeting of the NSC, Gordon Gray, special assistant for National Security Affairs, posed the question "what action would the US take if the USSR sought to intervene militarily in the Congo?" Secretary Herter referred the attendees to the report by the Joint Chiefs of Staff (the JCS) and informed Gen. Twining that, for the most part, he agreed with it. Gray then read the critical paragraph of the JCS report for those present:

> In addition to the United Nations actions, effective or otherwise, the United States must be prepared at any time to take appropriate military action as necessary to prevent or defeat Soviet military intervention in the Congo. Multilateral action would be preferable but unilateral action may be necessary. In the present Soviet belligerent mood, the USSR could estimate that the United States would not oppose them. We must be prepared to oppose and defeat them. In order to prevent their making such a rash move, they must be made to understand that we will not tolerate a Soviet military takeover of the Congo.[76]

This military stance neatly dovetailed with economic policy: intervention was tolerable only if it served American interests.[77]

Long before the sovereignal crisis in the Congo, White interests had dominated the political scene in Katanga. Moise Tshombe's CONAKAT party was founded with Belgian advice and financing. In particular, the huge mining concern, Union Miniere, and other White settlers exercised overweening power in the province. They knew that losing the Congo's wealth could have ripped the heart out of the Belgian economy. Thus, Belgians led the Katanga secession, not Tshombe.[78]

Equally important was the support for Tshombe and Katanga throughout the West. The Belgian military presence, which arrived in Katanga before Tshombe declared the secession, was bolstered by White mercenaries from different European and southern African nations. Supplies were shipped into Katanga through bordering North Rhodesia and Portuguese-controlled Angola. In fact, during a military strike against Katanga, Tshombe fled the province for Rhodesia with the aid of the British consul.[79] In this vein, Washington, hoping to disguise its true intent, worked with individual Western countries and through the United Nations to reduce Lumumba's power and reestablish Belgian dominance. However, the United States began to turn on the United Nations once it no longer served American purposes.

**Interloper Two: The United Nations**

Recognizing the limitations of their power as well as the political risks of engaging in a diplomacy that kept the colonies linked to the metropoles, American officials thought that working through multilateral organizations was the best strategy for controlling economic, political, and military developments on the continent. Such an approach had multiple benefits because it concealed American objectives from the Africans while appeasing European allies who disliked America's rhetorical anticolonialism. Well before the Congo crisis, Clarence Randall informed the president that "[American] assistance to the colonies was often less offensive [to the metropoles] if offered in the framework of a multilateral organization, so that it appeared as a mutual effort." Because the president was not convinced that "U.S. military activity in the area would be beneficial," American strategy with regard to the Congo was to provide troops and support through the United Nations.[80]

The American strategy to use the United Nations as an instrument of its own diplomacy was challenged by the nature of the international body as a united front which included Communists and an increasing number of allegedly primitive nations.[81] With respect to African support for Lumumba, the United States was cautious not to antagonize African nationalists.[82] Cautiously, some American officials encouraged Nkrumah to influence Lumumba in the hopes of offsetting Soviet influence. Nevertheless, they monitored Black support for the Congolese nationalist in response to the efforts of nations like Guinea, Ghana, and the United Arab Republic to aid Lumumba in the United Nations and within the Congo itself.[83] Whenever possible, American officials tried to emphasize any disagreements within the Congo, real or imagined, or between Lumumba and other Africans. Notably, they also feared Egyptian radicalism in the area. What they especially feared was the type of African autonomy and control over the Congo crisis espoused by Nkrumah in his September 23, 1960, U.N. speech.[84]

Despite praise for U.N. Secretary-General Dag Hammarskjold, early American concerns about the growth and changing character of the United Nations evolved into concerns about his leadership as well.[85] An initial concern with the United Nations as a tool of American foreign policy was that U.N. development aid to small countries necessarily meant that "the Soviets would . . . become involved." Consequently, it was argued that "the best recourse for the U.S. was to be found within the framework of the World Bank." This was a viable option because the World Bank effectively was an American institution.[86] Later, American trepidation was aroused by the growing number of non-White participants in the international body. For instance, representatives from Tunisia, Ceylon, and Indonesia, among others, pressured the Belgians and argued for greater U.N. support of Lumumba. Furthermore, it was the U.N. permanent representative in the Congo, Rajeshwar Dayal of India, who refused to allow Mobutu to arrest Lumumba in September 1960, then issued a November 1960 progress report that recommended a political solution to the crisis which would have included Lumumba, opposed recognition of Mobutu's government, and blamed Katangan and Belgian soldiers for atrocities in the Congo. "If we continue to bank on the UN as we had in the past," declared Secretary Herter, "we must make every effort to hold the emerging African nations on our side of the fence."[87] The president's experience with Francophone Africans confirmed this imperative.[88]

As the Congo crisis evolved, the United States decided to support the June 14, 1960, U.N. resolution to assist the Congo as a means of getting Western troops into the area and deterring the Soviet Union from moving unilaterally to the same end. Initially, the Lumumba government had welcomed U.N. assistance as a means of maintaining national unity. Although only a handful of American soldiers actually went to the Congo, most of the U.N. force consisted of soldiers from African states; the U.S. military helped with advice and an airlift of other troops and matériel. Early on, American officials were pleased with the U.N. response to the crisis. Although Washington felt that Soviet Premier Khrushchev was exploiting the opportunity to use propaganda to discredit American leadership of the Free World, U.N. resolutions which were perceived as anti-West were defeated. Additionally, the United Nations had agreed to the American suggestion of seeking exclusive rights to send technicians to the Congo, with the understanding that America would funnel all of its technicians through the United Nations.[89]

By late August 1960, Hammarskjold opined to American officials that the Congo crisis could be resolved once Lumumba was broken. When on September 5, 1960, American Andrew Cordier, Hammarskjold's temporary representative in Leopoldville, used U.N. troops to close the airport and seize the government radio station, moves aimed at marginalizing Lumumba during the Kasavubu coup, the relationship between the United States and the United Nations seemed sweet.[90]

However, American optimism soured as the United Nations veered away from American interests. Secretary-General Dag Hammarskjold knew that maintaining the United Nations' appearance of impartiality was paramount if the Congo, and his organization, were to survive the crisis. In addition, Hammarskjold, though not a fan of Lumumba, was interested in a political solution that might assuage the Congolese and the new Afro-Asian members of the United Nations. He maintained this position as Soviet Premier Khrushchev assailed him and as Lumumba requested that the United Nations withdraw its peacekeeping force. Although he agreed with the American position that Kasavubu had a right to oust Lumumba, Hammarskjold was unwilling to go to the extremes envisioned by the Belgians and the White House.[91]

When Mobutu's soldiers tried to break through U.N. troops to arrest Lumumba, Hammarskjold encouraged Dayal to stand firm. By mid-October 1960, Hammarskjold requested that the Belgians withdraw all personnel from the Congo, much to the dismay of Washington. Concerned to some extent with the appearance of legality, Secretary-General Hammarskjold was unwilling to condemn Lumumba publicly, even if it meant that Lumumba's political triumph might end the U.N. mission—and official U.S. presence—in the Congo. Once the United States had secured the services of Mobutu through the provision of information and significant financial support, the U.N. troops effectively shielded Lumumba from elimination. Just as troubling to the United States was the possible adoption of a UAR-Guinea-Ghana proposal to send a delegation to the Congo. Such a delegation aimed to seek political reconciliation, which to Washington meant a return to power for Lumumba.[92]

Hammarskjold also seemed concerned about the issue of African national boundaries and, thus, sovereignal integrity. At the beginning of the crisis, the Secretary-General seemed open to recognizing the legitimacy of the Katanga government. Accordingly, another shock to the Eisenhower administration came as Hammarskjold denounced the Katanga secession, sending a stiff letter to Moise Tshombe asking him to oust the Belgians. Furthermore, Hammarskjold wanted to have the Congolese parliament return to session, although Mobutu (as the new president) had considered, then rejected, this idea.[93]

Although there had been discussions about the development of a U.S. plan to encourage African nations to adopt four-year free elections, this idea was rejected in the National Security Council with regard to the Congo. The sole purpose of such elections was to eliminate imagined Communist influence in emerging governments. American officials, despite the lack of evidence, were convinced of Lumumba's Communist status, and they feared that elections in the Congo simply would formalize an anti-West government in the new country. In October 1960 as Secretary Herter reiterated the concern over Hammarskjold's new line and the potential reemergence of Lumumba as the principal figure in the Congo, Special Assistant Gordon Gray cryptically wondered aloud about the administration's limit in terms of dealing with Hammarskjold. Although the United States determined to continue pressuring the Secretary-General, Secretary Herter was not optimistic about the outcome. He reflected the general sentiment in the meeting by saying, "For Lumumba to get back in would just not be the answer."[94] Three months later, as the hour of Lumumba's demise neared, Eisenhower remarked, "One of our most serious problems soon would be the determination of our relations with the UN."

The president was convinced that the United Nations had made a mistake "in admitting to membership any nation claiming independence."[95] To avoid a repeat of the Congo crisis, the Eisenhower administration hoped to keep matches away from the kindling of African independence.

## Blacks with Guns: The Politics of Self-Abnegation in the Congo

As noted previously, American officials worried about the need to control the military in Africa. This was of particular significance in the Congo because the Black troops of the *Force Publique* rebelled against their Belgian officers.[96] Generally, explicit American military support of various African governments was very limited. Although there was some disagreement in NSC meetings regarding the provision of military equipment to African nations, Gen. Lemnitzer reflected the majority view that it was desirable for the United States to provide arms for internal security only.[97] Consistent with this view, the White House eventually supported an international arms control agreement for Africa. Although arguments can be made that the motivations for this stand were economic or geopolitical—Africa, after all, was not Latin America—the more powerful concern regarded the race of those who might be armed.[98]

The Whites who dictated foreign policy were very insecure during the early Cold War. Based on their misconceptions of Blacks, the Eisenhower administration believed that Africans were emotional, irrational, and prone to violence against Whites. They concluded that putting guns in the hands of such people could lead to unpredictable results, harmful to American interests. This was true particularly if those Africans were unwilling to discipline, coerce, or kill their own people in order to further U.S. objectives. It should be noted that these official discussions took place within the context of radicalized, largely nonviolent Black protests in America which directly challenged the comfortable notions of White Supremacy and America's pretense to freedom and equality.[99] Exacerbating the problem was the fact that American intelligence in Africa was extremely poor and Western media reporting on the Congo crisis focused on the handful of attacks on White settlers.[100] Therefore, the Eisenhower administration knew few Africans and trusted even less.[101]

Months before Congolese independence, Americans did not feel threatened because the Congolese were so poorly armed. Perhaps the riots in January 1960 and the Cuban revolution began to change American minds. By February 1960 NSC members discussed the need to pursue aggressively an international agreement to limit arms in Africa.[102]

American officials initially rejected the idea of restoring the *Force Publique* as a tool for political and social control in the Congo, likely because of the mutiny of Black troops, men who had responded predictably to the assertion by their White commanders that independence would not change their subordinate status in the military.[103] American calm further dissipated as Lumumba warned of the possibility of Black troops fighting Whites to defend African freedom. The composition of the U.N. peacekeeping troops only heightened the dilemma: Dulles was convinced that "the Government of Guinea . . . had told the Guinean troops they were to shoot Belgians in the Congo."[104] Even Charles DeGaulle communicated to the White House his fear about the presence of Blacks troops in the Congo and the message it would send to other colonial subjects. Although American officials supported "the creation of a general UN Emergency Force," they "did not favor the development of a special African military force."[105]

With specific regard to the Congo, the Eisenhower administration knew that military and technological might would dictate the political realities in Central Africa. The Belgians led the way by increasing the numbers of their soldiers in the Congo, trying to intimidate the newly elected Lumumba and his president and, perhaps, attempting to kill Lumumba as early as July 1960. Belgian financial and military support for Katanga allowed Moise Tshombe to issue a threat to U.N. representative Ralph Bunche that his troops would fire on any U.N. forces seeking to enter the province. The United States had helped Mobutu gain credibility and control over much of the Army by allowing him to take credit for the $1 million in aid that the Americans provided through the United Nations. Even Justin Bomboko, the pro-Western Congolese representative to the United Nations, cried that the U.N. forces had ordered loyal Congolese soldiers to disarm while the Belgians looted the nation's garrisons in the early days of the crisis.[106] Yet, because of the determination of African nationalists, military might cut both ways.

As Lumumba's calls for aid fell on deaf ears in the United States, the Congolese prime minister also was dismayed that U.N. forces were not ending the Katanga secession and forcing Belgian troops out of the country. By August 1960, Lumumba launched a two-pronged military attack on Kasai and Katanga provinces, an approach which met with stunning success until Kasavubu deposed him. Even as he was trapped in his residence, Lumumba survived, physically and politically, because many of the non-White troops in the U.N. force protected him. Following Lumumba's capture and just days before his death, soldiers loyal to him fought effectively against both Mobutu and Tshombe. In fact, the mutiny at the army barracks in Thysville forced his Belgian captors to transfer him from that military camp to Elisabethville as a way to avoid Lumumba's possible rescue by Congolese troops or sympathetic U.N. forces.[107]

Thus, in the context of the Congo, the Eisenhower administration could not follow its traditional approach of providing military support to an African government for internal security. To do so would mean giving Lumumba the power to stay in office and suppress the secessionist revolt instituted by outside agitators. The fluidity of the situation further complicated matters; the White House was unwilling to risk sending arms to leaders whose obedience they could not confirm. Although Mobutu fit the mold of their African strongman, his ability to dominate the Congo in 1960 was hardly assured. Many of the Congolese, whether nationalists or separatists, moderates or radicals, refused to engage in the self-abnegation required by Washington. Moreover, because the United States feared that Lumumba and other African radicals could gain succor from other sources—Egypt, China, the Soviet Union—the best hope for African pacification lay in turning off the arms spigot.

The hope for an arms control agreement in Africa had both military and psychological warfare implications. A July 1960 letter from Mansfield Sprague to members of the President's Committee on Information Activities Abroad (PCIAA) enumerated recommendations to the president for the "taking of early action on a number of issues concerning Africa." One of the items urged the president to press the United Nations for an Arms Control Commission for Africa.[108] Indeed, the final report to the president echoed this theme. The very first line of the subsection on Africa reads "we do not want to encourage an arms race in Africa."[109] Notably, the sentiment towards arms control appears nowhere else in the document.

Strategically, arms control for Africa meant that the United States could monopolize violence by directly supporting its European allies, manipulating the United Nations, or, as a last resort, invoking the Eisenhower Doctrine. Consequently, it was hoped, the West would remain the unchallenged power on the continent and Blacks would remain subject to White firepower, even if that firepower were in Black hands.[110] Specifically, it meant keeping Lumumba subject to Western forces, either state-sponsored or mercenary.

Arms control for Africa reflected grave insecurities in Washington. The American push for African arms control also translated into a psychological statement to Blacks that they would have to remain subject to the overweening military might of the West. This was significant because nineteenth-century Ethiopia had been able to maintain its sovereignty, in part, because "more than any other place in Africa, there were more firearms imported from Europe to Ethiopia."[111] Although probably unaware of this historical detail, the Eisenhower administration feared that arming blacks they did not control could lead to unpredictable or undesirable results. The American willingness to defend a White monopoly on power and violence, while protecting its strategic and economic interests, was pivotal in maintaining the essential ties between Belgium and the Congo.

## Conclusion: To Use My Body as a Nowhere's Road Map

U.S. foreign policy toward the Congo during the early Cold War was based upon the American desire for the continued sustenance of Western nations upon African wealth. The political, economic, and strategic concerns were influenced by the racial legacy of White Supremacy. Thus, a fundamental prerequisite to America's proprietary interest in African resources was the maintenance of a hierarchy of nations with Africans chained to the bottom.

As with South Africa, the White House's interpretation of events in the Congo heavily rested upon familiar racial tropes. Where the Congolese were emotional, unstable, and primitive, the Belgians were rational and sophisticated.[112] Unrest in the Congo was blamed on the provocations of agitators, the incompetence of Black leadership, or the blind hatred of Blacks for Whites. Again, the experiences of African women as a part of the Black collective belie the promises of African autonomy within the Free World.

## In the Search for Leadership, No Strong Women Need Apply

President Eisenhower and his advisers agreed that America needed the African strongman on its side in order to guarantee a pro-Western posture for the continent's emerging nations. Such a stricture eliminated African women, not simply because the White House believed that they were not strong, but because it could not conceive of Black female political leadership. Consequently, in the quest to influence the course of African independence, the White House felt it needed to appeal to African men only.

To say that the Eisenhower administration knew little about African women would be an understatement. Nowhere do the policy papers regarding Africa mention African women. The invisibility of Black women is so familiar as to appear natural.[113] This American attitude resulted in large part from the presence of an all-male decision-making staff and was nurtured by centuries of European misogyny imposed on the continent.

African women as a whole had a long, proud history of political activism buried by cultural chauvinism and the misinterpretation of historical phenomena. For example, Black women played significant political and military roles during Shaka's leadership of the Zulus. Dona Beatrice was one of the seminal political figures in the Kingdom of the Kongo in the seventeenth century, preaching a rejection of European customs and resistance to Portuguese meddling. Similarly, Nehanda wielded power in Zimbabwe at the end of the nineteenth century, urging resistance to the murderous expansion of Cecil Rhodes's British South African Company and serving as a war chief in the Shona's first *chimurenga* (war of liberation).[114] In the twentieth century, African women continued to exhibit their willingness to confront male domination, even as subjects of imperialism.

Audrey Wipper, describing three rebellions which occurred during or just before the Cold War, noted that "in all [three] societies women were formally subordinate to men, yet on these occasions they challenged, sometimes successfully, not only male but colonial authority."[115] Black women in Kenya (1922), Nigeria (1929), and the British Cameroons (1958-1959) rebelled against the suppression of African cultural, political, or economic activism. Their nerve and success were rooted in traditions of autonomy, which they had lost during colonialism. Their militancy was stimulated both by the corruption of colonial administrations and the weaknesses of African male leadership.[116] For instance, following the arrest of Kenyan activist Harry Thuku, it was Kikuyu women who insisted on fighting state repression:

A deputation of six leading African men went to see Sir Charles Bowring, the Colonial Secretary. Sir Charles assured them that Thuku would be given a full hearing by the Government before any decision was taken as to what was to be done with him . . . He urged them to return to the Police Station and disperse the crowd [of Africans]. They tried but the members of the crowd were in no mood to leave and the delegation was accused of being bribed. The women were particularly militant . . . *Mary Muthoni Nyanjiru . . . leapt to her feet, pulled up her dress over her shoulders and shouted to the men, "You take my dress and give me your trousers. You men are cowards. What are you waiting for? Our leader is in there. Let's get him."*[117]

Although little has been written about Congolese women, nothing suggests that they were less courageous or capable than their sisters. Although they "had a very hard time escaping the double oppression of their role as beasts of burden in traditional rural societies and the narrow conformism of the Belgian Catholic church," guerillas like Leonie Abo proved the existence of political potential.[118] Feminist revolutionary Andree' Blouin, a member of Lumumba's government, offered another template of Black female power.[119]

None of this history mattered to the White House. In the Congo, the need for the African strongman meant the need for a person willing to exercise violence and coercion in order to subdue African nationalism. Of course, the Eisenhower administration could not conceive of women playing this role since women did not serve as combat soldiers in the U.S. military.[120] Because Congolese women operated outside of direct Western influence, the White House could not rely upon the traditional forms of manipulation to bend indigenous female leadership to its will. Moreover, the lessons of modern African history suggest that African female activists were too antiauthoritarian to be trusted by the United States.

## Educational Policy as Reinforcement of Oppression

In discussing the problems faced by contemporary activists who challenge patriarchy, legal scholar Martha Chamallas notes, "Most large institutions follow practices and policies saturated with implicit male bias. Simply to follow these 'neutral' rules and ignore gender reproduces patterns of exclusion and paradoxically assures that gender will continue to matter in the world."[121] American officials repeatedly expressed the notion that the best way for the United States to help Africa was through the provision of educational assistance. This was considered significant because education was the path to political maturity. If education was the passport to political power, colonial policy had left Black women wanting.

On a consistent basis across the African continent, women received less education than men. Although the numbers of educated Africans in the early Cold War period were appallingly low, the number for women was shocking. For example, at the time of its independence, the Congo had one female high-school graduate.[122]

Leaving aside the insincere assurances of Belgian officials about uplifting the Africans, the Eisenhower administration believed that Africans could not function as responsible leaders until they gained at least formal, Western-style education.[123] Many African men supported this type of gender subordination as well. For the White House to accept this supposedly objective position meant completely excluding African women from leadership roles. Consequently, such an approach virtually assured a uniform cadre of African male leadership.

## The Narrow U.S. Focus on African Problems

American blandishments about creating responsible governments in Africa centered on very limited, sometimes vague, notions regarding Black access to political power and Black economic development which ultimately would benefit the West. At no point in policy planning did members of the Eisenhower administration consider the problems unique to African women.

Although the idea of creating Western-style democracy in Africa sounded appealing, it likely would have had little immediate benefit for women in the Congo. For the Congolese, the most significant issues centered around the destruction of families through forced migrant labor schemes; a lack of educational, economic, or housing preferences; and subjugation to male dominion.[124] Female access to the ballot might have helped to some degree because Lumumba insisted upon an equitable distribution of the Congo's gross national product, which might have addressed these issues.

Interestingly, Patrice Lumumba envisioned a society in which men and women could exist as peers. Although he did not have ample time to flesh out his views on gender equity, his early sentiments suggest that Congolese women at least would have enjoyed the right to vote. Accordingly, the Eisenhower administration's manipulation of the Congolese Parliament, through Mobutu, fractured the formal exercise of democracy as well as the potential social and economic benefits derived therefrom.

Ultimately, U.S. policy demanded Black sycophancy. This is not to say that all U.S. opinion regarding the Congo or the Belgians was uniform. Moreover, some American officials expressed dismay at Belgian ambivalence in wanting either a unified Congo or a separate Katanga, as well as the Belgians' constant flaunting of their military muscle throughout the crisis. Regardless, Washington's impression of the Congolese justified intervention to undermine the nation-state as conceived by Africans. Significantly, the tale of American crisis management in Africa during the latter half of 1960 demonstrated that American foreign policy toward Africa clearly worked against the Africans.

# CHAPTER SEVEN

# CONCLUSION: OVERRUNNING THE BEST INTERESTS OF THOSE CONCERNED

The Eisenhower administration painted the picture of a promise to Africa, then broke it. This result was preferable to destroying the global racial hierarchy that spawned America's racial caste system. As one scholar has noted, "Governments tend to share the perspectives and limitations of the societies from which they emerge."[1] Yet, all of the blame cannot be attributed to a single administration.

Although the impetus for American competition with the Soviet Union blossomed from the ashes of World War II, many of the roots of early Cold War foreign policy can be found in the centuries-old American project of racial and national formation. In sum, Whites are actors in the drama of race as much as Blacks. This book has highlighted the ways in which White officials sought to protect their racialized interests. Thus, as American diplomacy toward Africa evolved during the mid-twentieth century, Eisenhower foreign policy reflected both the long-standing impulses from previous periods and the exigencies of a rapidly changing world.

This book examined both the explicit and implicit power of race within U.S. diplomacy. The lessons from this analysis of American foreign policy are threefold. The first set of issues emerged explicitly from policy papers, planning sessions, and bureaucratic exchanges. The second set of issues laid buried beneath the jargon of public and private statements and executive decisions. These themes relate directly to the ghost that animated the shell of discourse and action. A final set of issues pertained to conundrums with which we struggle in the twenty-first century.

## Aspects of "Third Wave" Policy under the Eisenhower Administration

### Blacks as a "Problem" People

The president and his advisers, friends, and private confidants accepted the notion that Black people were inferior to Whites. Yet, they conceded that the notion of racial progress was critical to winning the Cold War. In Eisenhower's view, progress in race relations could be achieved only when Whites and non-Whites were prepared for such change. Additionally, because the Cold War was a site within which the reputational value of Whiteness was under repair, the administration saw the United States essentially as a fair and open nation with a justifiable racial hierarchy. Accordingly, Black agitation for racial reforms, rather than White oppression and resistance to reform, was the cause for domestic unrest. Black protest for both equality of opportunity and result were social issues that were secondary to the main tasks facing America.[2] When the president, for example, encouraged federal judges in the South to "operate moderately and with complete regard for the sensibilities of the population," he meant for them to consider the concerns and feelings of White southerners.[3]

The sanctuary of the Cold War taught that the European imperialists were actually civilized, peace-loving democracies who maintained the best of intentions toward their colonial subjects. Accordingly, Blacks in Africa were the source of friction and turmoil with their allegedly petty, inarticulate, emotional demands for freedom. During a discussion about the potential for democracy in Africa, Eisenhower remarked that "if you go and live with these Arabs, you will find that they simply cannot understand our ideas of freedom or human dignity." This view was applied to the Africans as well and brought to mind the inherent trouble in giving freedom to people without also giving them a sense of the responsibility that comes with freedom.[4]

Since the Eisenhower administration considered Blacks to be unfit for self-rule, Black insistence on self-determination forced the White House to construct a facade of support for self-determination which masked its intention of maintaining the bonds necessary for ensuring responsible Black behavior and the continued economic and political welfare of Europe.[5] Instead of pursuing a sensible approach of waiting twenty-five to fifty years before championing independence, the United States was forced to intervene in colonial affairs during the 1950s to transform an obsolete form of White privilege and control in order to secure what it considered to be orderly development.[6]

The Eisenhower administration assumed White superiority and Black primitivism to be indelible facts. This belief, and concomitant action, meant that the supreme military and economic power of the Western [White] world had to strictly monitor and control the behavior of Third World [non-White] peoples. As articulated by scores of Eisenhower strategists, staffers, and advisers, Free World preeminence necessarily relied upon the continued exploitation of the human and natural resources of Africa. Furthermore, America's superordinate political status in relation to the rest of the world rested on its ability to steer Africa's emerging nations into the Western camp. America's binary view of the Cold War world meant that African freedom was conditioned by the needs, fears, and insecurities of America and its European allies.

The oft-repeated apprehensions regarding Soviet penetration of the continent veiled the major concern: whether or not Africans would continue to supply the economic, political, strategic, and psychological needs of the West. Eisenhower officials were unwilling to distinguish between Marxist dogma or propaganda and African protest and resistance to exploitation. Thus, American fears regarding neutrality or Communist conversion had little to do with ideology. Essentially, any African nation unwilling to submit completely to Western hegemony was a threat to American security.[7]

America's experience in Haiti taught that dominion over non-Whites overseas could be maintained without resort to long-term formal micro- or macromanaged control.[8] Washington's discourse on decolonization masked its effort to create an informal Western empire in Africa. Additionally, because allies in Europe and the colonial-settler societies like the one in South Africa were invested with the property right of Whiteness, the Eisenhower administration was able to selectively intervene in African affairs in order to ensure orderly development.

First, American policy undermined the economic viability of African nations. U.S. diplomacy toward Ethiopia forced that relatively poor nation to pay dearly for military assistance that the United States earmarked solely for internal security. The Eisenhower administration's unwillingness to mitigate Ethiopia's staggering human suffering with favorable economic assistance is all the more revealing when contrasted with its grant military aid to Belgium.[9] Likewise, American reluctance to support Ghana's Volta River Project was a reactionary response to Nkrumah's quest for autarky. The Eisenhower administration's aloofness toward the project came as Nkrumah made a determined effort to create a positive relationship with the United States, the West, and—later—the Congo. Eisenhower officials refused American largesse without assurances of Ghanaian acquiescence to Western domination.

Second, American intervention was consistently antidemocratic. In the Congo, this meant destabilizing the legitimate government, then assassinating the democratically elected prime minister, while undermining the nascent nationalism that might have united the various ethnic groups of the former Belgian colony. In South Africa, it meant providing much-needed financial, political, and psychological support for an overtly violent, racist, antidemocratic minority regime that increasingly isolated itself from the rest of the world. Further, Washington was aware of Haile Selassie's iron-fisted modernization project and provided him weapons to protect his regime from internal threats.

Third, American culture and, in particular, White fantasies and images of Africa and its people shaped U.S. foreign policy. The White House justified the need for informal empire through its belief in African primitivism. In other words, because Africans were incompetent, America needed to choose their leaders for them, leaders who could guide the nation-building process in a manner satisfactory to the West. Any resistance to this seemingly natural, obvious solution was simply the result of either incoherent radicalism or Communist manipulation. In this way, American officials construed African demands for liberty as either incomprehensible or illegitimate. Consequently, if America was going to do anything, it was going to save the Africans from themselves before they hurt anyone else. As one group of contemporary scholars has put it, "Empire and colonialism can be viewed as monocultural regimes amplified globally, as in *mission civilisatrice*, White Man's Burden, and modernization as Westernization."[10] The Eisenhower administration's mission in the mid-twentieth century bore a strong resemblance to earlier White missions in Africa. Therefore, U.S. diplomacy was shaped by, and reinforced, long-standing racial hierarchies.

## The (White) Masculine Triumph through Transformation

From the American perspective, Africa lagged behind the rest of the world because of inherent human, political, and cultural flaws. For example, Clarence Randall argued that one of the great impediments to the development of free market systems in Africa was the communal ownership of land. Likewise, other supposed impediments to the development of Western-style democracy in Africa were African superstition, emotionalism, and complete reliance on an authoritarian figure, the tribal chief. A final supposed impediment to the advancement toward self-rule was the lack of formal education across the continent. In these ways, Africa was viewed as a woman who had to be trained to survive in a man's world; in the patriarchal view, "she" was a woman to be acted upon by men.[11]

The vast, diverse histories of centuries of African self-rule prior to European contact were meaningless to modern, Western man. White elites could not imagine a world in which Blacks competently governed their own affairs. The lack of scholarly research or CIA intelligence was meaningless in this respect. As Marion O'Callaghan theorizes:

> [Because] imagination is socially created and follows, not precedes, the structure of social relations . . . knowledge is not necessarily affected by access to information, since information is placed within a particular framework that is hardly ever explicit. This is not to say that it is not understood. Social significance is shared, but not openly acknowledged. Nor indeed challenged. The decolonization of the imagination, then, is closely linked to structural change, at a level at which, no matter the seeming historical or cultural continuity, new types of legitimation and, therefore, imagination occur. It is this structural change that has not happened in spite of the end of direct colonial rule.[12]

Thus, American guidance was seen as necessary to shepherd Africa safely along her voyage to independence. The taking up of this civilizing burden is another extension of nineteenth-century racial ideology and, as such, was not unique to Africa or the United States.[13]

The height of gendered imagery is evidenced in the discourse of Soviet penetration of a supposedly weak, defenseless Africa. The governments of Haile Selassie and Nkrumah attempted to convince the United States that they could engage Communist-bloc nations without becoming thralls of global Communism. What each leader stressed and what Washington failed to heed was that theirs were competent governments with valid, homegrown ideas about development. In this regard, the symbolic emasculation of Africans continued with the Eisenhower administration's insistence upon an international arms agreement for Africa. This development cannot be viewed accurately within the context of the isolated events of 1960. Rather it should be seen against the backdrop of America's history of violence toward non-Whites, the Eisenhower administration's willingness to supply arms to European colonial powers and South Africa, as well as the Soviet Union's superiority in conventional weapons. By trying to prevent Africans from gaining the weapons necessary to forcibly extricate themselves from their exploitive relationship with the West, the Eisenhower administration figuratively maintained the Free World's monopoly on African penetration.[14] Literally, U.S. policy not only denied Africans the option of choosing diplomatic or military solutions to problems but also deprived them of the figurative ability to rehabilitate their humanity through self-defense and self-determination.[15] Those Blacks who received weapons were, in the American mind, those willing to commit political self-abnegation.

Just as important as the symbolism of the effeminate African was the erasure of the significant, unique demands of non-White women. In the United States, historical Black-White convergences generally negotiated a truce in explicitly [White] masculine terms. The Eisenhower administration's emphasis on supporting authoritarian governments in African countries that it considered unprepared for democracy excluded African women from consideration as leaders. American support for, and anointing of, the African strongman completely excluded female activists from positions of authority. Moreover, the narrow American focus on pro-Western political and economic development removed from consideration social reforms that would have aided a substantial portion of Africa's population. Again, this is not to suggest that African men would have shared power comfortably with their sisters. However, America's Cold War diplomacy hardened existing gender disparities. Given the historical centrality of African women in their societies, this deliberate exclusion begs a fuller treatment.

## Washington's Conception of the African Nation-State

Much to the chagrin of the European metropoles, Washington openly supported closing the curtain on colonialism. Although cautious, many Africans strove for independence hoping that America's actions would match its rhetoric. What numerous observers abroad did not realize immediately was that the Eisenhower administration conceived of a free Africa in dramatically different terms than the Africans.

Based on the aforementioned racial convictions, American policymakers envisioned African states that served their interests. The ideal African state was pro-West, willingly accepting its peripheral status in world affairs, and collaborating in the revitalization of Western economies. Under this rubric, responsible African governments did not pretend that their goals and interests were as important as the struggle between East and West. Consequently, American diplomacy toward Africa was antidemocratic in two ways.

As alluded to earlier in this section, Washington acted to defeat democratic movements in every region of the continent. More specifically, on one level,

Eisenhower policy held that the paramount purpose of African state formation was to service the United States and its allies, not African peoples. At another level, because the White House did not trust African people to meet this threshold, American administrators created, tolerated, or helped perpetuate autocratic regimes to ensure compliance with the aforementioned purpose. Thus, even in the transformative atmosphere of the 1950s and early 1960s, U.S. diplomacy subverted the very freedoms it espoused.

## The Racial Sanctuary of the Early Cold War

### The Construction of White Innocence

A significant part of American Cold War rhetoric was the discourse on American traditions of democracy, freedom, and respect for the rule of law. This discourse ignored the experiences of people of color in the United States, omitted the traditional disfranchisement of millions of Blacks over the course of centuries, and hid the patterns of state-sponsored and vigilante violence needed to police the nation's various hierarchies. As successive administrations constructed a purified narrative of the nation's historical origins, they simultaneously offered a revision of European imperial behavior while concealing their affinities to the European imperialist project. This peculiar construction of identity also extended to an exculpation of the metropolitan powers that had savaged the African continent. Consequently, one of the most important functions of American foreign policy toward Africa was the creation and maintenance of the image of White innocence.

American propaganda suggested to world listeners that the United States was a trustworthy advocate for decolonization because it was a freedom-loving nation with a long-standing anticolonial tradition.[16] This image elided the history of European appropriation of Native American land and resources which had its roots in the same political and economic phenomena that had scarred Africa. Although it was true that the United States was formed by a secession from British control, its eighteenth-century formative stages were strikingly similar to twentieth-century South Africa.

American claims of equality, justice, and fairness were undermined by the reality of racial strife, de facto segregation, and government efforts to silence its harshest Black critics.[17] The Eisenhower administration highlighted advances in race relations through the State Department's goodwill ambassador tours, international exhibits, and its participation in civil rights litigation, among other things. The effort was to portray an America making natural and rational progress toward racial tolerance and inclusion. The international project of racial rehabilitation, however, did not rest there.

An additional element of American strategy was to emphasize the credibility of European powers which claimed that they were interested in civilizing Africa. The State Department's efforts in this regard were akin to the Justice Department's insistence upon the existence of segregationist goodwill in *Brown*. To suggest that Africa's best chance for development was a form of independence that kept Africans tied to their former oppressors implied the goodwill of those same oppressors. Much as in *Brown*, American officials wanted Blacks to renounce their memories of genocide and exploitation and trust that the authorities and transnational businesses that exploited them would be genuinely interested in their self-directed growth and prosperity.

## The Privileging of Whiteness

American decision-makers refused to hear evidence of African competence or complaints. They constructed an image of the African based upon White Supremacists' fantasies of Blacks. Additionally, they constructed a policy toward non-American Whites that was equally fantastical.

To the American mind, the Africans who denounced capitalism or embraced, or even sympathized with, Marxism were more than thralls of the Soviet siren; they were naive or unstable and endangered the world. On the other hand, the Whites who were anti-Communist and expressed a desire to guide Africans to independence were shrewd or logical. Both constructions rested on racial archetypes. In the case of the former, African analyses of and responses to the global situation were varied and, generally speaking, reasonable; as the NSC noted, Africans would do what they perceived to be in their best interests.[18] In the case of the latter, European platitudes about mutual cooperation for African uplift had no historical basis. There was little evidence from which to draw the conclusion that European interests in a decolonized Africa would allow for African self-determination. Equally instructive is the contrast between American interpretations of the behavior of the Lumumba government and the apartheid governments of South Africa.

The White House considered Lumumba to be emotionally unstable—a child, in the words of Ralph Bunche.[19] Part of the evidence of his instability was his separate requests for aid to the United States, the United Nations, and the United Soviet Socialist Republic. The desperate situation Lumumba faced, caused by the duplicity, thievery, and violence of the Belgians, warranted him seeking assistance from all available sources. Had the White House acceded to the Congolese request for aid, it is possible that Lumumba would have taken it in order to preserve the integrity of his fledgling country.

Another compelling piece of evidence against Lumumba was his speech during the independence ceremonies of June 30, 1960. He enraged many Westerners with his willingness to discuss openly the atrocities committed against the Congolese at the hands of the Belgians, as well as Congolese resistance to colonialism. Had he glossed over these events in favor of the typical diplomatic banter, he would have obscured the very basis for the landmark occasion. Again, his actions were understandable, even if they violated the veneer of White innocence and the demand for Black self-abnegation.

By comparison, the apartheid regimes of South Africa seem utterly insane. To believe that a racial minority, no matter how well-armed or funded, could indefinitely control and develop a frustrated majority was to, again, engage in fantasy. American officials recognized the riskiness of the apartheid project but continually aided and abetted it. The president and vice president were out of town when Lumumba arrived in the United States.[20] Thus, they offered no greeting, no assurances that cooperation with America could lead to economic, political, or social prosperity. When they greeted South African representatives, they refused to assail the Afrikaners as the villains they were. Likewise, American officials refused to demand reforms to ensure a truly democratic state in order to maintain continued U.S. cooperation. Undoubtedly, many in Washington viewed the Afrikaners as anachronistic yet civilized.

One of the greatest privileges of White Supremacy is the assumption of White normalcy.[21] The Eisenhower administration implemented an aggressive policy against the Lumumba government after nineteen days of his administration. With scant evidence, which was contradicted by Lumumba's numerous speeches and press conferences, as well as Soviet assessments of the Congolese leader, CIA Director Allen Dulles reported that "in Lumumba we were faced with a person who was Castro or worse and that 'it is safe to go on the assumption that Lumumba has been bought by the Communists.'"[22] In contrast, the administration invested politically in the Afrikaners after decades of evidence suggested that they should do otherwise.[23] As one would expect, the burden of this assumption fell heavily upon Black shoulders.

Equally significant was the American refusal to grant significant aid to emerging African nations. Although the Eisenhower administration imposed these limitations in response to a concern for European nations carrying their share of the development burden, it was not only the quantity but the quality of aid that was important. When American officials suggested that limited agricultural and educational aid would best serve the continent, their refusal to provide much-needed aid for technological development mirrored a centuries-old process of underdevelopment. Even the material the United States provided to Ethiopia, for example, was so substandard that the Ethiopians made little use of it. Like the European colonizers of the sixteenth, seventeenth, and eighteenth centuries, the United States refused to provide Africa with technology transfers that could have buoyed the continent's self-development.[24] This American refusal followed the internal logic of ensuring that the newly independent countries remained dependents of their former overlords.

## Inverted Relationships and the Protection of White Property Interests

The Eisenhower administration justified its policy of maintaining the essential ties between Europe and Africa, in part, by its concern for the dependence of backward Africans upon European trade and influence. The general attitude was reflected by the comments of Maurice Stans at the April 18, 1960, NSC meeting: "Through the years . . . anything that the [B]lacks had got had come from the [W]hites and they were going to continue to look to the [W]hites for assistance."[25] Stans's faith in Black dependence conflicted with the overt statements of Black self-determination during this period.

In fact, it was Europe and the rest of its progeny that were hopelessly dependent upon Africa and its resources.[26] The need to affirm Africa to the West emerged from the reality that Western aggrandizement relied upon the prevailing contrived, asymmetrical relationship.[27] The exploitation of African resources had been critical to European development and economic enhancement during the early stages of capitalism. As early as the Truman administration, the exploitation of African resources was deemed critical for Free World survival against global Communism. Even if certain African resources could be found in other Free World dominions, the West was unwilling to allow these resources to move beyond its control. Additionally, Western elites needed Third World wealth to mask serious class conflict within their own societies, among other problems.

Yet, as reflected in NSC discussions, "maintaining the essential [exploitive] ties" between Africa and Europe was the American means of saving Africa from political chaos, economic impoverishment, and social regression. Such a rationalization was a twentieth-century extension of the doomed races thesis that was central to scientific racism, social Darwinism, and nineteenth-century imperialism.[28] As a security blanket for European social health, Africa thus enabled capitalist governments to repress or co-opt reform-minded or revolutionary elements within their own societies. Europe's economic recovery and empowerment were essential to preventing the masses of Europeans from revolting from elite control. Furthermore, Washington maintained that a strong Europe was essential for Western security.[29]

Additionally, White psychological wealth was vested in its imperialism, whether in European or American form. The momentary success of Japan in World War II, as well as the victories of non-White troops against their German and Italian counterparts, discredited the idea of White superiority. The psychological devastation continued with the dismantling of the British Empire in the East. A crucial part of what the NSC referred to as the essential ties between Europe and Africa was the hierarchical master-servant bond. Since White Supremacy was based upon a historical denial of equality between White and non-White, an African move toward delinking from Europe meant that Whites would have to confront Blacks on a supposedly even plane.[30] The United States, as the White superpower, could not allow that to happen; it had to shield Whiteness and White privilege from the flux of decolonization. The American struggle with the Ghanaians regarding the Volta River Project exemplifies this pattern.

The American interest in the Volta River Project was not sufficient to provide support for a broad-based electrical transmission system that could spread power from the dam to larger parts of the fledgling nation. In addition to refusing to help Ghana supply power to other business interests and its own consumers, members of the administration inverted the roles of potential victims and victors. In their minds, the federal government had to "give . . . an even shake" to American businessmen who were already the beneficiaries of over $100 million in loans guaranteed by four sovereign governments. Equally incredible was the assertion that the United States, rather than Ghana, should be able to determine the distribution of electrical power from the dam, even though Ghana's commitment to the project, numerically, was at least four times larger than Washington's.[31]

Keeping in mind that Ghana was responsible for repaying the American loan, as well as the $40 million loan from the World Bank, it seems ludicrous to suggest that the White House's interest in the Volta River Project was greater than Accra's. Nevertheless, this attitude was consistent with other statements regarding aid to Africa. As Secretary Dillon stated in another NSC meeting, U.S. aid needed to be limited and focused because Black Africa was a relatively low priority. Secretary Gates augmented this statement by suggesting that modest American assistance in agriculture and education was best; after all "it was better than pouring money into the pockets of people who could not handle it."[32]

Many critics of America's foreign policy toward Africa complained that the Eisenhower administration ignored Africa.[33] Although this statement is true to a certain extent, the United States did pay close attention to some changes in Africa. America's growing interest was stimulated by Africans who articulated a vision of freedom that would place them on the world stage alongside, rather than beneath, Western powers. Eisenhower administration officials did not ignore this; in fact they were puzzled because such a vision seemed inconceivable. Therefore, the Eisenhower White House observed Africa and acted so as to prevent the dawning of a world in which global White hegemony was rendered obsolete.

## Lessons from the Early Cold War

### "Why Do They Hate Us?":
### White Normalcy and the Creation of Foreign Policy

Following a ten-week tour of Africa, Special Assistant to the Secretary of State Julius Holmes wrote a memo to his boss, Foster Dulles. Although acknowledging that generalizations about Africa were risky, Holmes warned that the virus of self-government was sweeping the continent. This pandemic was problematic because the "vast, primitive population is largely illiterate, more than half Pagan, and is practically leaping from the Iron Age into the Twentieth Century." Although the continent featured a number of thoughtful African leaders, these men were powerless because of the momentum toward independence and were seen as "themselves often the captives of their own political actions, declarations, and ambitions."

Another critical factor that Holmes argued needed always to be kept in mind was that "the [B]lack African's attitude toward the [W]hite man shades from universal envy through mistrust and fear to burning hate." As a result, Africa was ripe for Soviet penetration, and only one tack could save the future:

> I see no way to meet this threat except by concerted action with other Western powers, especially those having possession in Africa. This will require an understanding on their part of our objectives, and a higher degree of confidence in our motives in Africa, than now exists. The genuine danger with which we are all confronted should make this possible, for *it is clear that if Africa is lost to the West, Europe will be so weakened and out-flanked as to make its defense impossible.*[34]

Holmes's rhetoric is strikingly familiar in post-9/11 America.

As Americans tried to make sense of the attacks on the World Trade Center and the Pentagon in September 2001, many people were drawn to question, in reference to Islamic fundamentalists and other discontented populations around the world, "Why do they hate us?" Conservative pundits suggested that America was a target for attack because *they* envied our freedoms and way of life.[35] Others suggested that the attacks were nothing short of a blow at civilization.[36] This analysis of Eisenhower administration policy toward Africa suggests why such a myopic approach can lead to tragic results.

Holmes's report, like the administration's policy papers, absolved Europeans for their role in Africa's retrogression. In addition to masking the achievements of African history, Holmes described Africans as static, emotional, and unsteady. Furthermore, the atmosphere of sullen hostility led to plenty of "troubled waters for Communist fishing." Thus, envy and resentment were prime forces behind the push for freedom. Based on this construction, the Black quest for independence, not always well-reasoned, lacked legitimacy and deserved no real examination.[37] As a result, the United States missed a golden opportunity to work directly toward African self-determination, a move that may have netted a greater sense of global interdependence and security. Instead, the Eisenhower administration remained wedded to a view that privileged Whiteness and began anew a process of de-stabilization in Africa whose effects continue to be felt.

In our current crisis environment, it behooves Americans to treat as legitimate the grievances of people in Africa, Southwest Asia, and Central/South America. The question should not be, "Why do they hate us?" but, "Why do they continue to struggle?" Not only does one remove the examination from the venue of emotion, but one opens the possibility for understanding and reconciliation which cannot come from self-delusion. To do otherwise is to invite further violence and instability. As the legitimacy and relevance of African-centered diplomacy collapsed under the weight of the Cold War binary, current struggles and responses in the non-White world will lose their legitimacy under the crush of a war to defend White civilization.

## Control of Non-Whites, Globally

Notably, the global struggles of the late 1940s through the late 1980s are described as a Cold War between the United States and the Soviet Union. This designation itself privileges the experiences of officials and peoples from two nations and obscures the ideas, goals, and perspectives of the majority of the world's people. The supposed backwardness of Africans meant, to the American observer, that they were especially susceptible to Communist influence. The Africans' lack of political maturity meant that the United States had to control the transition from colonialism to independence so as to safeguard against harm to the West. As mentioned in several places above, the administration's view of all non-Whites was generally the same. Consequently, America took on the role of racial referee to negotiate between the West and the colonized world. This role was critical because the overwhelming majority of the world's people were unfit for freedom but, nevertheless, insistent upon it. The Eisenhower administration's position as a racial referee in global affairs mirrored its position as racial referee during the domestic social transformations of the 1950s.[38]

Although the Cold War never turned into an open shooting match between the United States and the Soviet Union, their proxy wars in Africa, Central America, and Southeast Asia cost the lives of millions of people of color. What this implies is that the real battles of the Cold War were always between North and South, with the Soviets playing the role of an outside agitator, spurring on non-White resistance. Although not a perfect analogy, the example of America's slave society is instructive. The Free World was equivalent to the antebellum slave society desperately clinging to its human property without whom it would be poorer economically, politically, and psychologically. The Soviet Union, at times like John Brown, was effectively a race traitor, willing to arm non-Whites to kill Whites in search of their freedom.

The real fight was not simply between the two camps. Had the United States been assured that non-Whites could govern themselves responsibly, there would have been no need to intervene in the colonial transformation. Yet, the experiences with Ghana—along with China, India, and Cuba, to name a few—suggested that non-White peoples might not be so self-effacing. The American struggle with the Soviet Union was about the ability of the Free World, especially the United States, to keep its neo-slaves and thus maintain its economic, political, and social superiority over the rest of the world, White or non-White. As such, the East-West dichotomy is insufficient to describe the efforts of the United States and its European allies to preserve their control of the global economic and political structure by transforming Western imperialism. Admittedly, the Soviet Union-as-John Brown analogy is not exact. Nonetheless, this description is helpful, though perhaps more provocative than definitive.

Also of interest is the consistent American reluctance to concede the authenticity of non-White resistance to its refined enslavement. When the president remarked that "most [Third World] nationalist sentiment was really camouflaged Communist agitation,"[39] he was denying that non-White captives had any real grievances about their treatment. To admit as much would be to admit that the entire Western system of freedom and democracy was at worst a sham, that the Free World was not free, and that the responsible tack for emerging non-White states was to seek a development path according to their needs.

The prevailing American view was that almost all of the neo-slaves were content and that any potential rebellion was sparked by an outside force bent on the total destruction of the neo-slave society, that necessary incubator toward civilization. "The fear outside the Soviet Union, however, was not simply the spread of communism . . . The issue was the possibility of a parallel and alternative international economy creating a threat that there would indeed be 'others.'"[40] Thus, the concession of decolonization was meant to relieve some of the pressure on a system fast becoming self-destructive. In so doing, the Northern [White] collective's subordination of the Southern [non-White] collective survived by altering its form.[41] By masking the contradictions of the racist, capitalist exploitation of the colonized World, Cold War decolonization allowed the Free World to continue to demand non-White obedience to a world order primarily dictated by race.

If the Cold War is no longer an appropriate phrase to describe the period from 1947-1989, what should we use? Perhaps any new terminology should place all of the world's civilizations on par or, at least, remove the particularized experience of the West from the discursive center. The global South is the home of the world's oldest cultures, as well as the overwhelming majority of the world's population. In addition, its people provided the germ for modern European development and bore the brunt of imperialism; its natural riches and ideas were the economic and intellectual engines that allowed for the creation and expansion of capitalism.[42] Moreover, the competitive quest for control of the resources throughout the non-White world resulted in numerous wars and conflicts between European powers.[43] Accordingly, what we once commonly referred to as the Third World is better understood as the First World.[44] During the 1950s, the Eisenhower administration defended a global hierarchy constructed over the course of nearly five hundred years. Therefore, the period beginning in 1946 perhaps is best described as the modern battle for the First World and conceived of as the most recent link in post-Columbian imperialism.

## The Failure of Contemporary "Third World" Nation-States

Throughout the various regions of Africa lie the rubble of failed nations. Undoubtedly, political corruption, ethnic rivalries, and shattered economies contributed mightily to the collapse of governments from Somalia to Liberia. These same dysfunctions exist in other parts of the former colonized world. Equally significant are the responses of people to the collapses of sovereign authorities. The rise of religious, ethnic, and economic fundamentalism across the globe witnesses to the skepticism of millions regarding the viability of their governments. Indeed, if as in Cold War Africa, the emerging states existed primarily to serve the interests of the West, then these states were doomed to failure. Perhaps the failure of these governments was one of the few things that was truly inevitable during the Cold War. More to the point, it is compelling that the United States faces its greatest international security threats from people responding to the collapse, or corruption, of sovereign authority. Thus, the privileging of Whiteness has not made the West safer, but has created new enemies as it fans old animosities.

## Postscript

Throughout the 1950s, the United States was part of an evolving world. Africa insisted on being part of that world. The Eisenhower administration refused to take this desire seriously. Examining the continent from a racial perspective developed over the course of centuries, the White House acted in a manner that it considered reasonable. From this perspective, one can understand how the Eisenhower administration "held the line" against structural changes that had the potential to topple global White Supremacy.

However, decisions that seemed obvious from Washington's perspective were problematic from many other vantage points. The flaws of America's Cold War diplomacy seemed most apparent to those observers who noted the distance between the language of freedom and respect for sovereignty and international law and conduct which belied such lofty abstractions. At that historical moment when Africa demanded that its global humanity be recognized, the Eisenhower administration balked under the weight of racial fantasies and expectations. Its shattering of the potential of this historical moment was such that neither truth nor transcendence have been able to undo the harm or the future.

Bones were crying in the Congo in 1961. The shrieking privileges of the Eisenhower administration inflected a dirge for ghosts. In turn, the dirge's arrhythmia muffled the march of new masters and mistresses. Yes, bones were crying in Africa, and a million dreams snapped under the weight of that terrible chorus.

# NOTES

## Chapter One

1. Frantz Fanon, *The Wretched of the Earth* (New York: Grove Press, 1968), p. 236.

2. W. E. B. DuBois, *The Souls of Black Folk* (New York: Signet Classic Series, 1982), p. 54.

3. See, e.g., "Interview of Senator Trent Lott, on Hannity and Colmes," December 11, 2002, www.foxnews.com [partial transcript]; Jesse Holland, "New Apology, New Views: Sen. Lott Apologizes on BET, Takes New Views on Martin Luther King Birthday and Affirmative Action," December 16, 2002, www.abcnews.com; "A Man Out of Time," *Newsweek*, December 23, 2002, www.msnbc.com; Jennifer Lawson, "Highlander Center's Aim Unchanged After 71 Years," *Knoxville News Sentinel*, January 16, 2003 (accompanied by a photograph of the billboard of King attending Highlander's Twenty-fifth anniversary celebration in a racially integrated setting; the caption of the billboard reads "Martin Luther King at Communist Training School").

4. See generally Derrick A. Bell, *Faces at the Bottom of the Well: The Permanence of Racism* (New York: Basic Books, 1992); Frances Cress-Welsing, *The Isis Papers: The Keys to the Colors* (Chicago: Third World Press, 1981); Neely Fuller, *The United Independent Compensatory Code/System/Concept: A Textbook/Workbook for Thought, Speech, and/or Action for Victims of Racism (White Supremacy)* (Washington, DC: Neely Fuller Jr., 1969); bell hooks, *Killing Rage: Ending Racism* (New York: Henry Holt & Co., 1995); Peggy McIntosh, "Unpacking the Invisible Knapsack," *Creation Spirituality*, January-February 1992, p. 33; Thandeka, *Learning to Be White: Money, Race, and God in America* (New York: Continuum, 1999).

5. See generally Ian F. Haney Lopez, *White By Law: The Legal Construction of Race* (New York: New York University Press, 1996); Karen Brodkin, *How Jews Became White Folks* (New Brunswick, NJ: Rutgers University Press, 2000); Noel Ignatiev, *How the Irish Became White* (New York: Routledge, 1995); Robert Chang, "Toward an Asian American Legal Scholarship: Critical Race Theory, Post-Structuralism, and Narrative Space," 81 *California Law Review* 1241 (1993); Paul Finkelman, "The Crime of Color," 67 *Tulane Law Review* 2063 (1993); Richard Ford, "Urban Space and the Color Line: The Consequences of Demarcation and Disorientation in the Postmodern Metropolis," 9 *Harvard Blackletter Journal* 117 (1992); Lisa Ikemoto, "Traces of the Master Narrative

in the Story of African American/Korean American Conflict: How We Constructed 'Los Angeles,'" 66 *Southern California Law Review* 1581 (1993).

6. Thandeka, *Learning to Be White*, pp. 3-17; Richard Dyer, *White* (New York: Routledge, 1997); Grace E. Hale, *Making Whiteness: The Culture of Segregation in the South, 1890-1940* (New York: Vintage Books, 1999); George Lipsitz, *The Possessive Investment in Whiteness: How White People Profit From Identity Politics* (Philadelphia: Temple University Press, 1998), pp. 1-9.

7. Reginald Horsman, *Race and Manifest Destiny: The Origins of American Racial Anglo-Saxonism* (Cambridge, MA: Harvard University Press, 1981), pp. 9-42, 81-115, 189-207; see also Thomas R. Hietala, *Manifest Design: Anxious Aggrandizement in Late Jacksonian America* (Ithaca, NY: Cornell University Press, 1985).

8. Carter A. Wilson, "Exploding the Myths of a Slandered Policy," *Black Scholar*, May/June 1986, p. 20; Cheryl I. Harris, "Whiteness As Property," 106 *Harvard Law Review* 1767 (June 1993), p. 1770; see also Lipsitz, *The Possessive Investment in Whiteness*, pp. 35-38.

9. Bruce Wright, *Black Robes, White Justice: Why Our Legal System Doesn't Work for Blacks* (New York: Carol Publishing Group, 1990), pp. 24-25.

10. See, e.g., Melvin L. Oliver and Thomas M. Shapiro, *Black Wealth/White Wealth: A New Perspective on Racial Inequality* (New York: Routledge, 1997), pp. 107-108 (where the authors address and refute the notion that conspicuous consumption is the explanation for Black poverty); Joe R. Feagin, Vera Hernan, and Pinar Batur, eds., *White Racism: The Basics* (New York: Routledge, 2nd edition, 2001), pp. 36-53.

11. Frantz Fanon, *Black Skin, White Masks* (New York: Grove Weidenfeld, translated by Charles L. Markmann, 1967), pp. 214-215; Joe R. Feagin and Melvin P. Sikes, *Living With Racism: The Black Middle-Class Experience* (Boston: Beacon Press, 1994), pp. 163-164; for personal accounts of Black individuals serving as "credits to their race," see David L. Lewis, *W.E.B. DuBois: Biography of a Race, 1868-1919* (New York: Henry Holt Co., 1993), pp. 102-103, 120, 124-126; Malcolm X and Alex Haley, *The Autobiography of Malcolm X* (New York: Ballantine Books, first edition, 1973), pp. 26-31.

12. See Fuller, *The United Independent Compensatory Code*, pp. 23-32.

13. For a recent example of the White reactionary response to Afrocentricity and multiculturalism, see Arthur Schlesinger Jr., *The Disuniting of America: Reflections on a Multicultural Society* (New York: Norton, 1991).

14. Here I borrow from a Japanese science fiction film, Mamoru Oshii, *Ghost in the Shell*, Bandai Visual and Manga Entertainment, 1996.

15. See generally Theodore W. Allen, *The Invention of the White Race: Racial Oppression and Social Control* (New York: Verso Books, 1994); Jack D. Forbes, *Africans and Native Americans: The Language of Race and the Evolution of Red-Black*

*Peoples* (Urbana: University of Illinois Press, 1993); Michael H. Hunt, *Ideology and U.S. Foreign Policy* (New Haven, CT: Yale University Press, 1987); Noel Ignatiev and John Garvey, *Race Traitor* (New York: Routledge, 1996); Gary B. Nash, *Red, White, and Black: The Peoples of Early America* (Englewood, NJ: Prentice Hall, 1974); Theda Perdue, *Slavery and the Evolution of Cherokee Society, 1540-1866* (Knoxville: University of Tennessee Press, 1979); David R. Roediger, *The Wages of Whiteness: Race and the Making of the American Working Class* (London: Verso, 1991); Ronald Takaki, *Iron Cages: Race and Culture in Nineteenth Century America* (New York: Knopf, 1979); Richard White, *The Middle Ground: Indians, Empires, and Republics in the Great Lakes Region, 1650-1815* (Cambridge: Cambridge University Press, 1991).

16. Kenneth C. Clark, *Dark Ghetto: Dilemmas of Social Power* (New York: Harper Torchbook, 1967); St. Clair Drake and Horace R. Cayton, *Black Metropolis: A Study of Negro Life in a Northern City* (New York: Harper and Row, 1962); Steven Gregory, *Black Corona: Race and the Politics of Place in an Urban Community* (Princeton, NJ: Princeton University Press, 1998); Arnold R. Hirsch, *Making the Second Ghetto* (Cambridge: Cambridge University Press, 1983); Alexander Keyssar, *Out of Work: The First Century of Unemployment in Massachusetts* (Cambridge: Cambridge University Press, 1986); Malcolm X and Alex Haley, *The Autobiography of Malcolm X*, pp. 23-38; Thomas J. Sugrue, *The Origins of the Urban Crisis: Race and Inequality in Postwar Detroit* (Princeton, NJ: Princeton University Press, 1996).

17. See Philomena Essed, *Understanding Everyday Racism: An Interdisciplinary Theory* (Newbury Park, CA: Sage Publications, 1991), pp. 6-7, 12-16; as to continuing disparities in criminal justice, education, environmental justice, automobile shopping, and other commercial activities, see Robert D. Bullard, *Dumping in Dixie: Race, Class, and Environmental Quality* (Boulder, CO: Westview Press, 1990); Steven R. Donziger, ed., *The Real War On Crime: The Report of the National Criminal Justice Commission* (New York: Harper Perennial, 1996); Jonathan Kozol, *Savage Inequalities: Children in America's Schools* (New York: Harper Perennial, 1992); Ian Ayers, "Further Evidence of Discrimination in New Car Negotiations and Estimates of Its Cause," 94 *Michigan Law Review* 190 (Oct. 1995); Ian Ayers, "Unequal Racial Access to Kidney Transplantation," 46 *Vanderbilt Law Review* 805 (May 1993); Michele L. Johnson, "Your Loan is Denied But What About Your Lending Discrimination Suit?: *Latimore v. Citibank Federal Savings Bank*," 68 *University of University of Cincinnati Law Review* 185 (Fall 1999); Deseriee A. Kennedy, "Consumer Discrimination: The Limitations of Federal Civil Rights Protection," 66 *Missouri Law Review* 275 (Spring 2001).

18. Alan Hendrickson, "Mental Maps," in Micahel J. Hogan and Thomas G. Patterson, eds., *Explaining the History of American Foreign Relations* (Camrbidge: Cambridge University Press, 1991), pp. 177-192; Philomena Essed, *Understanding Everyday Racism: An Interdisciplinary Theory* (Newbury Park, CA.: Sage Publications), pp. 75-76 (where the author discusses how victims of racism use "scripts" of past experience to understand new assaults).

19. C. L. R. James, *A History of Pan-African Revolt* (Chicago: C. H. Kerr, 1995), pp. 39-46, 103; Tim Matthewson, "Jefferson and Haiti," *Journal of Southern History*, 62, no. 2 (1995), pp. 209-248; Howard Zinn, *A People's History of the United States: 1492-present* (New York: HarperCollins, 1999), p. 125; see also Anna Julia Cooper, *Slavery and the*

*French Revolutionists (1788-1805)* (Lewiston, NY: The Edwin Mellen Press, trans., with an introduction by Frances R. Keller, 1988), pp. 149-155.

20. Tim Matthewson, "Jefferson and the Non-Recognition of Haiti," *Proceedings of the American Philosophical Society*, vol. 140, no. 1 (1996), pp. 22-48.

21. Eduardo Galeano, *The Open Veins of Latin America: Five Centuries of the Pillaging of a Continent*, trans. by Cedric Belfrage (New York: Monthly Review Press, 1973), pp. 78-79.

22. See, e.g., Cooper, *Slavery and the French Revolutionists*; C. L. R. James, *The Black Jacobins; Toussaint L'Ouverture and the San Domingo Revolution* (New York: Vintage Books, 2nd revised edition, 1963); Rayford W. Logan, *The Diplomatic Relations of the United States with Haiti, 1776-1891* (Chapel Hill: The University of North Carolina Press, 1941); Rayford W. Logan, *Haiti and the Dominican Republic* (New York: Oxford University Press, 1968); Brenda Gayle Plummer, *Haiti and the United States: The Psychological Moment* (Athens: University of Georgia Press, 1992); Brenda Gayle Plummer, *Haiti and the Great Powers, 1902-1915* (Baton Rouge: Louisiana State University Press, 1988).

23. For a contemporary assessment of U.S. foreign policy toward Haiti and the continued racial animus of American military personnel, see Stan Goff, *Hideous Dream: A Soldier's Memoir of the US Invasion of Haiti* (Winnipeg, Manitoba: Soft Skull Press, 2000).

24. Galeano, *The Open Veins of Latin America*, p. 78; see also J. Michael Dash, *Haiti and the United States: National Stereotypes and the Literary Imagination* (Houndsmill, Basingstoke: Macmillan Press, 1997).

25. Brenda G. Plummer, *Haiti and the United States: The Psychological Moment* (Athens: University of Georgia, 1997), p. 35.

26. Ibid., p. 43.

27. Ibid., p. 44.

28. George M. Fredrickson, *The Arrogance of Race: Historical Perspectives on Slavery, Racism, and Social Inequality* (Middletown, CT: Wesleyan University Press, 1988), pp. 62-65; James D. Lockett, "Abraham Lincoln and Colonization: An Episode That Ends in Tragedy at L'ile a Vache, Haiti, 1863-1864," *Journal of Black Studies* 21, no. 4 (1991), pp. 428-444; see also Logan, *The Diplomatic Relations of the United States with Haiti*, pp. 296, 298-303.

29. Plummer, *Haiti and the Great Powers*, p. 49.

30. Ibid., pp. 81-89.

31. Ibid., pp. 95-103.

32. Logan, *The Diplomatic Relations of the United States with Haiti*, pp. 368-383.

33. Plummer, *Haiti and the Great Powers*, pp. 103-113.

34. Logan, *Diplomatic Relations of the United State with Haiti*, pp. 415-457.

35. Plummer, *Haiti and the United States*, p. 101 (the U.S. government cited "widespread violence, anarchy, and imminent danger to foreigners' lives and property" to justify the landing of Marines at Port-au-Prince).

36. James McCorklin, *Garde d'Haiti, 1915-1934; Twenty Years of Organization and Training by the United States Marine Corps* (Annapolis, MD: U.S. Naval Institute, 1956), p. 232.

37. Plummer, *Haiti and the United States*, p. 107.

38. Ibid., p. 108.

39. David Healy, *Gunboat Diplomacy in the Wilson Era: The U.S. Navy in Haiti, 1915-1916* (Madison: University of Wisconsin Press, 1976), pp. 141-142.

40. Plummer, *Haiti and the United States*, p. 108.

41. Plummer, *Haiti and the United States*, pp. 105-120; see also Alex Dupuy, *Haiti in the World Economy: Class, Race, and Underdevelopment since 1700* (Boulder, CO.: Westview Press, 1989), p. 162.

42. Healy, *Gunboat Diplomacy*, pp. 81-84, 133-137; Plummer, *Haiti and the United States*, pp. 101-102.

43. Plummer, *Haiti and the United States*, p. 102; see also Myriam A. J. Chancy, *Framing Silence: Revolutionary Novels by Haitian Women* (New Brunswick, NJ: Rutgers University Press, 1999), pp. 53-56.

44. McCorklin, *Garde d'Haiti*, pp. 54-59.

45. Galeano, *Open Veins of Latin America*, p. 78.

46. Plummer, *Haiti and the United States*, pp. 102-104.

47. Plummer, *Haiti and the United States*, pp. 103-106; see also *Second Annual Report of the American High Commission of Haiti to the Secretary of State, December 31, 1923* (Washington, DC: U.S. Government Printing Office, 1924), p. 12.

48. Plummer, *Haiti and the United States*, pp. 114-117.

49. McCorklin, *Garde d'Haiti*, pp. 232-233.

50. Dupuy, *Haiti in the World Economy*, p. 144.

51. Mats Lundahl, *Politics or Markets? Essays on Haitian Underdevelopment* (London: Routledge Press, 1992), p. 350.

52. Dupuy, *Haiti in the World Economy*, p. 145; see also Simon Fass, *Political Economy in Haiti: The Drama of Survival* (New Brunswick, NJ: Transaction Books, 1990), p. 14.

53. Plummer, *Haiti and the United States*, p. 145; but, cf., Lundahl, *Politics or Markets?* p. 350.

54. Plummer, *Haiti and the United States*, p. 145.

55. Dupuy, *Haiti in the World Economy*, p. 145; Plummer, *Haiti and the United States*, pp. 145-146.

56. Plummer, *Haiti and the United States*, pp. 145-146; see also Dupuy, *Haiti in the World Economy*, 144-145 (where the authors describe SHADA's fifty-year monopoly on rubber production, its purchase of railroad lines and other private businesses, its ability to control its overhead by laying off any number of its 70,000 poorly paid employees while retaining its well-paid expatriate staff, and by having a detachment of fifty to sixty members of the Garde d'Haiti posted at every SHADA plantation).

57. Lundahl, *Politics or Markets?* p. 350.

58. Plummer, *Haiti and the United States*, p. 146.

59. See, e.g., *United Nations Mission of Technical Assistance to Haiti* (Lake Success, NY: United Nations, 1949), pp. 131-137, 141-143.

60. McCorklin, *Garde d'Haiti*, pp. 55-59, 137-141, 223-234; see also Dupuy, *Haiti in the World Economy*, p. 117.

61. Healy, *Gunboat Diplomacy*, pp. 68-69, 173-175, 196-197, 220; see also Chancy, *Framing Silence*, p. 48.

62. Plummer, *Haiti and the United States*, p. 134.

63. Ibid., pp. 154-159.

64. In this regard, I would like to thank Kathryn Statler who raised the issue of "models of nation-building" in the Eisenhower era in her paper "Committing to South Vietnam:

The Eisenhower Administration, Alliance Politics, and Nation Building, 1953-1961," delivered at the 2002 Society for Historians of American Foreign Relations annual conference, as well as the audience comments by George Herring.

65. Plummer, *Haiti and the United States*, p. 120.

66. Thomas J. Noer, *Cold War and Black Liberation: the United States and White Rule in Africa, 1948-1968* (Columbia: University of Missouri Press, 1985), pp. 34-60; see also Derrick A. Bell, "*Brown v. Board of Education* and the Interest Convergence Dilemma," 93 *Harvard Law Review* 518 (1980).

67. Lerone Bennett, Jr., *Before the Mayflower: A History of Black America* (Chicago: Johnson Publishing Co., 1987), p. 541. The report cites, among others, the eye-gouging, blow-torching lynching of a Black soldier returning from the war; the report stated, in part, that "negroes in America have been disillusioned over the wave of lynchings, brutality and official repression from all of the flamboyant promises of post war democracy and decency."

68. Brenda Gayle Plummer, *Rising Wind: Black Americans and U.S. Foreign Affairs, 1935-1960* (Chapel Hill: University of North Carolina Press, 1996), pp. 80-85, 87, 100, 171-181, 219.

69. See, e.g., October 31, 1957 Eisenhower reply letter to Mrs. William T. Mason, National Council of Negro Women, Ann Whitman File, DDE Diary Series; see also Mary Dudziak, "Desegregation As A Cold War Imperative," 41 *Stanford L. Rev.* (November 1988), pp. 111-112.

70. 163 U.S. 537 (1896).

71. 347 U.S. 483, 74 S. Ct. 686, 98 L.Ed. 873 (1954). The *Brown* case actually combined litigation from several federal courts into one appeal. The common thread in all of the cases was the effort by Black children and their families to integrate racially exclusive schools. For instance, *Bolling v. Sharpe*, 347 U.S. 497 (1954), a companion case to *Brown*, was of particular significance because it involved school segregation in the District of Columbia. The Department of Justice attorneys noted "the treatment of colored persons [in the nation's capital] is taken as the measure of our attitude toward minorities generally." DOJ brief, p. 4.

72. See, e.g., *Shelley v. Kraemer*, 334 U.S. 1 (1948), and *Henderson v. United States*, 339 U.S. 816 (1950). The term *amicus curiae* means "friend of the court."

73. DOJ brief in *Brown*, p. 6.

74. 345 U.S. 972-973. (Of the five questions enumerated in the order, the first two pertained to whether there was any evidence of congressional intent with regard to the application of the Fourteenth Amendment to school segregation. The third question asked if the Court had authority to construe the Fourteenth Amendment in such a way as to abolish segregated schools. Finally, the fourth and fifth questions pertained to the

appropriate remedy if the Court should determine that state-sponsored racially segregated schools are unconstitutional. Specifically, the Court wondered if it should grant immediate or gradual relief to the plaintiffs and whether the Supreme Court or local district courts were the appropriate place for detailed decrees.) See also Richard Kluger, *Simple Justice: The History of Brown v. Board of Education and Black America's Struggle for Equality* (New York: Vintage Books, 1977), pp. 726-727.

75. Phillip B. Kurland and Gerhard Casper, eds., *Landmark Briefs and Arguments of the Supreme Court of the United States: Constitutional Law*, vol. 49 (Bethesda, MD: University Publications of America, Inc., 1975), pp. 866, 1019-1023; see also March 5, 1965, interview of Herbert Brownell, John Foster Dulles Oral Histories Collection, Seeley G. Mudd Library, Princeton University, pp. 28-31.

76. Kurland and Casper, eds., *Landmark Briefs and Arguments*, vol. 49A, p. 523 (p. 22 of the transcript of oral arguments).

77. Ibid., pp. 534-537 (pp. 33-36 of the transcript of oral arguments; see especially p. 537 for this exchange: "MR. JUSTICE REED: And is this a denial of liberty or property, segregation? MR. RANKIN: Well, I would think it would be a denial of part of liberty rather than property.").

78. Ibid., p. 538 (p. 37 of the oral transcript; emphasis added).

79. 347 U.S. 483, at 495.

80. Kurland and Casper, eds., *Landmark Briefs and Arguments*, vol. 49A, p. 749 (p. 8 of the brief), pp. 773-790.

81. Ibid., p. 759 (p. 18 of the brief; see also footnote 11 on the same page, where the government states: "The well-publicized student disturbances which occurred recently in some localities certainly provide no basis for such a presumption."). See also p. 769 (where the attorneys argue that an injunction should be issued only after the school districts have had an opportunity to submit a desegregation plan).

82. Ibid., p. 761 (p. 20 of the brief; where the Justice Department alludes to the desegregation of New Jersey schools); but cf. Kluger, *Simple Justice*, pp. 124, 446, 706 (where the sociologist E. Franklin Frazier, as part of an NAACP brief, indicated that his evidence showed that public support was not necessary for successful desegregation).

83. Ibid., pp. 1213-1317 (the states represented included Arkansas, Maryland, North Carolina, Oklahoma, Texas, and Virginia).

84. See, e.g., Ibid., pp. 1245-1246 (pp. 31-32 of the transcript of the oral arguments, where Tom Gentry, Arkansas attorney general, presented this position with regard to gradual integration to avoid unpleasant incidents).

85. Ibid., p. 1285 (p. 71 of the transcript of the oral argument).

86. Ibid., pp. 1286-1287 (pp. 72-73 of the transcript of the oral argument, emphasis added).

87. Ibid., p. 1288 (p. 74 of the transcript of the oral argument, emphasis added).

88. Ibid., p. 1295 (p. 3 of the transcript of the oral argument, where the solicitor general stated that "the important thing . . . is to make clear to the lower courts and to the parties that there must be a bona fide advance toward the goal of desegregation. *That doesn't mean that people ought to be ridden over, roughshod; it doesn't mean that conditions ought to be ignored.* Adjustments have to be made, and allowance should be made for the time.").

89. Ibid., p. 1298 (p. 6 of the transcript of the oral argument).

90. 349 U.S. 294, at 299-300; May 31, 1955, diary entry re: phone call from Brownell to Eisenhower, DDE Diary Series, Ann Whitman File.

91. Cheryl I. Harris, "Whiteness as Property," 106 *Harvard Law Review* 1707 (1993).

92. Harris, "Whiteness as Property," p. 1750; see also Bell, "*Brown v. Board of Education* and the Interest Convergence Dilemma," 93 *Harvard Law Review* 518 (1980) pp. 520-522.

93. Harris, "Whiteness as Property," p. 1753.

94. Harris, "Whiteness as Property," pp. 1751-1756; Sumi Cho, "Redeeming Whiteness in the Shadow of Internment: Earl Warren, Brown, and a Theory of Racial Redemption," 19 *Boston College Third World Law Journal* 73, 75 (Fall 1998); see also C. Vann Woodward, *The Strange Career of Jim Crow* (New York: Oxford University Press, 1974), p. 162 (where the author counted 106 tactics southern states used to evade the ruling in *Brown I*).

95. Cho, "Redeeming Whiteness," p. 75.

96. Cho, "Redeeming Whiteness," p. 139.

97. Ibid. pp. 139-140; see also Thomas Ross, "The Rhetorical Tapestry of Race: White Innocence and Black Abstraction," 32 *William & Mary Law Review* (1990) 1, 22-23 (quoting John W. Davis's oral argument before the Court).

98. See, e.g., Kluger, *Simple Justice*, pp. 406-409; the PBS documentary series "The Rise and Fall of Jim Crow," vol. 4 (2002) (which focused on the efforts of attorney Charles H. Houston to record on film the desperate physical conditions of schools for Black children throughout the South and firsthand accounts from Black children in Farmville, Virginia).

99. Kluger, *Simple Justice*, p. 729 (regarding the oral arguments of Robert Carter, Spotswood Robinson, and others on behalf of the Black children).

100. Kurland and Casper, eds., *Landmark Briefs and Arguments*, vol. 49A, p. 1305 (p. 13 of the transcript of the April 14, 1955, oral argument where Marshall makes specific reference to *Sweatt v. Painter*, 339 U.S. 629 [1950], and *McLaurin v. Oklahoma*, 339 U.S. 637 [1950]).

101. Ibid., pp. 1305-1307 (pp. 13-15 of the transcript of the April 14, 1955, oral argument).

102. Ibid., pp. 1308-1309 (pp. 16-17 of the transcript of the April 14, 1955, oral argument).

103. Ibid., p. 1309 (p. 17 of the transcript of the April 14, 1955, oral argument).

104. Stephanie M. Wildman, et al., *Privilege Revealed: How Invisible Preferences Undermine America* (New York: New York University Press, 1996), p. 88.

105. Wildman, et al., *Privilege Revealed*, p. 91.

106. Kurland and Casper, eds., *Landmark Briefs and Arguments*, vol. 49A, p. 759 (p. 18 of the Justice Department's April 1955 brief on the question of relief).

107. Cho, "Redeeming Whiteness," p. 140. See also James T. Patterson, *Brown v. Board of Education: A Civil Rights Milestone and Its Troubled Legacy* (New York: Oxford University Press, 2001), pp. 61-63.

108. Ross, "The Rhetorical Tapestry," 32 *Wm & Mary L. Rev.* at 24-25.

109. Ibid., p. 26.

110. Kluger, *Simple Justice*, p. 735.

111. Ibid., pp. 730-732.

112. Ibid., p. 732.

113. Ibid.

114. Ibid.

115. Cho, "Redeeming Whiteness," p. 141.

116. Kurland and Casper, eds., *Landmark Briefs and Arguments*, vol. 49A, p. 758 (p. 17 of the Justice Department's April 1955 brief on the question of relief).

117. Kluger, *Simple Justice*, pp. 746-747.

118. Kurland and Casper, eds., *Landmark Briefs and Arguments,* vol. 49A, p. 1280 (p. 66 of the transcript of the April 13, 1955, oral argument).

119. 349 U.S. 294 at 299 (1955); see also Cho, "Redeeming Whiteness," p.141.

120. Harris "Whiteness as Property," p. 1754; but see Robert Weisbrot, *Freedom Bound: History of America's Civil Rights Movement* (New York: Plume Books, 1991), pp. 11-12.

121. Thomas Noer, *Cold War & Black Liberation: The United States and White Rule in Africa, 1948-1968* (Columbia: University of Missouri Press, 1985), p. 35.

122. Stephen Ambrose and Richard Immerman, *Ike's Spies: Eisenhower & the Espionage Establishment* (Garden City, NJ: Doubleday, 1981), pp. 220-22; but cf. generally, Piero Gleijeses, *Shattered Hope: The Guatamalan Revolution & The United States, 1944-1954* (Princeton, NJ: Princeton University Press, 1991).

123. Gordon Chang, *Friends and Enemies: The United States, China, and the Soviet Union, 1948-1972* (Stanford, CA: Stanford University Press, 1990), p. 171.

124. David F. Schmitz, *Thank God They're On Our Side: The United States and Right-Wing Dictatorships, 1921-1965* (Chapel Hill: University of North Carolina Press, 1999), p. 182. For an insider's perspective on the administration's racial views, see E. Frederic Morrow, *Forty Years A Guinea Pig,* (New York: Pilgrim Press, 1980); see also July 22, 1964, interview of James P. Mitchell, John Foster Dulles Oral History Collection, Seeley G. Mudd Library, Princeton University, pp. 3-4 (where Mitchell, the former secretary of labor, stressed that Foster Dulles was in full support of the principle of equality of job opportunity). With regard to works interpreting the impact of race on U.S. foreign relations generally, see the recently published series of anthologies, Michael Krenn, ed., *Race and U.S. Foreign Policy From the Colonial Period to the Present,* five volumes (New York: Garland Publishers, 1998).

125. Chang, *Friends and Enemies,* p. 170.

126. See Robert Bowie and Richard Immerman, *Waging Peace: How Eisenhower Shaped An Enduring Cold War Strategy* (Oxford: Oxford University Press, 1998), p. 220.

127. Chang, *Friends and Enemies,* pp. 170, 173.

128. July 22 and 27, 1965, interview of William Sebald, John Foster Dulles Oral History Collection, Seeley G. Mudd Library, Princeton University, p. 110.

129. Chang, *Friends and Enemies,* pp. 172-173.

130. August 16, 1954, memorandum from Max Rabb to Eisenhower re: the first "Negro" to attend a Cabinet meeting in the history of the United States, Ann Whitman File, ACW Diary Series, DDE Library.

131. The list of attendees at presidential "stag dinners" included: Howard Cullman (chairman of the New York Port Authority), William R. Hearst, Jr. (chairman of Editorial

Board, Hearst Newspapers), Charles Hook (chairman of Armco Steel Corp.), Morehead Patterson (chairman of American Machine & Foundry Co.), C. R. Smith (president of American Airlines), and Gen. Cornelius Wickersham (lawyer and partner, Cadwalader, Wickersham & Taft); Ellis Slater (president and director, Frankfort Distillers Corp., NYC), Toddie Lee Wynne (oil-cattleman, Dallas), Sid Richardson (oil-cattleman, Ft. Worth), Aksel Nielsen (president, The Title Guaranty Co., Denver), among others. December 10, 1953, and November 22, 1954, lists of stag dinner guests, Ann Whitman File, DDE Diary Series, DDE Library.

132. See, e.g., March 23, 1956, diary entry regarding meeting between Eisenhower, Secretaries Humphrey and Mitchell, and David J. McDonald of the United Steelworkers of America, Ann Whitman File, DDE Diary Series, DDE Library.

133. See, e.g., January 25, 1956, diary entry, Ann Whitman File, DDE Diary series; undated pre-press conference briefing note, Ann Whitman File, ACW Diary, DDE Library.

134. November 23, 1958, diary entry re: meeting between Eisenhower and General Gruenther, Ann Whitman File, ACW Diary Series, DDE Library.

135. See, e.g., Charlene E. McGee-Smith, *Tuskegee Airman: The Biography of Charles E. McGee, Air Force Fighter, Combat Record-Holder* (Boston: Branden Publishing, 2nd edition, 2000); Lawrence P. Scott and William M. Womack Sr., *Double V: The Civil Rights Struggle of the Tuskegee Airmen* (East Lansing: Michigan State University Press, 1994); see also Alan P. Gropman, *The Air Force Integrates, 1945-1964* (Washington, DC: Smithsonian Institution Press, 2nd edition, 1998), pp. 2-3.

136. July 22, 1957, letter from Eisenhower to Swede Hazlett, Ann Whitman File, DDE Diary Series, DDE Library.

137. March 30, 1956, letter to Rev. Billy Graham; March 21, 1956, phone conversation with Ovetta Culp Hobby; August 14, 1956, afternoon discussion about *Brown* decision and Ike's "alternate course" on desegregation, Ann Whitman File, ACW Diary Series, DDE Library.

138. George Fredrickson, *The Arrogance of Race: Historical Perspectives on Slavery, Racism, and Social Inequality* (Middletown, CT: Wesleyan University Press, 1988), pp. 29, 35-44; Horsman, *Race and Manifest Destiny*, pp. 122-137.

139. 347 U.S. 483 (1954); March 20, 1956, memo re: Eisenhower's congratulations to A. G. Brownell for his statement on segregation, Ann Whitman File, ACW Diary Series, DDE Library; see also January 25, 1954, diary entry of phone conversation between Eisenhower and Brownell, Ann Whitman File, DDE Series, DDE Library (in which the president remarked that "the best interest of the U.S. demands a [ruling] in keep[ing] with past decisions").

140. Arthur Larson, *Eisenhower: The President Nobody Knew* (New York: Charles Scribner's Sons, 1968), pp. 124-126.

141. Ibid.; see also Robert F. Burk, *The Eisenhower Administration and Black Civil Rights* (Knoxville: University of Tennessee Press, 1984), pp. 16-18.

142. Darlene C. Hine, ed., *Black Women in America: An Historical Encyclopedia*, vol. II (Brooklyn, NY: Carlson Publishing, Inc., 1993), p. 912.

143. Leon Litwack, *North of Slavery: The Negro in the Free States, 1790-1860* (Chicago: University of Chicago Press, 1961), pp. 77-79.

144. Paula Giddings, *When and Where I Enter: The Impact of Black Women on Race and Sex in America* (New York: William Morrow & Co., Inc., 1984), pp. 27-31; see also Pearl Cleage, *Deals With the Devil; And Other Reasons to Riot* (New York: Ballantine Books, 1993) pp. 8-43; Lani Guinier, *The Tyranny of the Majority: Fundamental Fairness in Representative Democracy* (New York: The Free Press, 1994), pp. 188-191; bell hooks, *Talking Back: Thinking Feminist, Thinking Black* (Boston: South End Press, 1989), pp. 84-91.

145. See Department of State Staff Notes' reference to Lucy's international celebrity in discussion of global reaction to Little Rock Nine; chapter 2, below.

146. Undated memo in series of National Security Council meeting notes, Ann Whitman File, NSC Series, DDE Library (probably duplicate from 440th NSC meeting, April 7, 1960).

147. February 26, 1959, memorandum regarding 397th NSC meeting, Ann Whitman File, NSC Series, DDE Library.

148. See Richard Immerman, *The CIA In Guatemala* (Austin: University of Texas, 1982), p. 74. As to the links between the Eisenhower administration and United Fruit Company, see Ambrose and Immerman, *Ike's Spies*, pp. 218-223.

149. April 7, 1960, memorandum regarding 440th NSC meeting, Ann Whitman File, NSC Series, DDE Library, p. 15.

150. NSC 5818 and 5920 discussed American foreign policy toward southern, central, and east Africa collectively.

151. March 31, 1960, memorandum regarding 423rd NSC meeting, Ann Whitman File, NSC Series, DDE Library.

152. Ibid.; Dwight D. Eisenhower, *Waging Peace, 1956-1961: The White House Years* (Garden City, NY: Doubleday Press, 1965), p. 582.

153. April 7, 1960, memorandum regarding 440th NSC meeting, Ann Whitman File, NSC Series, DDE Library.

154. May 9, 1958, memorandum regarding 365th NSC meeting, Ann Whitman File, NSC Series, DDE Library.

155. See Ambrose and Immerman, *Ike's Spies*, p. 216; see also Victor Marchetti and John D. Marks, *CIA and the Cult of Intelligence* (New York: Alfred A. Knopf, Inc., 1974), p. 26.

156. August 25, 1960, memorandum regarding 456th NSC meeting, Ann Whitman File, NSC Series, DDE Library, p. 12.

157. Ibid.

158. See August 23, 1957, NSC memorandum 5719/1, OSANSA Series, Subject subseries, paragraphs, 7, 9, 23-25; see also July 29, 1958, memorandum from Lay to NSC, OSANSA Series, Subject subseries, DDE Library (regarding proposed revisions to paragraphs 21-27 of NSC 5719/1); see also Clarence Randall diary of 1958 trip to Africa, entry numbers 3, 8, 10-12, Clarence Randall Papers, Public Policy Papers, Department of Rare Books and Special Collections, Seeley G. Mudd Library, Princeton University.

159. August 25, 1960, memo regarding 456th NSC meeting, Ann Whitman File, NSC Series, DDE Library, p. 9.

160. Lisa Ikemoto, *Traces of the Master Narrative in the Story of African American/Korean American Conflict: How We Constructed "Los Angeles,"* 66 S. Cal. L. Rev. 1581 (1993), p. 1582-3.

161. As to the colonial caricature of African women, see Catherine Coquery-Vidrovitch, *African Women: A Modern History* (New York: Westview Press, 1997, trans. Beth G. Raps), p. 196; see also David Sweetman, *Women Leaders in African History* (London: Heinemann Educational Books, Ltd., 1984).

162. See Emily S. Rosenberg, "Revisiting Dollar Diplomacy: Narratives of Money and Manliness," *Diplomatic History* 22, no. 2 (Spring 1998), pp. 155-176.

163. Catherine Coquery-Vidrovitch, *Africa: Endurance and Change South of the Sahara* (Berkeley: University of California Press, 1988, trans., David Maisel), pp. 89-98, 130-134, 140-141, 146-147, 166-167, 298-308; Barbara Lewis, "Getting Women on the African Agricultural Development Agenda," in Harvey Glickman, ed., *The Crisis and Challenge of African Development* (New York: Greenwood Press, 1983), pp. 176-200; Ali Mazrui, "Afrostroika and Planned Governance: Economic Adjustment and Political Engineering," in Aguibou Y. Yansane, ed., *Development Strategies in Africa: Current Economic, Social-Political and Institutional Trends and Issues* (Westport, CT: Greenwood Press, 1996), pp. 100-102; Stephen Younger, "Labor Market Consequences of Retrenchment for Civil Servants in Ghana," in David E. Sahn, ed., *Economic Reform and the Poor in Africa* (Oxford: Clarendon, 1996), pp. 185-202.

164. See Derrick A. Bell, *"Brown v. Board of Education* and the Interest Convergence Dilemma," 93 *Harvard Law Review* 518 (1980), for Prof. Bell's "interest-convergence theory."

165. See undated "The Psychological Dimensions of American Foreign Policy," Presidential Committee on Information Activities Abroad (Sprague Committee) File, Box #15, Public Opinion folder, DDE Library, p. 3.

# Chapter Two

1. Ebere Nwaubani, *The United States and Decolonization in West Africa, 1950-1960* (Rochester, NY: University of Rochester Press, 2001), pp. 1-2.

2. The peaceful transition from colonial to independent state for Ghana is contrasted with the bloody revolutions in Guinea Bissau, Cape Verde, Angola, and (to a lesser degree) Kenya and the Congo. See, e.g., Basil Davidson, *No Fist is Big Enough to Hide the Sky: The Liberation of Guinea-Bissau and Cape Verde* (London: Zed Press, 1981); Mustafah Dhada, *Warriors at Work: How Guinea Was Really Set Free* (Niwot: University Press of Colorado, 1993); John A. Marcum, *The Angolan Revolution* (Cambridge, MA: MIT Press, 1978); George S. Mwase, *Strike a Blow and Die: A Narrative of Race Relations in Colonial Africa* (Cambridge, MA: MIT Press, 1967); Cora A. Presley, *Kikuyu Women, The Mau Mau Rebellion, and Social Change in Kenya* (Boulder, CO: Westview Press, 1992).

3. December 3, 1955, John Cowles letter to Eisenhower, Ann Whitman File, DDE Diary Series, DDE Library, pp. 1-2.

4. December 7, 1955, Eisenhower reply letter to John Cowles, Ann Whitman File, DDE Diary Series, DDE Library.

5. December 3, 1955, Cowles to Eisenhower, p. 1.

6. See, e.g., Darryl C. Thomas, *The Theory and Practice of Third World Solidarity* (Westport, CT: Praeger, 2001); Francois Godement, *The New Asian Renaissance: From Colonialism to the Post-Cold War* (London: Routledge, 1997); R. A. Longmire, *Soviet Relations With South and South-East Asia: An Historical Survey* (London: Kegan Paul, International, 1989); A. W. Stargaardt, *Australia's Asian Policies: The History of a Debate, 1839-1972* (Hamburg: The Institute of Asian Affairs in Hamburg, 1977); George McT. Kahin, *The Asian-African Conference: Bandung, Indonesia, April 1955* (Ithaca, NY: Cornell University Press, 1956); Carlos P. Romulo, *The Meaning of Bandung* (Chapel Hill: University of North Carolina Press, 1956); Richard Wright, *The Color Curtain: A Report on the Bandung Conference* (Cleveland: The World Publications, Co., 1956); Christopher Waters, "After Decolonization: Australia and the Emergence of the Non-Aligned Movement in Asia, 1954-55," *Diplomacy and Statecraft* [Great Britain] 12, no. 2, (2001), pp. 153-174; Yan Zhang, "I Wish I Had Met Richard Wright at Bandung in 1955: Recollections on a Conference Attended by Both Wright and the Author," *Mississippi Quarterly* 50, no. 2 (1997), pp. 277-287.

7. Warren F. Kimball, *The Juggler: Franklin Roosevelt as Wartime Statesman* (Princeton, NJ: Princeton University Press, 1991), pp. 43-60; Thomas J. McCormick, *America's Half-Century: United States Foreign Policy in the Cold War and After* (Baltimore, MD: Johns Hopkins University Press, 1995), pp. 33, 113; Thomas Paterson, *On Every Front:*

*The Making of the Cold War* (New York: W. W. Norton & Co., 1979), pp. 36-37, 91; Emily Rosenberg, *Spreading the American Dream,* pp. 202-228; Laurence Shoup and William Minter, "Shaping A New World Order: The Council on Foreign Relations' Blueprint for World Hegemony," in Holly Sklar, ed., *Trilateralism: The Trilateral Commission and Elite Planning for World Management* (Boston, MA: South End Press, 1980), pp. 135-151; see also Robert D. Schulzinger, *The Wise Men of Foreign Affairs: The History of the Council on Foreign Relations* (New York: Columbia University Press, 1984), and Michael Wala, *The Council on Foreign Relations and American Foreign Policy in the Early Cold War* (Providence, RI: Bergahn Books, 1994).

8. Warren F. Kimball, *Forged in War: Roosevelt, Churchill, and the Second World War* (New York: W. Morrow, 1997), pp. 300-305; Kimball, *The Juggler,* pp. 134-145; Paterson, *On Every Front,* p. 37; Penny Von Eschen, *Race Against Empire: Black Americans and Anti-Colonialism, 1937-1957* (Ithaca, NY: Cornell University Press, 1994), pp. 25-27, 100-101; Kenneth Maxwell, "The Portuguese Colonies and Decolonization," *Africana Journal* 15 (1990), p. 62.

9. Walter LaFeber, "Roosevelt, Churchill, and Indochina, 1942-5," *American Historical Review* 80 (December 1985), pp. 1277-1295; William R. Louis, *Imperialism at Bay, 1941-1945: The United States and Decolonization of the British Empire* (New York: Oxford University Press, 1978), pp. 3-10, 91-94; William Minter, *King Solomon's Mines Revisited: Western Interests and the Burdened History of Southern Africa* (New York: Basic Books, 1986), pp. 116-117; but cf. Kimball, *The Juggler,* pp. 130, 145.

10. Brenda G. Plummer, *Rising Wind: Black Americans and U.S. Foreign Affairs, 1935-1960* (Chapel Hill, NC: University of North Carolina Press, 1996), pp. 86-89, 102-104, 107, 116-118; Von Eschen, *Race Against Empire,* pp. 30, 42; see also Kenneth O'Reilly, *Racial Matters: the FBI's Secret File on Black America, 1960-1972* (New York: Free Press, 1989), p. 357 (where the author excerpts Paul Robeson's article "Negroes in the Ranks of the World Front in the Fight for Peace and Progress" published in *Trybnua Luda* [Poland], June 2, 1949).

11. Melvyn Leffler, *A Preponderance of Power: National Security, the Truman Administration, and the Cold War* (Palo Alto, CA: Stanford University Press, 1992), pp. 121-127, 142-146, 194-195, 214 (regarding the popular support for the Truman Doctrine, among other things); Paterson, *On Every Front,* p. 58, 106; see also William Blum, *The CIA: A Forgotten History* (London: Zed Books, Ltd., 1986), pp. 33-37.

12. Leffler, *Preponderance of Power,* pp. 159-161.

13. Ibid., pp. 164-165; see also Gabriel Kolko, *Confronting the Third World: United States Foreign Policy, 1945-1980* (New York: Pantheon Books, 1988), pp. 53, 111-112.

14. David Fieldhouse, "Arrested Development in Anglophone Black Africa?" in Prosser Gifford & William Roger Louis, eds., *Decolonization and African Independence: The Transfers of Power, 1960-1980* (New Haven, CT: Yale University Press, 1988), p. 139.

15. See, e.g., Andrew J. Rotter, *The Path to Vietnam: Origins of the American Commitment to Southeast Asia* (Ithaca, NY: Cornell University Press, 1987), pp. 49-69, 165-166.

16. Leffler, *Preponderance of Power*, p. 166.

17. Leffler, *Preponderance of Power*, pp. 166-167; see also July 7, 1953, letter from Eisenhower to Senator Ralph Flanders, Ann Whitman File, DDE Diary Series, DDE Library, pp. 1-2.

18. Leffler, *Preponderance of Power*, p. 314.

19. McCormick, *America's Half-Century*, p. 91.

20. Paterson, *On Every Front*, p. 67.

21. William Roger Louis and Ronald Robinson, "The United States and The Liquidation of the British Empire in Tropical Africa, 1941-1951," in Prosser Gifford and William Roger Louis, eds., *The Transfer of Power in Africa: Decolonization, 1940-1960* (New Haven, CT: Yale University Press, 1982), pp. 45-46.

22. Leffler, *Preponderance of Power*, pp. 355-356, quoting NSC 68.

23. National Security Council Memorandum 68, as reproduced in Ernest R. May, ed., *American Cold War Strategy: Interpreting NSC 68* (Boston, MA: Bedford Books of St. Martin's Press, 1993), pp. 25-27.

24. NSC 68, as reproduced in May, ed., *American Cold War Strategy*, pp. 49-50.

25. Thomas Borstelmann, *Apartheid's Reluctant Uncle: The United States and Southern Africa in the Early Cold War* (New York: Oxford University Press, 1993), pp. 122-131; Minter, *King Solomon's Mines Revisited*, pp. 113-118.

26. Von Eschen, *Race Against Empire*, p. 125.

27. Ibid., p. 133.

28. William A. Williams, *The Tragedy of American Diplomacy* (New York: W. W. Norton, 1972), pp. 18-22; see also Michael R. Hall, *Sugar and Power in the Dominican Republic: Eisenhower, Kennedy and the Trujillos* (Westport, CT: Greenwood Press, 2000); Gilbert M. Joseph, Catherine C. LeGrand, and Ricardo D. Salvatore, eds., *Close Encounters of Empire: Writing the Cultural History of U.S.-Latin American Relations* (Durham: Duke University Press, 1998).

29. Robert Bowie and Richard Immerman, *Waging Peace: How Eisenhower Shaped an Enduring Cold War Strategy* (New York: Oxford University Press, 1998), pp. 213-214; McCormick, *America's Half-Century*, pp. 55-57, 112-113; but cf. Kolko, *Confronting the Third World*, pp. 53.

30. Bowie and Immerman, *Waging Peace*, p. 213; John L. Gaddis, *Strategies of Containment: A Critical Appraisal of Postwar American National Security Policy* (New York: Oxford University Press, 1982), pp. 149-152.

31. Bowie and Immerman, *Waging Peace*, p. 213.

32. Noer, *Cold War and Black Liberation*, pp. 35-36.

33. Interview of Ambassador William Sebald, John Foster Dulles Oral History Collection, Public Policy Papers, Department of Rare Books and Special Collections, Seeley G. Mudd Library, Princeton University, p. 98; see also Richard H. Immerman, *John Foster Dulles: Piety, Pragmatism, and Power in U.S. Foreign Policy* (Wilmington, DE: Scholarly Resources, 1999), pp. 31-32, 65-68, 88, 109-111, 117-119.

34. Kolko, *Confronting the Third World*, p. 49.

35. NSC 68, as reproduced in May, ed., *American Cold War Strategy*, p. 54.

36. February 27, 1956, Eisenhower letter to Edgar Eisenhower, Ann Whitman File, DDE Diary Series, pp. 1-2; as to general distinctions in the foreign policy views of Eisenhower and Dulles, see Immerman, *John Foster Dulles*, pp. 42-44.

37. August 23, 1957, memorandum re: 355th NSC meeting, Ann Whitman File, NSC Series, DDE Library, p. 1; Noer, *Cold War and Black Liberation*, p. 49; see also Dwight D. Eisenhower, *Waging Peace: The White House Years; A Personal Account, 1956-1961* (Garden City, NY: Doubleday & Co., Inc., 1965), p. 573.

38. August 8, 1958, memorandum re: 375th NSC meeting, Ann Whitman File, NSC Series, DDE Library, pp. 10-14.

39. August 25, 1960, memorandum re: 456th NSC meeting, Ann Whitman File, NSC Series, DDE Library, p. 3.

40. Ibid.; see also August 23, 1957, memorandum re: 355th NSC meeting, p. 9.

41. February 5, 1954, diary entry of phone conversation between Eisenhower and General Bedell Smith re: military situation in Indo China, Ann Whitman File, DDE Series, DDE Library; with respect to the general mistrust within the administration for Third World nationalism, see David F. Schmitz, *Thank God They're On Our Side: the United States and Right-Wing Dictatorships, 1921-1965* (Chapel Hill: University of North Carolina Press, 1999), pp. 180-187.

42. Eisenhower, *Waging Peace*, p. 572.

43. November 1955, "Psychological Aspects of United States Strategy: Source Book of Individual Papers," White House Staff Secretary File, NSC Staff Papers, Executive Secretary Subject File Series, pp. iv-vi, 88, 93. PCG members included Paul Linebarger from Johns Hopkins University, William Webber from New England Electric Systems, and a young Henry Kissinger.

44. August 23, 1957, National Security Council memorandum 5719/1, OSANSA records, NSC Series, Policy Papers Sub-series, DDE Library, pp. 2, 13; see also Rotter, *The Path to Vietnam: Origins of the American Commitment to Southeast Asia* (Ithaca, NY: Cornell University Press, 1987), pp. 69, 172-186.

45. August 12, 1958, memorandum from James Lay to NSC re: Presidential approval of revisions to NSC 5719/1, etc.

46. See August 1, 1958, memorandum from N.F. Twining, Chairman Joint Chiefs to Staff to Secretary of Defense re: revisions to NSC 5719/1, OSANSA Records, NSC Series, Policy Papers Sub-series and August 5, 1958, memorandum from Lay to NSC re: JCS views on revisions to NSC 5719/1, OSANSA Records, NSC, Policy Papers Sub-series, DDE Library.

47. NSC 5719/1, p. 6.

48. Ibid., p. 9.

49. Ibid., pp. 7-8, 10 (¶ 13 Policy Guidance); see also January 19, 1960, National Security Council memorandum 6001 (NSC 6001), "U.S. Policy Toward South, Central, and East Africa," White House Office, National Security Council Staff Papers, Disaster File, Box #44, DDE Library, p. 4 (where nearly identical language appears).

50. July 29, 1958, memorandum from Lay to NSC re: proposed revisions to 5719/1, OSANSA Records, NSC Series, Policy Papers Sub-series, DDE Library, pp. 14-15.

51. March 31, 1960, memorandum re: 432nd NSC meeting, Ann Whitman File, NSC Series, DDE Library, p. 3.

52. NSC 5719/1, p. 12 (¶18, Policy Guidance).

53. Ibid. (¶17, The Communist Threat).

54. NSC 5719/1, p. 18 (¶28, Detribalization).

55. Ibid., (¶29, Policy Guidance).

56. August 8, 1958, memorandum re: 375th NSC meeting, Ann Whitman File, NSC Series, DDE Library, p. 11.

57. NSC 5719/1, p. 10; see also July 29, 1958, memorandum from Lay to NSC, p. 7; see also NSC 6001, pp. 5-6.

58. NSC 5719/1, p. 19.

59. March 21, 1958, OCB Progress Report on NSC 5719/1, OSANSA Records, NSC Series, Policy Papers Sub-series, DDE Library, p. 3.

60. Ibid., pp. 8-9.

61. April 22, 1958, memorandum from Elmer Staats, Executive Officer of OCB to James Lay Jr., Executive Secretary of NSC, OSANSA Records, NSC Series, Policy Papers Subseries, DDE Library, p. 1; see also NSC 5719/1, p. 19.

62. April 8, 1955, memorandum re: 244th NSC meeting, p. 17; see also interview of Ambassador William Sebald, John Foster Dulles Oral History Collection, Public Policy Papers, Department of Rare Books and Special Collections, Seeley G. Mudd Library, Princeton University, pp. 108-109.

63. February 12, 1960, briefing note re: U.S. Policy Toward West Africa, White House Office, Office of the Special Assistant for National Security Affairs Records, 1952-1961, NSC Briefing Notes Sub-series, DDE Library, p. 3, ¶ 11(b); see also NSC 6001, p. 4 (where the drafters recommend that the United States should "encourage participation of the moderate leaders in regional or Pan-African movements").

64. Eisenhower, *Waging Peace*, pp. 27, 115-116.

65. See NSC memorandum 6001, U.S. Policy Toward South, Central, and East Africa, NSC Series, Policy Papers Sub-series, DDE Library.

66. Kenneth Maxwell, "*The Portuguese Colonies and Decolonization,*" *Africana Journal* 15 (1990), 59-73, p. 61.

67. Minter, *King Solomon's Mines Revisited*, p. 116.

68. March 24, 1958, memorandum from Staats to Lay re: March 22, 1958 OCB Report on NSC 5719/1, p. 5, ¶16, OSANSA Records, NSC Series, Policy Papers Sub-series, DDE Library.

69. Ibid., p. 6 (where the authors note "that Africans in Angola consider the Belgian colonial policies in the Congo as liberal and the Portuguese look on them as dangerously so").

70. See, e.g., August 8, 1958, memorandum re: 375th NSC meeting, pp 12-13.

71. August 18, 1959, John H. Morrow Foreign Service Dispatch to Department of State, Ann Whitman File, International Series, Cameroun Sub-series, DDE Library.

72. Ibid. (p. 1 of the official translation attached to Foreign Service Dispatch).

73. Ibid. (p. 2. of the official translation); see also Richard Joseph, "Radical Nationalism in French Africa: The Case of Cameroon," in Gifford and Louis, eds., *Decolonization and African Independence*, pp. 335-341.

74. Ibid. (pp. 2-3 of the official translation).

75. Ibid. (pp. 3-4 of the official translation).

76. Ibid.

77. September 14, 1959, memorandum from Calhoun, Department of State, to Brig. Gen. A. J. Goodpaster, the White House, Ann Whitman File, International Series, Cameroun Sub-series, DDE Library.

78. Joseph, "Radical Nationalism in French Africa, " pp. 328-329, 341.

79. November 12, 1959, Department of State Memorandum of Conversation re: "The French Community and the West," Ann Whitman File, International Series, Ivory Coast folder, DDE Library, pp. 1, 3.

80. Ibid., pp. 1-2.

81. Ibid., p. 2.

82. Ibid.

83. Anna J. Cooper, *Slavery and the French Revolutionists (1788-1805)*, with an introduction by Frances R. Keller (Lewiston, NY: The Edwin Mellen Press, 1988), pp. 31-43.

84. Fieldhouse, "Arrested Development," p. 138.

85. For Foster Dulles's "genuine" support for decolonization, see Immerman, *John Foster Dulles*, pp. 154-155.

86. March 31, 1960 Memorandum re: 423rd NSC meeting re U.S. Policy Toward South, Central, and East Africa (NSC 5818 and NSC 5920), Ann Whitman File, NSC Series, DDE Library, p. 2.

87. As an example of this construction, within the context of the Suez Canal crisis, see Immerman, *John Foster Dulles*, p. 150 (where the author writes: "As Dulles said privately to the president, U.S. efforts to disassociate the free world alliance from the history of European imperialism would suffer immeasurable damage from [a joint British-French attack on Egypt]").

88. George White Jr., "Little Wheel Blues: John Lee Hooker, the Eisenhower Administration, and African Decolonization," *Cercles* 5 (2002), pp. 109-126.

89. Eisenhower, *Waging Peace*, p. 576; perhaps this dim view of non-White leadership resulted from the trying experiences U.S. officials had with men like Chiang Kai-shek (Immerman, *John Foster Dulles*, pp. 118-119).

90. See, e.g., Ibrahim K. Sundiata, "The Roots of African Despotism: The Question of Political Culture," in Gregory Maddox, ed., *African Nationalism and Revolution* (New York: Garland Publishers, 1993), pp. 35-54.

91. Walter Rodney, *How Europe Underdeveloped Africa* (Washington, DC: Howard University Press, 1981), pp. 128-135, 228, 250.

92. Jan N. Pieterse, *White On Black: Images of Africa and Blacks in Western Popular Culture* (New Haven, CT: Yale University Press, 1992), p. 235; see also David R. Roediger, *The Wages of Whiteness: Race and the Making of the American Working Class* (London: Verso 1991), pp. 98-99.

93. Alan K. Henrickson, "Mental Maps," in Michael Hogan and Thomas Paterson, eds., *Explaining the History of American Foreign Relations* (Cambridge: Cambridge University Press, 1991), pp. 177-192; see also February 2, 1959, briefing note re: Horn of Africa, White House Office, Office of the Special Assistant for National Security Affairs Records, 1952-1961, NSC Briefing Note subseries, p. 3, ¶ 5 (use of the term "West").

94. Interview of Ambassador Julius C. Holmes, John Foster Dulles Oral History Collection, Public Policy Papers, Department of Rare Books and Special Collections, Seeley G. Mudd Library, Princeton University, pp. 14-20.

95. Aguibou Yansane, *Decolonization in West African States with French Colonial Legacy* (Cambridge, MA: Schenkman, 1984), pp. 18-29, 136-139, 309-314; see also Richard Lobban and Marilyn Halter, *Historical Dictionary of the Republic of Cape Verde* second edition (Metuchen, NJ: The Scarecrow Press, 1988), pp. 26-28; Kevin Danaher, "Educational Inequality in South Africa and Its Implications for U.S. Foreign Policy," *Harvard Educational Review* 54, no. 2 (May 1984, pp. 166-174).

96. Eric Foner, *Reconstruction: America's Unfinished Revolution, 1863-1877* (New York: Harper & Row, 1988), p. 251.

## Chapter Three

1. Margaret M. Russell, "Race and the Dominant Gaze: Narratives of Law and Inequality in Popular Film," in Richard Delgado, ed., *Critical Race Theory: The Cutting Edge* (Philadelphia: Temple University Press, 1995), p. 57.

2. B. Asfaw et al., "Australopithecus Garhi: A New Species of Early Hominid from Ethiopia," *Science* 284 (1999), pp. 629-635; E. Abbate et al., "A One-Million-Year-Old Homo Cranium from the Danakil (Afar) Depression of Eritrea," *Nature* 393 (May-June 1998), p. 458; Alison S. Brooks, "What's New in Early Human Evolution," *Journal of the National Museum of Natural History* 18, no. 2 (Spring 1996) (online version); but cf. the recent discovery of "Toumai" in Chad and the argument of multiple sites of humanoid evolution in Africa.

3. Teshale Tibebu, *The Making of Modern Ethiopia, 1896-1974* (Lawrenceville, NJ: Red Sea Press, 1995), pp. 30-52.

4. For a review of the Italian historiography, rationalizations of the "lack of success" at Adwa, and a revisionist account of the battle, see Romain H. Rainero, "The Battle of Adowa on 1st March, 1896: A Reappraisal," in J. A. DeMoor and H. L. Wesseling, eds.,

*Imperialism and War: Essays On Colonial Wars in Asia and Africa* (Lieden, The Netherlands: E. J. Brill/Universitaire Pers Leiden, 1989), pp. 189-200.

5. Tibebu, *Modern Ethiopia*, p. 48.

6. Ibid., pp. 31, 47-49.

7. Asafa Jalata, *Oromo Nationalism and the Ethiopian Discourse: The Search for Freedom and Democracy* (Lawrenceville, NJ: The Red Sea Press, Inc., 1998), pp. 2-3; see also Tibebu, *Modern Ethiopia*, pp. 37-39; Herbert S. Lewis, "The Development of Oromo Political Consciousness from 1958 to 1994," in P. T. W. Baxter, Jan Hutlin, and Alessandro Triulzi, eds., *Being and Becoming Oromo: Historical and Anthropological Enquiries* (Lawrenceville, NJ: The Red Sea Press, Inc., 1996), pp. 39-40.

8. Rainero, "The Battle of Adowa," pp. 194-198.

9. Tibebu, *Modern Ethiopia*, pp. 107-114.

10. Ibid., pp. 137-138.

11. Ibid., pp. 134-138.

12. Ibid., pp. 116-132.

13. September 25, 1953, letter from R. D. Muir, Acting Chief of Protocol, Department of State, to Thomas E. Stephens, Secretary to the President, re: appointment of Deressa as Ethiopian Ambassador (with a brief bio attached), White House Central Files, Official File Series, Box #860, DDE Library; see also Tibebu, *Modern Ethiopia*, pp. 16, 38, 45 (on the latter, the author asserts that "Galla" was not an ethnic slur as much as a designation referring to one's lack of power and was applied to Oromo, Gurage, Walayta, and other peoples subjugated by the Amhara).

14. October 11, 1954, letter from Harold Stassen, Director-Foreign Operations Administration, to Eisenhower transmitting the July 21, 1954, letter from Marcus Gordon, Director-U.S.A. Operations Mission to Ethiopia [Point 4] and the original undated letter [including photograph] from Yassin Mohamed Aberra, Saleh Kebire, and Sayoum Haregot, White House Central File, Official File Series, Box #860, DDE Library.

15. Mohammed Hassen, "The Development of Oromo Nationalism," in Baxter, Hutlin, and Triulzi, eds., *Being and Becoming Oromo*, pp. 67-69.

16. Plummer, *Rising Wind*, pp. 39-56, 78; see also Von Eschen, *Race Against Empire*, p. 11; Basil Davidson, *Black Star: A View of the Life and Times of Kwame Nkrumah* (London: Allen Lane, 1973), pp. 89-90; James H. Meriwether, *Proudly We Can Be Africans: Black Americans and Africa, 1935-1961* (Chapel Hill: University of North Carolina Press, 2002), pp. 29-50.

17. Thomas Borstelmann, *Apartheid's Reluctant Uncle: The United States and Southern Africa in the Early Cold War* (New York: Oxford University Press, 1993), p. 18.

18. Harold Marcus, *Ethiopia, Great Britain, and the United States, 1941-1974: The Politics of Empire* (Berkeley: University of California Press, 1983), pp. 12-13, 28-34, 47.

19. Ibid., pp. 25-26.

20. Robert L. Harris Jr., "Racial Equality and the United Nations Charter," in Michael Krenn, ed., *Race and U.S. Foreign Policy During the Cold War* (New York: Garland Publishers, 1998), p. 15.

21. Ibid., p. 17.

22. See, e.g., Okbazghi Yohannes, *Eritrea, a Pawn in World Politics* (Gainesville: University of Florida Press, 1991), pp. 89-176.

23. Miscellaneous Records of the Bureau of Public Affairs, U.S. Department of State, Record Group 59, 1955-1959 Decimal File, 811.411/12-458, Box 4158, National Archives II, College Park, MD (hereinafter "NARA II"), pp. 1-7.

24. See, e.g., World Conference for Action Against Apartheid, *Report of the World Conference for Action Against Apartheid, Lagos, Nigeria*, 2 vols. (New York: United Nations, 1977), p. 28; Timothy M. Shaw, "The Non-Aligned Movement and the New International Division of Labour," in Ralph I. Onwuka and Timothy M. Shaw, eds., *Africa in World Politics: Into the 1990s* (Houndmills: Macmillan, 1989), p. 11.

25. Marcus, *Ethiopia, Great Britain, and the United States*, pp. 79-86.

26. See October 23, 1956, National Security Memorandum 5615 (superceded by NSC 5615/1, November 19, 1956), OSANSA Records, NSC Series, Policy Papers Sub-series, DDE Library, pp. 1-2, 6.

27. May 29, 1957, OCB Progress Report on NSC 5615/1, OSANSA Records, NSC Series, Policy Papers Sub-series, p. 1; December 18, 1957, OCB Progress Report on NSC 5615/1, OSANSA Records, NSC Series, Policy Papers Sub-series, p. 1, both documents from the DDE Library.

28. March 20, 1953, memorandum from W. B. Smith, Under Secretary of State to Eisenhower re: Appointment of the Ethiopian Ambassador, Ras Imru, 11:15 am, March 24, 1953, White House Central Files, Official Files Series, Box #860; July 23, 1953, letter from Haile Selassie with birthday greetings to Eisenhower, White House Central Files, Official File Series, Box #860, both documents from DDE Library.

29. July 11, 1954, letter from Haile Selassie to Eisenhower, White House Central Files, Official File, Series, Box #860, DDE Library.

30. Undated Proposed 1957 White House Press Release, White House Central Files, Official File Series, Box #594, DDE Library.

31. April 16, 1958, John Foster Dulles memorandum to Eisenhower re: acceptability of the appointment of Zaude Gabre Heywot as Ethiopian Ambassador to the United States [with attached biographical sketch and remarks], White House Central Files, Official File Series, Box #860, DDE Library.

32. Marcus, *Ethiopia, Great Britain, and the United States*, pp. 86-87.

33. April 5, 1957, "Report to the President on the Vice President's Visit to Africa," (hereinafter "Nixon's Africa Report"), DDE Library, Tab D, attachment no. 3, p. 1.

34. June 4, 1957, OCB "Highlights of Progress Report on Ethiopia," memorandum from James R. Gustin to Roy Melbourne, White House Office, NSC Staff Papers, OCB Central File Series, Box #29; April 5, 1957, "Nixon's Africa Report," Tab D, attachment no. 3, attachment no. 6, "Summary of the Remarks Made By His Imperial Majesty at the Audience Granted on March 12, 1957 to His Excellency the Vice-President of the United States of America," p. 1, all documents from DDE Library.

35. October 3, 1956, OCB "Analysis of Internal Security Situation in Ethiopia (Pursuant to NSC Action 1290-d) and Recommended Action," White House Office, NSC Staff Papers, OCB Central File Series, Box #28, DDE Library, p. 1; for Gustin's comments, see October 10, 1956, transmittal memorandum from James R. Gustin to Roy Melbourne, White House Office, NSC Staff Papers, OCB Central File Series, Box #28, DDE Library.

36. October 3, 1956, OCB "Analysis of Internal Security Situation in Ethiopia," p. 1.

37. April 30, 1957, OCB Progress Report on U.S. Policy Toward Ethiopia (NSC 6515/1), White House Office, NSC Staff Papers, OCB Central File Series, Box #29, DDE Library, p. 1.

38. July 22, 1958, Department of State Outgoing Telegram to the U.S. Embassy in Addis Ababa, conveying message from Eisenhower to Haile Selassie, Ann Whitman File, International Series, Box #9, DDE Library, p. 1; as to the nature of the Lebanese crisis of 1958, see William Blum, *The CIA: A Forgotten History: US Global Interventions Since World War 2* (London: Zed Books, 1986), pp. 103-107.

39. April 16, 1960, Department of State telegram to the U.S. Embassy in Addis Ababa conveying Eisenhower message to Haile Selassie re: Ethiopia's vote at the Law of the Seas Conference, Ann Whitman File, International Series, Box #9, DDE Library, pp. 1-2.

40. April 19, 1960, letter from Haile Selassie to Eisenhower; see also April 23, 1960, Herter "Memorandum for the President" re: Law of the Seas Conference and Acknowledgment of Message from the Emperor of Ethiopia; both documents from Ann Whitman File, International Series, Box #9, DDE Library.

41. September 27, 1960, "Memorandum of Conference with the President," Ann Whitman File, International Series, Box #9, DDE Library, p. 1.

42. November 2, 1960, memorandum from Herter to Eisenhower re: U.S. aid to Ethiopia; see also October 28, 1960, Department of State telegram to U.S. Embassy in Addis

Ababa conveying confidential message from Herter to Deputy Prime Minister Aklilou; both documents from Ann Whitman File, International Series, Box #9, DDE Library.

43. See November 19, 1956, National Security Council Memorandum 5615/1, OSANSA Records, NSC Series, Policy Papers Sub-series and National Security Council Memorandum 5903, DDE Library.

44. See October 3, 1956, OCB "Analysis of Internal Security Situation in Ethiopia (Pursuant to NSC Action 1290-d) and Recommended Action"; see also October 10, 1956 memorandum from James R. Gustin to Mr. Melbourne transmitting a paper on Ethiopia (in which Gustin refers to the "backwardness" of Ethiopia); both documents from White House Office, National Security Council Staff Papers, OCB Central Files Series, Box #28, DDE Library.

45. October 3, 1956, OCB "Analysis of Internal Security Situation in Ethiopia (Pursuant to NSC Action 1290-d) and Recommended Action," p. 1; see also October 10, 1956, memorandum from James R. Gustin to Roy Melbourne transmitting a paper on Ethiopia (in which Gustin refers to the "backwardness" of Ethiopia); both documents from White House Office, National Security Council Staff Papers, OCB Central File Series, Box #28, DDE Library.

46. February 28, 1957, OCB "Outline Plan of Operations with Respect to Ethiopia," White House Office, National Security Council Papers, 1948-1961, OCB Central File Series, Box #28, DDE Library, p. 3.

47. October 10, 1956, Gustin memorandum to Melbourne.

48. Eisenhower, *Waging Peace*, pp. 30-48, 145-146, 194.

49. NSC 5615, p. 1.

50. November 19, 1956, National Security Council Memorandum 5615/1, "U.S. Policy Toward Ethiopia," DDE Library.

51. Marcus, *Ethiopia, Great Britain, and the United States*, p. 87; see also Thomas J. McCormick, *America's Half-Century: United States Foreign Policy in the Cold War and After*, 2nd edition (Baltimore: Johns Hopkins Press, 1995), pp. 122-124, 137, 139.

52. April 5, 1957, "Nixon's Africa Report," pp. 2-3.

53. See, e.g., April 30, 1957, OCB Progress Report on NSC 5615/1, DDE Library, p. 4.

54. NSC 5615/1, p. 2.

55. Ibid, p. 3.

56. Marcus, *Ethiopia, Great Britain, and the United States*, pp. 88-94, 98-103; Plummer, *Rising Wind*, p. 260.

57. NSC 5615/1, p. 2.

58. October 3, 1956, OCB "Analysis of Internal Security Situation in Ethiopia," DDE Library, p. 14.

59. Ibid., pp. 6, 10.

60. April 30, 1957, OCB Progress Report on NSC 5615/1, DDE Library, p. 4.

61. Marcus, *Ethiopia, Great Britain, and the United States*, pp. 103-105; see also October 3, 1956, OCB "Analysis of Internal Security Situation in Ethiopia," DDE Library, p. 6 (where the authors write "there is no known indigenous Communist Party in Ethiopia").

62. October 3, 1956, OCB "Analysis of Internal Security Situation in Ethiopia," pp. 5-6.

63. NSC 5615/1, p. 4; see also October 3, 1956, OCB "Analysis of Internal Security Situation in Ethiopia," p. 3.

64. October 3, 1956, OCB "Analysis of Internal Security Situation in Ethiopia," p. 1.

65. August 13, 1958, memorandum from Melbourne to Lay as an attachment to OCB progress report on NSC 5615/1, OSANSA Records, NSC Series, Policy Papers, DDE Library.

66. July 9, 1958, OCB Progress Report on NSC 5615/1, OSANSA Records, NSC Series, Policy Papers subseries, DDE Library, p.4, head note 10.

67. February 26, 1959, memorandum regarding 397th NSC meeting, paragraph 4, "US Policy Toward Horn of Africa [NSC 5903]," Ann Whitman File, DDE Diary, NSC Series, DDE Library, p. 11.

68. October 23, 1956, Dulles memorandum to Eisenhower re: Appointment with Senator Green [with attached table listing assistance to Ethiopia from 1952-1956], White House Central Files, Official File Series, Box #860, DDE Library. The attached table contains three categories: "military," "technical," and "other." U.S. military aid to Ethiopia during the preceding five years was: 1952-$0; 1953-$5.0 million; 1954-$5.5 million; 1955-$0.5 million; 1956-$2.0 million.

69. July 9, 1958, OCB Progress Report on "U.S. Policy Toward Ethiopia (NSC 5615/1)," OSANSA Records, NSC Series, Policy Papers Sub-series, pp. 1, 3; for an earlier iteration of this sentiment, see November 15, 1956, memorandum from Herbert Hoover, Jr. to Eisenhower, Ann Whitman File, International Series, Box #9, and April 30, 1957, OCB Progress Report on NSC 5615/1, pp. 3-4, both documents from DDE Library.

70. November 15, 1956, Hoover memorandum to Eisenhower, Ann Whitman File, International Series, Box #9, DDE Library.

71. Eisenhower, *Waging Peace*, pp. 193-194.

72. "Nixon's Africa Report," Tab D, attachment no. 1, p. 1; attachment no. 2, p. 1; attachment no. 6, pp. 1-4; attachment no. 7.

73. "Nixon's Africa Report," Tab D, attachment no. 7, pp. 1-3.

74. Ibid.

75. Ibid., pp. 4-12.

76. Ibid., p. 6; attachment no. 6, pp. 3, 6-9; as to the British request directly communicated to the Ethiopians, that Ethiopia surrender a portion of its territory for "the viability of a united Somaliland," see Tab D, attachment no. 3: Memorandum of Conversation between Nixon et al. and Ato Aklilou Abte Wolde et al., p. 2.

77. Ibid., p. 9; Tab D attachment no. 8: "Imperial Ethiopian Government-Ministry of Foreign Affairs," pp. 1-2.

78. NSC 5615/1, p. 3.

79. April 15, 1957, OCB Progress Report on U.S. Policy Toward Ethiopia (NSC 5615/1), White House Office, National Security Council Papers, 1948-1961, OCB Central File Series, Box #29, DDE Library, p. 3.

80. May 29, 1957, OCB Progress Report on NSC 5615/1, OSANSA Records, NSC Series, Policy Papers Sub-series, p. 3.

81. June 4, 1957, James Gustin memorandum to Melbourne, White House Office, NSC Staff Papers, OCB Central File Series, Box #29, DDE Library.

82. July 9, 1958, OCB Progress Report on NSC 5615/1, p. 4.

83. Marcus, *Ethiopia, Great Britain, and the United States*, pp. 105-108.

84. October 3, 1956, OCB "Analysis of Internal Security Situation in Ethiopia," pp. 1, 9.

85. April 30, 1957, OCB Progress Report on NSC 5615/1, p. 3.

86. July 9, 1958, OCB Progress Report on NSC 5615/1, pp. 1-2.

87. Although the OCB Progress Reports on NSC 5615/1 generally praise the Ethiopians for their clear-sightedness with regard to Communism, American officials were concerned by Emperor Selassie's visit to Moscow. See July 23, 1959, memorandum re: 414th NSC meeting, Ann Whitman File, NSC Series, pp. 8-9; December 18, 1957, OCB Progress Report on NSC 5615/1, OSANSA Records, NSC Series, Policy Papers Sub-series, p. 2, ¶ 4 (entitled "Lack of Understanding Regarding Communist Threat"), but c.f. July 9, 1958, OCB Progress Report on NSC 5615/1, OSANSA Records, NSC Series, Policy Papers Sub-series, pp. 1, 9, all documents from DDE Library.

88. July 23, 1959, memorandum from 414th NSC meeting, Ann Whitman File, NSC Series, DDE Library, pp. 8-9.

89. Marcus, *Ethiopia, Great Britain, and the United States*, pp. 108-112.

90. Catherine Hoskyns, *The Congo: A Chronology of Events, January 1960-December 1961* (Oxford: Oxford University Press, 1962), pp. 32-33.

91. August 16, 1960, memorandum from 455th NSC meeting, p. 6.

92. December 18, 1957, OCB Progress Report on NSC 5615/1.

93. November 2, 1960, Department of State outgoing telegram to U.S. Embassy in Addis Ababa, DDE Library, p. 2.

94. November 21, 1960, Herter memorandum to Eisenhower, Ann Whitman File, International Series, Box #9; December 1, 1960, Haile Selassie letter to Eisenhower, Ann Whitman File, International Series, Box #9, both documents from DDE Library.

95. Bahru Zewde, *A History of Modern Ethiopia, 1855-1974* (Athens: Ohio University Press, 1991), pp. 211-215; Edmond J. Keller, *Revolutionary Ethiopia: From Empire to People's Republic* (Bloomington: Indiana University Press, 1988), pp. 132-136.

96. See generally Marcus, *Ethiopia, Great Britain, and the United States*; John Markakis, *National and Class Conflict in the Horn of Africa* (Cambridge: Cambridge University Press, 1987).

97. See generally Marcus, *Ethiopia, Great Britain, and the United States*; Markakis, *National and Class Conflict in the Horn of Africa*.

98. See bell hooks, "Moving From Pain to Power: Black Self-Determination," in *Killing Rage: Ending Racism* (New York: H. Holt and Co., 1995), p. 251 (where the author notes that Black revolutionary zeal often is coupled with a patriarchal impulse toward masculine rule).

99. "Nixon's Africa Report," p. 6.

100. "Nixon's Africa Report," pp. 5-6 (emphasis added).

101. October 3, 1956, OCB "Analysis of Internal Security Situation in Ethiopia," pp. 1, 7.

102. October 3, 1956, OCB "Analysis of Internal Security Situation in Ethiopia," p. 2.

103. See, e.g., February 4, 1959, NSC 5903 "U.S. Policy Toward the Horn of Africa," White House Office, National Security Council Staff Papers, Disaster File, Box #44, DDE Library, pp. 4-5.

104. October 3, 1956, OCB "Analysis of Internal Security Situation in Ethiopia," pp. 3, 11.

105. Bernard Magubane, "The Evolution of the Class Structure in Africa," in P. C. W. Gutkind and Immanuel M. Wallerstein, eds., *The Political Economy of Contemporary Africa* (Beverly Hills, CA: Sage Publications, 1976), p. 174.

106. Jane I. Guyer, "Women in the Rural Economy: Contemporary Variations," in Margaret J. Hay and Sharon Stichter, eds., *African Women South of the Sahara* (London: Longman, 1984), pp. 21-22, 27; Ann Whitehead, "Wives and Mothers: Female Farmers in Africa," in Aderanti Adepoju and Christine Oppong, eds., *Gender, Work, and Population in Sub-Saharan Africa* (Portsmouth, NH: Heinemann Publishers, 1994), pp. 49-52.

107. Jeanne K. Henn, "Women in the Rural Economy: Past, Present, and Future," in Hay and Stichter, eds., *African Women South of the Sahara*, p. 1.

108. Barbara A. Dicks and Eddie S. Bogle, "Sociocultural Aspects of Ethiopian Women's Contributions to Agriculture," in Valentine U. James, *Women and Sustainable Development in Africa* (Westport, CT: Praeger Publishers, 1995), p. 95.

109. Tsehai Berhane-Selassie, "Ethiopian Rural Women and the State," in Gwendolyn Mikell, ed., *African Feminism: the Politics of Survival in Sub-Saharan Africa* (Philadelphia: University of Pennsylvania Press, 1997) , pp. 184-201.

110. Catherine Besteman, "Out Migration," in Helen K. Henderson and Ellen Hansen, eds., *Gender and Agricultural Development: Surveying the Field* (Tucson: University of Arizona Press, 1995), p. 72.

111. Judith Warner and Ellen Hansen, "Agroforestry," in Henderson and Hansen, eds., *Gender and Agricultural Development*, p. 107.

112. See, e.g., Henn, "Women in the Rural Economy," p. 15; Berhane-Selassie, "Ethiopian Rural Women and the State," pp. 184-201.

113. Berhane-Selassie, "Ethiopian Rural Women and the State," pp. 187-192; Gracia Clark, *Onions Are My Husband: Survival and Accumulation by West African Market Women* (Chicago: University of Chicago Press, 1994), pp. 374-401; Robertson, *Comparative Advantage: Women in Trade in Accra, Ghana and Nairobi, Kenya*, in Bessie House-Midamba and Felix K. Ekechi, eds., *African Market Women and Economic Power: the Role of Women in African Economic Development* (Westport, CT: Greenwood Press, 1995), p. 118; Claire C. Robertson, *Sharing the Same Bowl?: A Socioeconomic History of Women and Class in Accra, Ghana* (Bloomington: Indiana University Press, 1994), p. 17.

114. Berhane-Selassie, "Ethiopian Rural Women and the State," p. 187.

# Chapter Four

1. See, e.g., Thomas Noer, "The New Frontier and African Neutralism: Kennedy, Nkrumah and the Volta River Project," *Diplomatic History* 8, no. 1 (1984), pp. 61-79; William Blum, *The CIA: A Forgotten History*, pp. 223-225.

2. Donald I. Ray, *Ghana: Politics, Economics and Society* (Boulder, CO: Lynne Rienner, 1986), p. 5.

3. Francis Agbodeka, *African Politics and British Policy in the Gold Coast 1868-1900* (Evanston, IL: Northwestern University Press, 1971), p. 5; see, generally, H. Meredith, *Account of the History of the Gold Coast* (London: Longman, 1812), and W. E. F. Ward, *A History of Ghana* (New York: Praeger, 1958).

4. Ray, *Ghana*, pp. 8-9; W. Walton Claridge, *A History of the Gold Coast and Ashanti: from the earliest times to the commencement of the twentieth century* (New York: Barnes & Noble, reprinted 1915), pp. 33-49; see also J. D. Fage, *Ghana: A Historical Interpretation* (Madison: University of Wisconsin Press, 1959), pp. 37-39; see generally, John Vogt, *Portuguese Rule on the Gold Coast, 1469-1682* (Athens: University of Georgia Press, 1979).

5. Agbodeka, *African Politics and British Policy in the Gold Coast*, pp. 10-11.

6. Ibid., pp. 12-14, 34-122; Ray, *Ghana*, p. 9; Alexander Holmes, "What Was the 'Nationalism' of the 1930s in Ghana?" in Paul Jenkins et al., eds., *Akyem Abuakwa and the Politics of the Inter-War Period in Ghana* (Frankfurt: Basler Afrika Bibliographien, 1975), pp. 15, 19-29.

7. Adu Boahen, "Ghana Since Independence," in Prosser Gifford and W. Roger Louis, eds., *Decolonization and African Independence: The Transfers of Power, 1960-1980* (New Haven, CT: Yale University Press, 1988), pp. 200-203; Davidson, *Let Freedom Come*, pp. 179-180; but, cf. Holmes, "Nationalism," pp. 17, 26-29.

8. Holmes, "Nationalism," pp. 21-24.

9. Ibid., pp. 26-29.

10. John Henrik Clarke, *Notes for An African World Revolution: Africans At the Crossroads* (Trenton, NJ: Africa World Press, 1991), p. 101.

11. Peter O. Esedebe, *Pan-Africanism: the Idea and Movement, 1776-1963* (Washington, DC: Howard University Press, 1982), pp. 156-157, 162-163.

12. Clarke, *Notes for An African World Revolution*, pp. 103-105.

13. Ray, *Ghana*, p. 10.

14. Basil Davidson, *Black Star: A View of the Life and Times of Kwame Nkrumah* (London: Allen Lane, 1973), pp. 72-83; Ray, *Ghana*, p. 10.

15. Davidson, *Black Star*, pp. 41-46, 68-69; see also Clarke, *Notes for An African World Revolution*, pp. 111-113; David Rooney, *Kwame Nkrumah: The Political Kingdom in the Third World* (London: I. B. Tauris, 1988), pp. 43-50.

16. Opoku Agyeman, *Nkrumah's Ghana and East Africa: Pan-Africanism and African Interstate Relations* (Cranbury, NJ: Associated University Press, 1992), pp. 12-13, 18-19, 58; see also J. A. Rogers, *World's Great Men of Color: Vol. 1* (New York: Macmillan, 1972), pp. 240-245 (for a comparison of Nkrumah's unification tactics with those of Askia the Great, leader of West Africa's multiethnic, religiously diverse Songhay empire).

17. May 9, 1958, memorandum re: 365th NCS meeting, Ann Whitman File, NSC Series, DDE Library, p. 2.

18. Clarke, *Notes for An African World Revolution*, pp. 107-108 (citing from Nkrumah's pamphlet "Towards Colonial Freedom").

19. Clarke, *Notes for An African World Revolution*, p. 112.

20. Agyeman, *Nkrumah's Ghana and East Africa: Pan-Africanism and African Interstate Relations*, pp. 27-28 (quoting from Jitendra Mohna, "Ghana Parliament and Foreign Policy, 1957-1960," *Economic Bulletin of Ghana* 6, no. 4 [1966]). I use the term "Nkrumahism" only as a means of distinguishing Nkrumah's line of thought from earlier and alternate forms of Pan-Africanism.

21. Davidson, *Black Star*, pp. 80-81; see also Ray, *Ghana: Politics, Economics and Society*, p. 10.

22. Olatunde Ojo, D. K. Orwa, and C. M. B. Utete, *African International Relations* (London: Longman Group, 1985), p. 143.

23. Ibid., p. 78.

24. Agyeman, *Nkrumah's Ghana and East Africa*, pp. 25-27.

25. Ibid.; see also Olajide Aluko, *Ghana and Nigeria, 1957-1970: A Study in Inter-African Discord* (New York: Barnes and Noble Books, 1976), pp. 98-101.

26. Ojo, Orwa, and Utete, *African International Relations*, p. 75; Agyeman, *Nkrumah's Ghana and East Africa*, pp. 60-61; Joseph Nye, *Pan-Africanism and East African Integration* (Cambridge, MA: Harvard University Press, 1966), p. 31; see also Ebere Nwaubani, "Eisenhower, Nkrumah, and the Congo Crisis," *Journal of Contemporary History* [London] 36, no. 4, pp. 607-608 (where the author argues that Patrice Lumumba was another participant in the conference who became a Pan-Africanist after sojourning in Accra in 1958), and Jean Van Lierde, ed., *Lumumba Speaks: The Speeches and Writings of Patrice Lumumba, 1958-1961* (Boston: Little, Brown & Co., 1972), pp. 55-58.

27. Olajide Aluko, *Ghana and Nigeria 1957-1970: A Study in Inter-African Discord* (New York: Barnes and Noble, 1976), pp. 39-62, 76-86.

28. Ojo, Orwa, and Utete, *African International Relations*, pp. 74-76, 130-132, 143-144; see remarks by the Ivory Coast's Felix Houphouet-Boigny to President Eisenhower, November 12, 1959, Department of State Memorandum of Conversation re: "The French Community and the West," Ann Whitman File, International Series, Ivory Coast folder, pp. 1, 3; Liberian President Tubman's speech, February 12, 1960, briefing note re: U.S. Policy Toward West Africa, White House Office, Office of the Special Assistant for National Security Affairs Records, 1952-1961, NSC Briefing Notes subseries, p. 3, ¶ 11(b), both documents from DDE Library.

29. Ojo, Orwa, and Utete, *African International Relations*, pp. 80-82.

30. Margaret M. Russell, "Race and the Dominant Gaze: Narratives of Law and Inequality in Popular Film, " 15 *Legal Studies Forum* 243 (1991), p. 257.

31. See, generally, Peter Hahn and Mary Ann Heiss, *Empire and Revolution: The United States and the Third World Since 1945* (Columbus: Ohio State University Press, 2001).

32. E. Frederic Morrow, *Black Man in the White House: a Diary of the Eisenhower Years by the Administrative Officer for Special Projects, the White House, 1955-1961* (New York: Coward-McCann, 1963), pp. 131-135; see also, e.g., March 1, 1960, Department of State telegram to the American Embassy in Accra with text of Eisenhower's congratulations on the acceptance of Ghana's new constitution, Ann Whitman File, ACW Diary Series, Ghana folder; June 27, 1960, Department of State telegram to American Embassy in Accra with the text of Eisenhower's congratulations to Nkrumah on becoming president of Ghana, Ann Whitman File, ACW Diary Series, Ghana folder, both documents from DDE Library; Nwaubani, "Eisenhower, Nkrumah, and the Congo Crisis," pp. 602-604 (where the author quotes from the August 4, 1958, *Time* article regarding the elaborate welcome for Nkrumah on his official state visit to Washington); see, e.g., April 22, 1958, OCB memorandum to James Lay, OSANSA Records, NSC Policy Papers series; see also July 29, 1960, Department of State memorandum from Herter to Eisenhower, Ann Whitman File, ACW Diary Series, Ghana folder (regarding a "thank you" message from Nkrumah for American airlift of Ghanaian troops into Congo), both documents from DDE Library; see also Nwaubani, "Eisenhower, Nkrumah, and the Congo Crisis," pp. 603-604 (where the author mentions Nkrumah's 1958 speech before the Council on Foreign Relations, in which he predicted a major place for the West in the economic development of decolonized Africa).

33. Davidson, *Black Star*, pp. 91-93.

34. March 21, 1958, Operations Coordinating Board Report to NSC on NSC 5719/1, OSANSA Records, NSC Policy Papers series, pp. 3, 10, DDE Library.

35. See August 1, 1958, memorandum from N. F. Twining, Chairman Joint Chiefs of Staff to Secretary of Defense re: revisions to NSC 5719/1, OSANSA Records, NSC Series, Policy Papers Sub-series; August 5, 1958, memorandum from Lay to NSC re: JCS

views on revisions to NSC 5719/1, OSANSA Records, NSC, Policy Papers Sub-series, pp. 6-10, both documents from DDE Library.

36. Davidson, *Black Star*, p. 94; see also David K. Fieldhouse, *Black Africa, 1945-1980: Economic Decolonization and Arrested Development* (London: Allen & Unwin, 1986), pp. 52-55.

37. October 14, 1959, Staff Notes #654, Ann Whitman File, DDE Diary Series, DDE Library, paragraph 1; see, e.g., March 31, 1960, memorandum re: 423rd NSC meeting, Ann Whitman File, NSC Series, DDE Library, p. 3.

38. September 21, 1960, State Department memorandum from Douglas Dillon to Eisenhower, Ann Whitman File, ACW Diary Series, Ghana folder, DDE Library, pp. 1-3.

39. Ibid., p. 4.

40. See, e.g., September 22, 1960, Secretary of State Memorandum of Conversation between Eisenhower/Herter and Nkrumah, Ann Whitman File, ACW Diary Series, Ghana folder, DDE Library.

41. Frantz Fanon, *The Wretched of the Earth* (New York: Grove Weidenfeld, 1968), pp. 42-64; bell hooks, "Whiteness in the Black Imagination," in *Killing Rage*, p. 35.

42. Aluko, *Ghana and Nigeria*, p. 98; Kwame Nkrumah, *Consciencism: Philosophy and Ideology for Decolonization* (New York: Monthly Review Press, 1964), p. 102.

43. Aluko, *Ghana and Nigeria*, p. 99; Nkrumah, *Consciencism*, pp. 102-105.

44. Aluko, *Ghana and Nigeria*, p. 98.

45. See NSC 5719/1, p. 19.

46. See March 31, 1960, memorandum re: 423rd NSC meeting, Ann Whitman File, DDE Diary Series, NSC Series, p. 4; June 30, 1960, memorandum re: 449th NSC meeting, Ann Whitman File, NSC Series, paragraph 2; July 18, 1960, memorandum re: 451stNSC meeting, Ann Whitman File, NSC Series, p. 6, all documents from DDE Library; Nwaubani, "Eisenhower, Nkrumah, and the Congo Crisis," pp. 603-605, 614-616.

47. April 28, 1960, outgoing telegram from State Department to American Embassy-Accra, *FRUS: Africa, 1958-1960*, vol. XIV, p. 271.

48. May 1, 1960, incoming telegram from American Embassy-Accra to Secretary of State, *FRUS: Africa, 1958-1960*, vol. XIV, p. 271, n. 2.

49. August 2, 1960, outgoing telegram from State Department to American Embassy-Accra, *FRUS: Africa, 1958-1960*, vol. XIV, pp. 379-380.

50. August 5, 1960, letter from Kwame Nkrumah to Dwight Eisenhower, Ann Whitman File, International Series, Ghana folder, DDE Library, pp. 1-2.

51. September 22, 1960, Secretary of State Memorandum of Conversation between Eisenhower/Herter and Nkrumah, Ann Whitman File, ACW Diary Series, Ghana folder, p. 2, DDE Library.

52. Richard D. Mahoney, *JFK: Ordeal in Africa* (New York: Oxford University Press, 1983), p. 50 (where the author quotes W. M. Q. Halm, Ghana's ambassador to the United States, who also attended the meeting); Nwaubani, *Eisenhower, Nkrumah, and the Congo Crisis,* p. 613.

53. Eisenhower, *Waging Peace,* p. 583.

54. Kwame Nkrumah, *Challenge of the Congo* (London: Panaf Books, 1967), pp. 70-73.

55. Nwaubani, "Eisenhower, Nkrumah, and the Congo Crisis," pp. 610-613.

56. W. Scott Thompson, *Ghana's Foreign Policy, 1957-1966: Diplomacy, Ideology, and the New State* (Princeton, NJ: Princeton University Press, 1969), p. 165.

57. Nkrumah, *Challenge of the Congo,* p. 71; Thompson, *Ghana's Foreign Policy,* p. 166.

58. Georges Abi-Saab, *The UN Operation in the Congo, 1960-1964* (Oxford: Oxford University Press, 1978), p. 115.

59. Ernest W. Lefever, *Crisis in the Congo: A UN Force in Action* (Washington, DC: The Brookings Institution, 1965), p. 50.

60. Nwaubani, "Eisenhower, Nkrumah, and the Congo Crisis," pp. 610-611 (citing the September 24, 1960 edition of *The New York Times*).

61. See, e.g., Ray, *Ghana,* p. 2; David K. Fieldhouse, *The West and the Third World: Trade, Colonialism, Dependence, and Development* (Oxford: Blackwell, 1999), pp. 198, 200-211.

62. July 29, 1958, memorandum from James Lay to NSC re: revisions to NSC 5719/1, OSANSA Records, NSC Policy Papers series, DDE Library; see specifically the updated version of Appendix D "U.S. policy with Respect to International Commodity Agreements." For an individual official's perspective, see April 1958 Clarence Randall "Memorandum To Council on Foreign Economic Policy," Clarence Randall Papers, Seeley G. Mudd Library, Princeton University, Box #11, p. 10.

63. June 19, 1958, NSC Action No. 1926 (as cited in July 29, 1958, memorandum re: revisions to NSC 5719/1, Annex D, p. 26), DDE Library.

64. Davidson, *Black Star,* p. 197; Thomas J. Noer, *The New Frontier and African Nationalism, Diplomatic History* (Winter 1984), pp. 90-91; Ebere Nwaubani, *The United States and Decolonization in West Africa* (Rochester, NY: University of Rochester Press, 2001), pp. 163-168.

65. Noer, "The New Frontier and African Neutralism," p. 92; see also David K. Fieldhouse, *Merchant Capital and Economic Decolonization: The United Africa Company, 1929-1987* (Oxford: Clarendon Press, 1994), p. 403; Nwaubani, *The United States and Decolonization*, pp. 171-173.

66. Noer, *The New Frontier and African Neutralism*, pp. 92-93; see also October 10, 1957, diary entry re: discriminatory treatment of African dignitary, Ann Whitman File, ACW Diary Series, DDE Library, and Nwaubani, *The United States and Decolonization*, pp. 124, 180-181.

67. 1956 "The Volta River Project, Vol. I: Report of the Preparatory Commission," Ann Whitman File, ACW Diary series, Ghana subseries, DDE Library.

68. November 12, 1957, letter from Kwame Nkrumah to Dwight Eisenhower, Ann Whitman File, DDE Diary, International series, DDE Library.

69. Nwaubani, *The United States and Decolonization*, pp. 128-130, 181-185, 191-194.

70. Nwaubani, *The United States and Decolonization*, pp. 128-130, 181-185, 191-194; March 21, 1958, OCB Report to the NSC on NSC 5719/1, DDE Library, p. 6.

71. Undated roster of individuals invited to July 23, 1958, lunch with Nkrumah at the White House, White House Central Files, Official File Series, Box #929; August 8, 1958, memorandum from 375th NSC meeting, Ann Whitman File, DDE Diary, both documents from DDE Library; Noer, "The New Frontier and African Neutralism," p. 63.

72. September 17, 1959, letter from Kwame Nkrumah to Dwight Eisenhower, Ann Whitman File, DDE Diary, International Series, DDE Library.

73. Noer, *The New Frontier and African Neutralism*, p. 93; see also Nwaubani, *The United States and Decolonization*, pp. 199-200.

74. July 19, 1958, memorandum from John Foster Dulles to Eisenhower with attached "Briefing Memorandum for the Official Visit of the Prime Minister of Ghana, July 23-26, 1958," p. 2 and accompanying reference paper on the Volta River Project, p. 3, Ann Whitman File, DDE Diary, Ghana folder, DDE Library.

75. Noer, *The New Frontier and African Neutralism*, pp. 93-94.

76. Noer, *The New Frontier and African Neutralism*, p. 94; see also Hussein M. Fahim, *Egyptian Nubians: Resettlement and Years of Coping* (Salt Lake City: University of Utah Press, 1983), p. 27; Plummer, *Rising Wind*, pp. 258-260.

77. Fahim, *Egyptian Nubians*, p. 29; McCormick, *America's Half-Century*, pp. 122-123; Nwaubani, *The United States and Decolonization*, p. 203.

78. Agyeman, *Nkrumah's Ghana and East Africa*, pp. 25-27; Clarke, *Notes for an African World*, pp. 107-108; Nkrumah, *Consciencism*, pp. 102-105.

79. Eisenhower, *Waging Peace*, p. 582.

80. Nwaubani, "Eisenhower, Nkrumah, and the Congo Crisis," p. 602-604 (where the author quotes from Padmore's book *Pan-Africanism or Communism*, pp. 375-376).

81. Noer, *The New Frontier and African Neutralism*, p. 63; September 21, 1960, Dillon memorandum to Eisenhower, p. 2, and January 7, 1958, memorandum re: 350th NSC meeting, Ann Whitman File, NSC Series, both documents from DDE Library; Nwaubani, "Eisenhower, Nkrumah, and the Congo Crisis," pp. 605-607 (where the author points to the fact that the Nkrumah administration waited almost a year before approving the Soviet line of credit; the Soviet offer of 160 million rubles represented 14.7 million of Ghana's dollars).

82. Noer, "The New Frontier and African Neutralism," p. 63.

83. August 30, 1960, Staff Notes #828, Ann Whitman File, DDE Diary, Toner Notes Series, DDE Library, p. 2.

84. August 25, 1960, memorandum re: 456th NSC meeting, Ann Whitman File, DDE Diary, NSC Series, DDE Library, p. 11 (emphasis added).

85. Ibid., p. 12.

86. See September 22, 1960, Secretary of State Memorandum of Conversation between Eisenhower, Herter, and Nkrumah, Ann Whitman File, ACW Diary Series, Ghana folder, pp. 1-2; see also October 22, 1960, letter from Kwame Nkrumah to Dwight Eisenhower, Ann Whitman File, DDE Diary, International series, regarding the Volta River Project, both documents from DDE Library.

87. September 22, 1960, Secretary of State Memorandum of Conversation between Eisenhower, Herter, and Nkrumah, Ann Whitman File, ACW Diary Series, Ghana folder, pp. 1-2; see also October 22, 1960, Nkrumah letter to Eisenhower, Ann Whitman File, DDE Diary, International Series, p. 2, both documents from DDE Library; see also Ray, *Ghana*, p. 13.

88. November 14, 1960, memorandum from Herter to Eisenhower, Ann Whitman File, DDE Diary series, Ghana folder, DDE Library.

89. November 11, 1960, memorandum from Herter to Eisenhower re: Nkrumah's request for American financial assistance for additional electric power transmission, Ann Whitman File, ACW Diary, Ghana series, and November 17, 1960, letter from Dwight Eisenhower to Kwame Nkrumah, Ann Whitman File, DDE Diary, International Series, both documents from DDE Library; see also Nwaubani, "Eisenhower, Nkrumah, and the Congo Crisis," pp. 608-615.

90. November 18, 1960, Department of State telegram to American Embassy, Accra, with Eisenhower reply to Nkrumah's letter requesting U.S. aid for additional transmission facility, Ann Whitman File, ACW Diary series, Ghana folder; see also

November 14, 1960, memorandum from Herter to Eisenhower, Ann Whitman File, DDE Diary series, Ghana folder, both documents from DDE Library.

91. Judith Marshall, *The State of Ambivalence: Right and Left Options in Ghana*, in Gregory Maddox, ed., *African Nationalism and Revolution* (New York: Garland, 1993), p. 96; as to Ghana's economic importance to Britain, see David K. Fieldhouse, *Merchant Capital and Economic Decolonization: The United Africa Company, 1929-1987* (New York: Oxford University Press, 1994), p. 451.

92. Marshall, *The State of Ambivalence*, p. 97; see also David K. Fieldhouse, *Black Africa, 1945-1980: Economic Decolonization and Arrested Development* (London: Allen and Unwin, 1986), pp. 140-141.

93. Tom Little, *Modern Egypt* (New York: Praeger, 1967), p. 162.

94. Herbert Brownell, *Advising Ike: The Memoirs of Attorney General Herbert Brownell* (Lawrence: University Press of Kansas, 1993), p. 204.

95. Stephen J. Whitfield, *A Death in the Delta: The Story of Emmet Till* (New York: Free Press, 1988); Ralph E. Luker, "Racial Matters: Civil Rights and Civil Wrongs," *American Quarterly* 43, no. 1 (March 1991), pp. 165-171.

96. See, e.g., October 15, 1955, resolution on Emmet Till case from the Norwegian Students Association; October 21, 1955, letter to the president and resolution on the Emmet Till case from the Greater Paterson (NJ) Council of Churches; November 25, 1955, letter to Sherman Adams from Vivian Mason of National Council of Negro Women transmitting to president copies of organization's resolutions re: murders of Emmet Till, Rev. George Lee, and Lamar Smith; all documents from White House Central File, Alphabetical File, Emmet Till folder, DDE Library.

97. September 28, 1955, Foreign Service dispatch, from American Embassy in Bern to State Department, Washington, transmitting a copy of the editorial from *Le Democrate*, a small local newspaper circulating in the Bernese Jura region, NARA II.

98. Robert F. Burk, *The Eisenhower Administration and Black Civil Rights* (Knoxville: University of Tennessee Press, 1984), pp. 24-28, 207, 217-226.

99. See, e.g., Amended Complaint in *United States v. Archbell, et al.*, Case #4065, United States District Court for the Western District of Tennessee; January 4, 1961, letter from James A. Hutchins Jr. to Martin D. Garber, United States Department of Agriculture, re: the need to send emergency food supplies to Black families evicted by White landowners; both from File of the Special Counsel to the President, David P. Kendall Papers, Box #6, DDE Library.

100. December 11, 1953, "Government Contracts Committee: Principles and Program for Compliance," James P. Mitchell Papers, Presidential Committee on Government Contracts, 1953-1957, Box #125, DDE Library, pp. 2-3; see also Burk, *The Eisenhower Administration and Black Civil Rights*, pp. 93-102.

101. June-July 1959 PCGC Newsletter #19, which includes an article about *The New Girl*, a thirty-minute film which traces the experiences of a Black clerical worker, the first ever hired by the fictional company, and her White colleagues during her first day on the job; April 15, 1959, speech by Secretary of Labor James P. Mitchell before the luncheon meeting of the PCGC, St. Louis Chamber of Commerce, and St. Louis Labor Council in St. Louis, MO, p. 3; November 20, 1958, minutes of PCGC meeting, which include a discussion of a seminar at PCGC's Chicago regional office, pp. 5-6; all documents from Office of the Special Assistant to the President for Personnel Management, Box #19, DDE Library; see also December 11, 1953, "PCGC Principles and Program for Compliance," pp. 2, 6-7, 11 (where the committee also was exhorted not to "undertake the job of securing compliance"); for a sample of a PCGC response to a discrimination complaint, see November 17, 1959, PCGC Summary of Case #887, Office of the Special Assistant to the President for Personnel Management, Box #19, DDE Library.

102. October 15, 1959, letter from Robert I. Biren, Compliance Officer–International Cooperation Administration to Jacob Seidenberg, Executive Director–PCGC re: ICA's request for policy guidance from PCGC regarding obligation to include "nondiscrimination provision" in contracts with foreign governments; November 12, 1959, memorandum from Seidenberg to PCGC re: ICA interpretation that PCGC requirement of nondiscrimination clause in federal government contracts did not apply to contracts with foreign governments; all from Office of the Special Assistant to the President for Personnel Managament, Box #19, DDE Library.

103. The PCGC absolved itself from any responsibility for Black business development through government contracting. For instance, when hearing a complaint by the Black-owned Watson Laundry and Cleaner Plant that the Defense Department refused to contract with that outfit because it was Black, the "Committee unanimously agreed that regardless of the merits of the case, it was not within its jurisdiction." See minutes of June 25, 1959, PCGC meeting, Office of the Special Assistant to the President for Personnel Management, Box #19, DDE Library, p. 5.

104. Burk, *The Eisenhower Administration and Black Civil Rights*, pp. 93-108.

105. Kenneth Jackson, *Crabgrass Frontier: The Suburbanization of the United States* (New York: Oxford University Press, 1985), 199-203.

106. 334 U.S. 1, 68 S. Ct. 836, 92 L. Ed. 1161 (1948); Douglas S. Massey and Nancy A. Denton, *American Apartheid: Segregation of the Making of the Underclass* (Cambridge, MA: Harvard University Press, 1993), pp. 51-55; Jackson, *Crabgrass Frontier*, pp. 204-208; Melvin L. Oliver and Thomas M. Shapiro, *Black Wealth/White Wealth: A New Perspective on Racial Inequality* (New York: Routledge 1995), pp. 15-18.

107. Burk, *The Eisenhower Administration and Black Civil Rights*, pp. 113-119.

108. See November 14, 1958, *New York Times*, p. 46; see also November 20, 1958, letter from Algernon D. Black, Chairman–National Committee Against Discrimination in Housing, to President Eisenhower, Office of the Special Assistant to the President for Personnel Management, Box #42, DDE Library, p. 1.

109. November 20, 1958, Algernon Black letter to Eisenhower, p. 2; see also Burk, *The Eisenhower Administration and Black Civil Rights*, pp. 114-115.

110. December 19, 1958, letter from Albert M. Cole, Administrator–HHFA, to Algernon D. Black, Office of the Special Assistant to the President for Personnel Management, Box #42, DDE Library, pp. 1-2.

111. See, e.g., the oral arguments by the Eisenhower administration's Solicitor General in the Supreme Court case *Brown v. Board of Education*, where Simon Sobeloff asserted that the federal government thought that the Court should not impose an injunction against state-sponsored racially segregated schools to force the admission of Black students. Phillip B. Kurland and Gerhard Casper, eds., *Landmark Briefs and Arguments of the Supreme Court of the United States: Constitutional Law*, vol. 49A (Bethesda, MD: University Publications of America, Inc., 1975), pp. 1278-1288 (pp. 64-74 of the transcript of April 13, 1955, oral arguments).

112. Oliver and Shapiro, *Black Wealth/White Wealth*, pp. 39-41, 147-151; Massey and Denton, *American Apartheid*, p. 189; John H. Franklin and Alfred A. Moss, *From Slavery to Freedom: A History of African Americans* (New York: McGraw-Hill, 7th edition, 1994), pp. 470-474; December 1, 1958, letter from Edna A. Merson, Chairman–Committee on Civil Rights in Manhattan, Inc., to Eisenhower, Office of the Special Assistant to the President for Personnel Management, Box #42, DDE Library.

113. Burk, *The Eisenhower Administration and Black Civil Rights*, pp. 112-113.

114. See Immanuel M. Wallerstein, *The Modern World-System: Capitalist Agriculture and the Origins of the European World-Economy in the Sixteenth Century* (New York: Academic Press, 1974); McCormick, *America's Half-Century*, pp. 50-52, 119; Fieldhouse, *Merchant Capital*, p. 552.

115. Rodney, *How Europe Underdeveloped Africa*, p. 108; see generally Basil Davidson, *The African Past; Chronicles from Antiquity to Modern Times* (Boston: Little, Brown & Co., 1964).

116. But cf. Nwaubani, "Eisenhower, Nkrumah, and the Congo Crisis," pp. 604-609 (where the author indicates that Wilson Clark Flake, American Ambassador to Ghana, did discuss the use of American aid as a means of smoothing relations between the two countries, particularly given Ghana's emphasis on "positive neutrality" and its insistence that it should be able to find economic partners anywhere in the world); to compare the American view of Nkrumah to that of British capitalists, see Fieldhouse, *Merchant Capital*, p. 453; March 31, 1960, memorandum re: 423rd NSC meeting re: U.S. Policy Toward South, Central, and East Africa (NSC 5818 and NSC 5920), Ann Whitman File, NSC Series, DDE Library, p. 2.

117. See, e.g., August 25, 1960, memorandum re: 456th NSC meeting, pp. 3-4, 8; March 24, 1960, memorandum re: 438th NSC meeting, pp. 9-11, both documents from DDE Library.

118. March 24, 1960, memorandum re: 438th NSC meeting, Ann Whitman File, DDE Diary, NSC Series, DDE Library, p. 9.

119. April 7, 1960, memorandum re: 440th NSC meeting, Ann Whitman File, DDE Diary, NSC Series, DDE Library, p. 2.

120. On the issue of enhancing American prestige in the Third World, see March 21, 1958, OCB report to NSC on 5719/1, p. 6.

121. See George White Jr. "Holding the Line: Race, Racism, and American Foreign Policy, 1953-1961," Ph.D. dissertation (Temple University, 2001), DAI: 61, no. 12A (2001) (see especially chapter 2 in which the author characterizes American foreign relations with Africa as evolving through different eras as U.S. power and European hegemony over Africa both grow and transform).

122. Claire Robertson, *Sharing the Same Bowl: A Socioeconomic History of Women and Class in Accra, Ghana* (Bloomington: Indiana University Press, 1984), pp. 12-18, 75-122; Robertson, *Comparative Advantage: Women in Trade in Accra, Ghana and Nairobi, Kenya*, in House-Midamba and Ekechi, eds., *African Market Women and Economic Power*, pp. 110-111; Clark, *Onions Are My Husband: Survival and Accumulation By West African Market Women*, pp. 375-380, 397-415.

123. Tsehai Berhane-Selassie, *Ethiopian Rural Women and the State*, in Mikell, ed., *African Feminism*, p. 187; Clark, *Onions Are My Husband*, pp. 376-377, 397; Robertson, *Sharing the Same Bowl*, pp. 39-41, 137-146.

124. Emily S. Rosenberg, "Revisiting Dollar Diplomacy: Narratives of Money and Manliness," *Diplomatic History* 22, no. 2 (Spring 1998), pp. 155-176.

125. September 22, 1960, Secretary of State Memorandum of Conversation between Eisenhower, Herter, and Nkrumah, Ann Whitman File, ACW Diary, Ghana series, DDE Library.

126. See, e.g., Frances Cress-Welsing, *The Isis Papers: The Keys to the Colors* (Chicago: Third World Press, 1991); W. E. B. DuBois, *The Souls of Black Folk* (Millwood, NY: Kraus-Thomson Organization, Ltd. reprint, 1973); George M. Fredrickson, *The Arrogance of Race: Historical Perspectives on Slavery, Racism, and Social Inequality* (Middletown, CT: Wesleyan University Press, 1988); bell hooks, *Black Looks: Race and Representation* (Boston: South End Press, 1992); Winthrop Jordan, *White Over Black: American Attitudes Toward the Negro, 1550-1812* (Baltimore, MD: Penguin Books, 1969); Kimberle W. Crenshaw, "Race, Reform, and Retrenchment: Transformation and Legitimation in Anti-Discrimination Law," 101 *Harvard Law Review* 1331, 1373-1374 (May 1988). As to women, see, e.g., Maria Mies, ed., *Women: The Last Colony* (London: Zed Books, 1989); Marta Weigle, *Creation and Procreation* (Philadelphia: University of Pennsylvania Press, 1989); Celina Romany, "Themes for a Conversation on Race and Gender in International Human Rights Law," and J. Clay Smith Jr., "United States Foreign Policy and Goler Teal Butcher," in Adrien K. Wing, ed., *Global Critical Race Feminism: An International Reader* (New York: New York University Press, 2000), pp. 53-66 and 192-203, respectively.

127. June 6, 1957, Adlai Stevenson letter to Walter Rice, vice president and a director of Reynolds Metal Co., Adlai Stevenson Papers, vol. 7, Public Policy Papers, Department of Rare Books and Special Collections, Seeley G. Mudd Library, Princeton University, pp. 24-27.

## Chapter Five

1. August 16, 1956, Department of State memorandum from John Simmons to Bernard Shanley re: scheduling of meeting between president and newly appointed ambassador from the Union of South Africa; pp. 1-2 of the attached remarks from the ambassador of Union of South Africa for the president, Ann Whitman File, International Series, South Africa folder, DDE Library.

2. George M. Fredrickson, *White Supremacy: A Comparative Study in American and South African History* (New York: Oxford University Press, 1981), pp. 21-28, 30-40; Tim Juckes, *Opposition in South Africa: The Leadership of Z. K. Matthews, Nelson Mandela, and Stephen Biko* (Westport, CT: Praeger Publishers, 1995), pp. 15-16; Christopher Saunders, *Historical Dictionary of South Africa* (Metuchen, NJ: The Scarecrow Press, 1983), pp. 73-74; Cas De Villiers, *African Problems and Challenges* (Sandton, South Africa: Valiant, 1976), p. 59; Simon A. de Villiers, ed., *Otto Landsberg, 1803-1905: Nineteenth-Century South African Artist* (Cape Town: C. Struik, 1974), p. 27; Bernard Magubane, *The Making of a Racist State: British Imperialism and the Union of South Africa, 1875-1910* (Trenton, NJ: Africa World Press, 1996), pp. 99-103.

3. Lynn Berat, *Walvis Bay: Decolonization and International Law* (New Haven, CT: Yale University Press, 1990), pp. 99, 108-109 (quoting from John Westlake's treatise *International Law*), pp. 120-121 (re: *terra nullus*); Magubane, *The Making of a Racist State*, pp. 144-148.

4. Bhikhu Parekh, "Liberalism and Colonialism: a Critique of Locke and Mill," in Jan N. Pieterse and Bhikhu Parekh, eds., *The Decolonization of Imagination: Culture, Knowledge, and Power* (London: Zed Books, 1995), pp. 82-88.

5. *FRUS, 1955-1957: volume XVIII*, Memorandum of Conversation, Department of State, Washington, July 5, 1956, p. 786.

6. Juckes, *Opposition in South Africa*, p. 19.

7. *FRUS, 1955-1957: volume XVIII*, Memorandum of Conversation, US-UK Discussions at Camp David: South African Race Problem, March 28, 1960, p. 747.

8. Borstelmann, *Apartheid's Reluctant Uncle*, pp. 10, 47-48.

9. See, e.g., NSC 5719/1, OSANSA Records, NSC Series, Policy Papers Sub-series, p. 13; March 31, 1960, memorandum re: 432nd NSC meeting, Ann Whitman File, NSC Series, DDE Library, p. 3.

10. *FRUS, 1955-1957*, dispatch from the Embassy in South Africa to the Department of State, April 11, 1957 ["U.S. Embassy Staff Study on the South African Race Problem I"], p. 815.

11. Magubane, *The Making of a Racist State*, pp. 384-386.

12. Juckes, *Opposition in South Africa*, p. 17.

13. Ibid., p. 19.

14. Ibid., pp. 19-20 (where the author describes the Mines and Work Act and Native Labour Regulation Act of 1911, the 1913 Land Act, the Apprentice Act of 1922, the Industrial Conciliation Act of 1924, the Native Administration Act of 1927, and the Native Services Contract Act of 1932); Catherine Higgs, *Ghost of Equality: the Public Loves of D. D. T. Jabavu of South Africa, 1885-1959* (Athens: Ohio University Press, 1997), pp. 99-104, 115-126. In the American context see Joe W. Trotter, *The African American Experience* (Boston: Houghton Mifflin, 2001), pp. 134-148, 218-226, 271-272 (re: nineteenth century restrictions on African Americans, including restrictions on their right to vote, own weapons, engage in commercial trade or crafts, and move freely throughout the nation); Paul Finkleman, Dred Scott v. Sandford: *A Brief History With Documents* (Boston: Bedford Books, 1997); Ian F. Haney-Lopez, *White By Law: the Legal Construction of Race* (New York: New York University Press, 1996) (re: the racial prerequisite of the 1790 Naturalization Act and its 1952 repeal); Derrick Bell, *Race, Racism, and American Law* (Boston: Little, Brown, 1975), pp. 15-20, 86-91 (re: the U.S. Supreme Court's support for nineteenth-century racial segregation).

15. Juckes, *Opposition in South Africa*, p. 32.

16. Ibid., p. 33.

17. Leo Marquard, *The Peoples and Policies of South Africa* (London: Oxford University Press, 1969), p. 136.

18. Frederick A. Johnstone, *Class, Race and Gold: A Study of Class Relations and Racial Discrimination in South Africa* (London: Routledge & K. Paul, 1976), pp. 135-136, 157-167.

19. Thomas Karis and Gwendolyn M. Carter, eds., *From Protest to Challenge: A Documentary History of African Politics in South Africa, 1882-1964* (Stanford, CA: Hoover International Press, 1972), vol. 1, pp. 339-344; Higgs, *Ghost of Equality*, pp. 32-49; James, *A History of Pan African Revolt*, pp. 88-92; Juckes, *Opposition in South Africa*, pp. 34-41, 43; Marquard, *The Peoples and Policies of South Africa*, pp. 120, 136.

20. Magubane, *The Making of a Racist State*, pp. 163-174.

21. Ibid., pp. 177-178.

22. Ibid., pp. 178-180.

23. William Minter, *King Solomon's Mines Revisited: Western Interests and the Burdened History of Southern Africa* (New York: Basic Books, 1986), pp. 76-83; Borstelmann, *Apartheid's Reluctant Uncle*, pp. 49-50, 138-139, 198 (citing Paul Nitze, "Minerals as a Factor in U.S. Foreign Economic Policy," *Department of State Bulletin*, February 16, 1947, p. 300).

24. NSC 5719/1, OSANSA Records, NSC Series, pp. 3-4, 25; for a South African defense perspective, see Gen. Walter Walker, *The Bear at the Back Door: The Soviet Threat to the West's Lifeline in Africa* (Sandton, Republic of South Africa: Valiant Publishers, 1978), pp. 10-14.

25. But c.f. Borstelmann, *Apartheid's Reluctant Uncle*, p. 128.

26. June 8, 1955, diary entry of president's itinerary, Ann Whitman File, ACW Diary series, DDE Library.

27. Borstelmann, *Apartheid's Reluctant Uncle*, pp. 33-34, 70-71, 74; Higgs, *Ghost of Equality*, pp. 129-145; Johnstone, *Class, Race, and Gold*, pp. 152-157; Juckes, *Opposition in South Africa*, pp. 33-34, 44, 46-49; Albert Luthuli, *Let My People Go* (New York: McGraw Hill, 1962), p. 101; Marquard, *The Peoples and Policies of South Africa*, p. 140.

28. Saunders, *Historical Dictionary of South Africa*, p. 17.

29. Saunders, *Historical Dictionary of South Africa*, p. 17; Magubane, *The Making of a Racist State*, p. 357; see also Johnstone, *Class, Race, and Gold*, p. 164.

30. Borstelmann, *Apartheid's Reluctant Uncle*, pp. 30, 74, 75-76, 142.

31. James, *A History of Pan-African Revolt*, pp. 88-92; Juckes, *Opposition in South Africa*, p. 34; Marquard, *The Peoples and Policies of South Africa*, p. 136.

32. Marquard, *The Peoples and Politics of South Africa*, p. 141; Borstelmann, *Apartheid's Reluctant Uncle*, p. 145; Juckes, *Opposition in South Africa*, p. 59; see also Saunders, *Historical Dictionary of South Africa*, pp. 132-133.

33. July 7, 1953, letter from Eisenhower to Flanders, Ann Whitman File, DDE Diary Series, DDE Library; NSC 5719/1, p. 12.

34. NSC 5719/1, p. 11.

35. *FRUS, 1958-1960, volume. XIV*, February 6, 1958, memorandum from Holmes to Dulles.

36. March 21, 1958, OCB Progress Report on NSC 5719/1, OSANSA Records, NSC Series, Policy Papers Sub-series, DDE Library p. 2; *FRUS, 1958-1960, volume XIV*, Memorandum of Conversation [between Eric Louw, South African Minister of External Affairs, and Secretary of State Herter], New York, September 21, 1959, p. 737; *FRUS, 1958-1960, volume XIV*, telegram from the Embassy in South Africa to the Department of State, Pretoria, June 30, 1960, p. 752.

37. Richard E. Lapchick and Stephanie Urdang, *Oppression and Resistance: The Struggle of Women in Southern Africa* (Westport, CT: Greenwood Press, 1982), p. 121; Karis and Carter, eds., *From Protest to Challenge*, vol. 3, pp. 335-340, 344-346.

38. Ibid., p. 346.

39. Ibid., pp. 347-349.

40. Ibid., pp. 347-349.

41. March 21, 1958, OCB Progress Report on NSC 5719/1, p. 2.

42. Ibid., pp. 3-4.

43. Borstelmann, *Apartheid's Reluctant Uncle*, p. 187.

44. See, e.g., March 21, 1958, OCB Progress Report on NSC 5719/1, p. 9, and *Progress Through Separate Development: South Africa in Peaceful Transition* (New York: Information Service of South Africa, 4th edition, 1973); see also *FRUS, 1955-1957, volume XVIII*, memorandum from the counselor of the Embassy in South Africa (Maddox) to the deputy assistant secretary of state for African affairs (Palmer), Washington, December 18, 1957, pp. 835-836; *FRUS, 1958-1960, volume XIV*, February 6, 1958, memorandum from Holmes to Dulles, p. 7.

45. May 9, 1958, memorandum re: 365th NSC mtg, Ann Whitman File, NSC Series, DDE Library, p. 3.

46. Higgs, *Ghost of Equality*, pp. 99-106, 112-120, 124-140; Karis and Carter, eds., *From Protest to Challenge*, vol. 2, pp. 13-60; Karis and Carter, eds., *From Protest to Challenge*, vol. 3, pp. 16-19.

47. May 6, 1953, telegram from Allen Dulles to Walter White, Allen W. Dulles Papers, Box #57, Folder 33, Public Policy Papers, Department of Rare Books and Special Collections, Seeley G. Mudd Library, Princeton University Library.

48. See Gerald Torres and Kathryn Milun, "Frontier of Legal Thought III: Translating 'Yonnondio' by the Precedent and Evidence: The Mashpee Indian Case," 1990 *Duke Law Journal* 660 (September 1990), pp. 664-686.

49. *FRUS, 1955-1957*, April 11, 1957, dispatch re: U.S. Embassy Staff Study on the South African Race Problem I, p. 808.

50. Ibid., p. 812.

51. May 6, 1960, memorandum from Waldemar Nielsen to the PCIAA ad hoc committee, OSANSA Records, Sprague Committee Files, Council on Foreign Affairs series, DDE Library, p. 3; *FRUS, 1955-1957*, dispatch from the Embassy in South Africa to the Department of State [re: U.S. Embassy Staff Study on the South African Race Problem II], Pretoria, April 12, 1957, p. 821; see also *FRUS 1955-1957, volume XVIII*, dispatch from the Embassy in South Africa to the Department of State, Pretoria, August 6, 1956, pp. 792-793.

52. See, generally, Brian Glick, *War At Home* (Boston: South End Press, 1989), and O' Reilly, *Racial Matters*.

53. See, e.g., *FRUS, 1955-1957*, letter from the assistant secretary of state for Near Eastern, South Asian, and African affairs (Rountree) to the ambassador in South Africa (Byroade), Washington, December 14, 1956, p. 803.

54. See, e.g., July 25, 1960, PCIAA #37, "Themes," OSANSA Records, Sprague Committee File, PCIAA Papers series, DDE Library.

55. See, e.g., *FRUS, 1958-1960*, telegram From the embassy in South Africa to the Department of State, Capetown [re: meeting between American Ambassador Crowe and Prime Minister Henrik Verwoerd], April 27, 1959, p. 733; *FRUS, 1958-1960*, September 21, 1959 Memorandum of Conversation between Herter et al., and Louw, p. 736.

56. April 2, 1960, memorandum re: 439th NSC meeting, Ann Whitman File, NSC Series, DDE Library, pp. 9-10.

57. See, e.g., June 4, 1958, letter from Randall to B. H. Larabee, president of Firestone Plantations in Liberia, U.S. Council on Foreign Economic Policy, Records File, (1954-1961), Policy Papers Series, Box #12, DDE Library.

58. See, e.g., April 19, 1960, Satterthwaite letter to Randall re: attached Department of State Airgam from Dar es Salaam which also mentions Julius Nyerere and a potential boycott of American films distributed through South Africa, U.S. Council on Foreign Economic Policy, Office of the Chairman: Records (1954-1961), Randall Series, Subject Subseries, Box #1, DDE Library.

59. *FRUS, 1958-1960*, March 28, 1960, memorandum of Conversation re: Camp David meeting between Eisenhower et al., and British Prime Minister Macmillan et al., pp. 745-746.

60. Walker, *The Bear at the Back Door*, pp. 81-82 (for the defense of the Afrikaner entitlement from a British military officer); see, e.g., *FRUS, 1955-1957*, letter from the

Acting Director of the Office of Southern Africa Affairs (Hadsel) to the Ambassador in Egypt (Byroade), Washington, August 3, 1956, pp. 786-790; *FRUS, 1955-1957*, April 11, 1957, dispatch, Embassy Staff Study on the South African Race Problem I, pp. 807-815; *FRUS, 1958-1960*, February 6, 1958, Holmes memorandum to Dulles, pp. 1-10; *FRUS, 1958-1960*, National Intelligence Estimate [NIE 73-60], July 19, 1960, "The Outlook for the Union of South Africa," pp. 753-755.

61. Frances Cress-Welsing, *The Isis Papers: the Keys to the Colors* (Chicago: Third World Press, 1991), pp. 178-180; see generally, Marimba Ani, *Yurugu: An African Centered Critique of European Cultural Thought and Behavior* (Trenton, NJ: Africa World Press, 1994), and Jared Diamond, *Guns, Germs, and Steel: The Fates of Human Societies* (New York: W. W. Norton, 1999).

62. John Lansdale, *Mau Maus of the Mind: Making Mau Mau and Remaking Kenya,"* *Journal of African History* 31 (1990), pp. 393-421; Meddi Mugyenyi, *The Sources of Collective Rebellion: Nationalism in Buganda and Kikuyuland,* in Gregory Maddox, ed., *The Colonial Epoch in Africa* (New York: Garland, 1993), pp. 364-368; for the reaction in the West Indies, see Horace Campbell, *Rasta and Resistance: From Marcus Garvey to Walter Rodney* (Trenton, NJ: Africa World Press, 1990).

63. *FRUS, 1958-1960*, July 19, 1960, NIE 73-60, p. 754

64. *FRUS, 1958-1960, volume XIV*, memorandum from the Acting Assistant Secretary of State for International Organization Affairs (Walmsley) to the Under Secretary of State (Herter), July 9, 1958, pp. 726-729; Borstelmann, *Apartheid's Reluctant Uncle*, p. 181.

65. Ibid.

66. Ibid., p. 191.

67. Ibid., pp. 164, 184-185; Minter, *King Solomon's Mines Revisited*, pp. 73-77.

68. Marquard, *The Peoples and Policies of South Africa*, p. 132.

69. Karis & Carter, eds., *From Protest to Challenge*, vol. 3, pp. 332-334; Richard E. Lapchick and Stephanie Urdang, *Oppression and Resistance: the Struggle of Women in Southern Africa* (Westport, CT: Greenwood, 1982), pp. 146-147.

70. April 2, 1960, memorandum re: 439th NSC meeting, Ann Whitman File, NSC Series, DDE Library, pp. 9-10 (emphasis added).

71. Karis and Carter, eds., *From Protest to Challenge*, vol. 3, pp. 336, 338-339.

72. *FRUS, 1958-1960: volume XIV*, Editorial Note, p. 741.

73. Ibid. (referring to March 22, 1960, telegram 49 to U.S. Embassy, Capetown).

74. Ibid., pp. 741-742 (referring to the Memorandum of the Meeting, taken by Gen. Goodpaster; emphasis added).

75. Ibid., p. 742.

76. *FRUS, 1958-1960: volume XIV*, telegram from the Embassy in South Africa to the Department of State, Capetown, March 25, 1960, pp. 743-744.

77. Ibid. p. 742 (referring to U.N. Ambassador Henry Cabot Lodge's report of favorable reaction from the Afro-Asian group of nations); March 25, 1960, telegram from the Embassy in South Africa, pp. 743-744.

78. August 4, 1960, memorandum regarding 454th NSC meeting, Ann Whitman File, NSC Series, DDE Library, p. 19 (emphasis in original).

79. July 29, 1960, Briefing Note for the NSC meeting, August 1, 1960, "Commitments For Grant Military Assistance To Certain Free World Nations With Well-Developed Economies," p. 1 (referring to a December 3, 1959, NSC meeting and NSC Action No. 2158), attached to August 4, 1960, memorandum re: the 454th NSC meeting, Ann Whitman File, NSC Briefing Notes Series, DDE Library.

80. Ibid. (referring to a State-Defense report in February 1960 and NSC Action No. 2187).

81. Ibid., p. 2.

82. See July 26, 1960, letter from Mansfield Sprague to PCIAA members re: draft letter to President with PCIAA recommendations for "early action on a number of matters concerning Africa," OSANSA Records, Sprague Committee Files, Presidential Report Series, DDE Library, p. 9.

83. See, e.g., *FRUS, 1955-1957*, August 3, 1956, letter From Hadsel to Byroade, p. 788.

84. February 12, 1960, Briefing Note for the NSC meeting, p. 2, Feb. 16, 1960, OSANSA Records, NSC briefing notes series, DDE Library.

85. *FRUS, 1955-1957*, telegram from the Mission at the United Nations to the Department of State [regarding conversation between Henry Cabot Lodge and South African Foreign Minister Louw], New York, November 19, 1956, pp. 798-799; *FRUS, 1958-1960*, February 6, 1958, Holmes memorandum to Dulles, pp. 6-7.

86. *FRUS, 1958-1960*, telegram from the Embassy in South Africa to the Department of State [re: meeting between Crowe and Verwoerd], Capetown, April 27, 1959, p. 733.

87. Karis and Carter, eds., *From Protest to Challenge*, vol. 3, pp. 339-344.

88. Ibid., pp. 335-336, 344-349.

89. *FRUS, 1958-1960*, July 19, 1960, NIE 73-60, p. 755.

90. *FRUS, 1955-1957*, April 12, 1957, dispatch, Embassy Staff Study on the South African Race Problem II, pp. 818-819; *FRUS, 1955-1957*, memorandum from the Deputy Director of the Office of Southern Africa Affairs (LaMont) to the Deputy Assistant Secretary of State for African Affairs (Palmer), Washington, May 16, 1957, p. 828; but cf. *FRUS, 1955-1957*, August 6, 1956, Edward Wailes dispatch to State Department.

91. See, e.g., David N. Gibbs, *The Political Economy of Third World Intervention: Mines, Money, and U.S. Policy in the Congo Crisis* (Chicago: University of Chicago Press, 1991).

92. Karis and Carter, eds., *From Protest to Challenge*, p. 346.

93. *FRUS, 1958-1960*, April 27, 1959, telegram, pp. 732-733 (regarding the description of Verwoerd) and September 1958, Phillip D. Block III, "Report on Africa," pp. 11-12, U.S. Council on Foreign Economic Policy, Office of the Chairman: Records (1954-1961), Randall Series, Subject Subseries, Box #1, DDE Library (regarding Afrikaners); cf., *FRUS, 1958-1960*, February 6, 1958, Holmes memorandum to Dulles, p. 7 (regarding descriptions of the Africans).

94. Lapchick and Urdang, *Oppression and Resistance*, pp. 118-164.

95. Coquery-Vidrovitch, *African Women*, pp. 59-64, 76-80, 119-120, 124-125; Lapchick and Urdang, *Oppression and Resistance*, pp. 17-85.

96. Anne McClintock, "'The Very House of Difference': Race, Gender, and Politics of South African Women's Narrative in *Poppie Nongena*," in Dominick LaCapra, ed., *The Bounds of Race: Perspectives on Hegemony and Resistance* (Ithaca, NY: Cornell University Press, 1991), pp. 202-203.

97. *FRUS, 1958-1960*, July 9, 1958, Walmsley memorandum to Herter, p. 728 (emphasis added).

## Chapter Six

1. NSC 5719/1, pp. 2-3.

2. Ibid., pp. 15-16 (paragraph 25, "Policy Guidance").

3. See, e.g., Chinweizu, *The West and the Rest of Us: White Predators, Black Slavers, and the African Elite* (New York: Random House, 1975), pp. 62-69; E. D. Morel, *The Black Man's Burden: The White Man in Africa from the Fifteenth Century to World War I* (New York: Monthly Review Press edition, 1969), pp. 109-126; Thomas Pakenham, *The Scramble for Africa: The White Man's Conquest of the Dark Continent From 1876 to 1912* (New York: Avon Books, 1991), pp. 398-399, 659.

4. David N. Gibbs, *The Political Economy of Third World Intervention: Mines, Money and U.S. Policy in the Congo Crisis* (Chicago: University of Chicago Press, 1991), pp. 39-49; see also Morel, *The Black Man's Burden*, and Chinwezu, *The West and the Rest of Us*.

5. George Martelli, *Leopold to Lumumba: A History of the Congo, 1877-1960* (London: Chapman & Hall, 1962), p. 150.

6. Thomas Borstelmann, *Apartheid's Reluctant Uncle: The United States and Southern Africa in the Early Cold War* (New York: Oxford University Press, 1993), p. 18; Basil Davidson, *Let Freedom Come: Africa in Modern History* (Boston: Little, Brown, 1978), p. 201; Gibbs, *The Political Economy of Third World Intervention*, pp. 54-62; see also Adam Hocschild, *King Leopold's Ghost: A Story of Greed, Terrorism, and Heroism in Colonial Africa* (New York: Houghton Mifflin, 1998).

7. William Minter, *King Solomon's Mines Revisited: Western Interests and the Burdened History of Southern Africa* (New York: Basic Books, 1986), p. 68.

8. May 9, 1958, memorandum re: 365th NSC meeting, Ann Whitman File, NSC Series, DDE Library, p. 3.

9. Martelli, *Leopold to Lumumba*, p. 193.

10. Rodney, *How Europe Underdeveloped Africa*, pp. 43, 80, 98-101, 134; see also Chinwezu, *The West and the Rest of Us*.

11. Gibbs, *The Political Economy of Third World Intervention*, pp. 52-54; Davidson, *Let Freedom Come*, pp. 158, 201-202; Lise A. Namikis, "Battleground Africa: The Cold War and the Congo Crisis, 1960-1965, vol. I" (Ph.D. Dissertation: University of Southern California, 2002), p. 33 (where the author notes that the small Batelela ethnic group, from which Patrice Lumumba emerged, prided itself on its resistance to Belgian colonial governance); Minter, *King Solomon's Mines Revisited*, pp. 68-69; James, *A History of Pan-African Revolt*, pp. 82-83; Borstelmann, *Apartheid's Reluctant Uncle*, p. 25.

12. Gibbs, *The Political Economy of Third World Intervention*, pp. 44-52, 60-69, 136-140; Alan James, *Britain and the Congo Crisis, 1960-1963* (New York: St. Martin's Press, 1996), p. 31; Crawford Young, *Politics in the Congo: Decolonization and Independence* (Princeton, NJ: Princeton University Press, 1964), p. 17; but cf. Namikis, "Battleground Africa," p. 69 (regarding the decline in American investment in the Congo after 1957).

13. March 21, 1958, OCB Progress Report on NSC 5719/1, OSANSA Records, NSC Series, Policy Papers Sub-series, DDE Library, p. 5.

14. Ibid.

15. Ibid.; see also Gibbs, *The Political Economy of Third World Intervention*, pp. 72-74, 203.

16. Davidson, *Let Freedom Come*, p. 274-275; Gibbs, *The Political Economy of Third World Intervention*, pp. 73-74; see also Smith Hempstone, *Rebels, Mercenaries, and Dividends: The Katanga Story* (New York: Praeger Publishers, 1962), pp. 22-23; Ilunga Kabongo, *The Catastrophe of Belgian Decolonization*, in Gifford and Louis, eds., *Decolonization and African Independence*, p. 384; Sean Kelly, *America's Tyrant: The CIA and Mobutu of Zaire: How the United States Put Mobutu in Power, Protected Him From His Enemies, Helped Him Become One of the Richest Men in the World and Lived to Regret It* (Washington, DC: The American University Press, 1993), p. 24.

17. November 5, 1959, memorandum re: 423rd NSC meeting, Ann Whitman File, NSC Series, DDE Library, pp. 6-7.

18. Madeline Kalb, *The Congo Cables: The Cold War in Africa—From Eisenhower to Kennedy* (New York: Macmillan, 1982), pp. xxi-xxiii; Namikis, "Battleground Africa," pp. 26-27 (referring to Antoine A. J. Van Bilsen's proposed thirty-year plan for the decolonization of the Congo and the angry reaction throughout Belgium to his liberal idea).

19. March 31, 1960, memorandum re: the 432nd NSC meeting [held January 14], Ann Whitman File, NSC Series, DDE Library, pp. 1-2.

20. Ibid., pp. 3-5 (emphasis added).

21. See, e.g., Kalb, *The Congo Cables*, p. 7.

22. March 31, 1960, memorandum re: 432nd NSC meeting, p. 4 (emphasis added).

23. October 6, 1960, memorandum re: 462nd NSC meeting, Ann Whitman File, NSC Series, DDE Library, p. 11.

24. For typical, negative Western reactions to Lumumba, see Eisenhower, *Waging Peace*, pp. 575-576; Gibbs, *The Political Economy of Third World Intervention*, pp. 92-93; Hempstone, *Rebels, Mercenaries, and Dividends*, pp. 131-132; Kalb, *The Congo Cables*, pp. 38-39; but cf. Jean van Lierde, ed., *Lumumba Speaks: The Speeches and Writings of Patrice Lumumba, 1958-1961* (Boston: Little, Brown and Co., 1972), pp. 3-52.

25. Gibbs, *The Political Economy of Third World Intervention*, p. 75; Hempstone, *Rebels, Mercenaries, and Dividends*, pp. 89-102; Kalb, *The Congo Cables*, p. 38.

26. See, e.g., October 6, 1960, memorandum from R. F. Peterson, U.S. Mission to the United Nations, to Ambassador Wadsworth for Cabinet Meeting, regarding an assessment of the proceedings of the U.N. General Assembly in September 1960, Ann Whitman File, Cabinet Series, Box #16, DDE Library; see also Carol Collins, "Fatally Flawed Mediation: Cordier and the Congo Crisis," *Africa Today* (3rd Quarter, 1992), pp.

5-22, and Ebere Nwaubani, "Eisenhower, Nkrumah, and the Congo Crisis," *Journal of Contemporary History* 36, no. 4 (2001), 599-622; but cf. October 8, 1960, Department of State incoming telegram from Flake, U.S. Embassy-Accra, to Herter regarding Flake's conversation with Nkrumah, Council on Foreign Economic Policy: Office of the Chairman Records, Randall Series, Subject subseries, Box #1, DDE Library.

27. Patrice Lumumba, *Congo, My Country* (New York: Praeger, 1962), pp. 15-68, 85-86, 93-124; van Lierde, ed., *Lumumba Speaks*, pp. 55-59, 157-185.

28. W. A. E. Surkin, ed., *African Political Thought: Lumumba, Nkrumah, and Toure* (Denver, CO: University of Denver, 1968), pp. 19, 24-25, 39-40, 54; Namikis, "Battleground Africa," pp. 34 (which describes Lumumba as being "anti-imperialist not anti-Western"), 45-47; see also Catherine Hoskyns, *The Congo Since Independence: January 1960-December 1961* (London: Oxford University Press, 1965), pp. 64-77.

29. van Lierde, ed., *Lumumba Speaks*, p. 62; Davidson, *Let Freedom Come*, pp. 232-233, 253-254.

30. van Lierde, ed., *Lumumba Speaks*, pp. 66, 73, 78-80, 87-88, 174, 222-223, 310-311.

31. Surkin, ed., *African Political Thought*, p. 19.

32. Ibid., pp. 19-20; van Lierde, ed., *Lumumba Speaks*, pp. 85-86; Namikis, "Battleground Africa," pp. 95, 100-104.

33. van Lierde, ed., *Lumumba Speaks*, p. 172 (emphasis added).

34. But cf. *FRUS 1958-1960, vol. XIV*, February 25, 1960, Memorandum of Conversation between Lumumba and U.S. Ambassador to Belgium William Burden, p. 263 (for a more complex portrayal of Lumumba by an American).

35. June 30, 1960, memorandum re: 449th NSC meeting, Ann Whitman File, NSC Series, DDE Library, p. 4.

36. Ibid., p. 5.

37. It should be noted that Kasavubu and Lumumba broke relations with Belgium after they learned of: (1) the Belgian's collaboration in the Katanga secession; (2) the refusal of the White officers in the *Force Publique* to assist in government-sponsored reforms of the military; and, (3) the assassination attempt on Lumumba. See Namikis, "Battleground Africa," p. 45, and van Lierde, ed., *Lumumba Speaks*, pp. 236-271; July 18, 1960, memorandum re: 451st NSC meeting, Ann Whitman File, NSC series, DDE Library, p. 6; but cf. Davidson, *Let Freedom Come*, pp. 120, 132; Gibbs, *The Political Economy of Third World Intervention*, pp. 53-57, 71-72; Lumumba, *Congo, My Country*, pp. 15-17.

38. July 18, 1960, memorandum re: 451st NSC meeting, pp. 6-9; but cf. van Lierde, ed., *Lumumba Speaks*, pp. 57, 298-306, 316-318; Namikis, "Battleground Africa," pp. 36, 46.

39. Surkin, ed., *African Political Thought*, p. 17.

40. van Lierde, ed., *Lumumba Speaks*, pp. 221-222.

41. Ibid., pp. 223-224.

42. Ibid., p. 220; see also Kelly, *America's Tyrant*, p. 16.

43. Eisenhower, *Waging Peace*, p. 573; see also Kalb, *The Congo Cables*, p. 3.

44. Kalb, *The Congo Cables*, pp. 3-4, 6-7, 24; Kelly, *America's Tyrant*, p. 24.

45. July 27, 1960, Department of State incoming telegram re: Congo, Ann Whitman File, ACW Diary Series, Congo folder, DDE Library. The Belgians also were stealing gold and diamonds from mines in the Kasai and Orientele provinces, postindependence. See van Lierde, ed., *Lumumba Speaks*, p. 328.

46. See, e.g., *FRUS, 1958-1960, vol. XIV*, April 7, 1960, memorandum from American Embassy, Brussels (Burden) to Dillon, pp. 266-270 (where Burden warned of the impoverished state in which the Congo would enter independence).

47. Kwame Nkrumah, *Challenge of the Congo* (London: Panaf, 1967), p. 2 (where the Ghanaian leader stated that his nation provided Lumumba with a "flying secretariat" during his July-August 1960 trips to the U.S. and across Africa); July 28, 1960, memorandum re: 453rd NSC meeting, Ann Whitman File, NSC Series, DDE Library, p. 5.

48. September 21, 1960, memorandum re: 460th NSC meeting, Ann Whitman File, NSC series, DDE Library, p. 14; Namikis, "Battleground Africa," p. 210.

49. Kalb, *The Congo Cables*, pp. 27 (quoting a July 19, 1960, memorandum from Burden to the State Department), 28-38, 51-55, 63-66; September 15, 1960, memorandum re: 459th NSC meeting, Ann Whitman File, NSC Series, DDE Library, p. 9.

50. March 15, 1960, notes from the second meeting of the PCIAA regarding American intelligence activities, OSANSA Records, Sprague Committee Files, Meeting Minutes series, DDE Library, p. 2.

51. June 18, 1959, memorandum re: 410th NSC meeting, Ann Whitman File, NSC Series, DDE Library, pp. 2-3.

52. March 31, 1960, memorandum re: 432nd NSC meeting, p. 3.

53. August 25, 1960, memorandum re: 456th NSC meeting, Ann Whitman File, NSC Series, DDE Library, p. 9.

54. March 31, 1960, memorandum re: 432nd NSC meeting, p. 3.

55. See, e.g., Phillip Agee, *Inside the Company: CIA Diary* (New York: Stonehill, 1975); Robert Bowie and Richard H. Immerman, *Waging Peace: How Eisenhower Shaped an Enduring Cold War Strategy* (Oxford: Oxford University Press, 2nd edition, 2000); Audrey R. and George McT. Kahin, *Subversion as Foreign Policy: the Secret Eisenhower and Dulles Debacle in Indonesia* (New York: New Press, 1995); Warner Poelchau, ed., *White Paper Whitewash: Interviews with Phillip Agee on the CIA and El Salvador* (New York: Deep Cover Books, 1981); and Ellen Ray et al., eds., *Dirty Work 2: The CIA in Africa* (Secaucus, NJ: Lyle Stuart, 1979); John Stockwell, *In Search of Enemies: A CIA Story* (New York: Norton, 1978).

56. William Blum, *The CIA: A Forgotten History: U.S. Global Interventions Since World War 2* (London: Zed Books, 1986), p. 175.

57. See, e.g., June 30, 1960, memorandum re: 449th NSC meeting, and July 18, 1960, memorandum re: 451st NSC meeting; see also Gibbs, *The Political Economy of Third World Intervention*, pp. 94-95, 132-135; Kalb, *The Congo Cables*, pp. 15, 25, 28-29; Namikis, "Battleground Africa," pp. 183-186 (regarding U.S. support of Kasavubu's coup).

58. August 4, 1960, memorandum re: 454th NSC meeting, Ann Whitman File, NSC Series, DDE Library, p. 16.

59. August 25, 1960, memorandum re: 456th NSC meeting, p. 7; October 6, 1960, memorandum re: 462nd NSC meeting, Ann Whitman File, NSC Series, DDE Library, p. 11; Namikis, "Battleground Africa," pp. 43-44.

60. Kelly, *America's Tyrant*, pp. 15-16

61. Kelly, *America's Tyrant*, pp. 15-16; September 21, 1960, memorandum re: 460th NSC meeting, p. 14; Namikis "Battleground Africa," pp. 33-34, 38 (regarding the long-standing philosophical differences between Lumumba the nationalist and Kasavubu the ethnic separatist); see also Thomas Franck and John Carey, *The Legal Aspects of the United Nations Action in the Congo* (Dobbs Ferry, NY: Oceana Publications, Inc. for the Association of the Bar of the City of New York, 1963), p. 9.

62. See, e.g., August 25, 1960, memorandum re: 457th NSC meeting, and September 21, 1960, memorandum re: 460tn NSC meeting; see also Kalb, *The Congo Cables*, pp. 142, 150, 158-164.

63. Van Lierde, ed., *Lumumba Speaks*, pp. 353-404; Kalb, *The Congo Cables*, pp. 89-97, 133-139; September 15, 1960, memorandum re: 459th NSC meeting, October 18, 1960, memorandum re: 463rd NSC meeting, pp. 8-10; October 24, 1960, memorandum re: 464th NSC meeting, p. 16, December 2, 1960, memorandum re: 468th NSC meeting, December 29, 1960, memorandum re: 472nd NSC meeting [all from Ann Whitman File, NSC Series, DDE Library]; *FRUS, 1958-1960, vol. XIV*, July 19, 1960, American Embassy, Brussels (Burden) to State Department, pp. 330-332 and editorial notes for the

Boggs Memoranda re: the September 15, 1960, and September 21, 1960, NSC meetings, pp. 489-490, 496-497.

64. "Alleged Assassination Plots Involving Foreign Leaders," *An Interim Report of the Senate Select Committee to Study Governmental Operations with Respect to Intelligence Activities*, United States Senate (Washington, DC: U.S. Government Printing Office, 1975), pp. 24-33, 39, 42-48, 75-76; see also Kalb, *The Congo Cables*, pp. 129-133, 149-152.

65. Namikis, "Battleground Africa," pp. 232-233.

66. December 2, 1960, memorandum re: 468th NSC meeting, p. 16; "Alleged Assassination Plots Involving Foreign Leaders," pp. 68-70; see also Blum, *The CIA*, pp. 174-176; Kalb, *The Congo Cables*, pp. 161-164; Kelly, *America's Tyrant*, pp. 38-42, 50-55; but cf. Ludo de Witte, *The Assassination of Patrice Lumumba* (Paris: Karthala, 2000), pp. 108-110, 172-179 (who places the ultimate blame for Lumumba's murder on the Belgians).

67. See, e.g., Amos N. Wilson, *The Falsification of Afrikan Consciousness: Eurocentric History, Psychiatry, and the Politics of White Supremacy* (New York: African World InfoSystems, 1993), p. 106; Fredrickson, *Arrogance of Race*, pp. 19, 22-24 (for a similar trait in antebellum U.S. history); and DuBois, *Black Reconstruction* (for a similar trait during the Reconstruction era in U.S. history); see also William H. Chafe, *Civilians and Civil Liberties: Greensboro, North Carolina and the Black Struggle for Freedom* (Oxford: Oxford University Press, 1981), pp. 64-70; Eugene D. Genovese, *Roll, Jordan, Roll: The World the Slaves Made* (New York: Pantheon Books, 1974), pp. 259-260, 587-597; Robin D. G. Kelly, *Hammer and Hoe: Alabama Communists During the Great Depression* (Chapel Hill: University of North Carolina Press, 1990), pp. 220-231.

68. Namikis, "Battleground Africa," pp. 119, 133, 135.

69. See, e.g., NSC 5719/1, p. 12, and March 21, 1958, OCB Progress Report on NSC 5719/1, p. 11 (regarding early perceptions of the Communist threat in Africa); August 23, 1957, memorandum re: 335th NSC meeting, p. 9 (regarding Nixon and Herter's subsequent evaluation). These and other changes were reflected in the administration's final position paper on Sub-Saharan Africa, NSC 6001.

70. March 24, 1960, memorandum re: 438th NSC meeting, Ann Whitman File, NSC Series, DDE Library, p. 9.

71. See March 31, 1960, memorandum re: 432nd NSC meeting.

72. March 24, 1960, memorandum re: 438th NSC meeting. p. 9, and March 31, 1960, memorandum re: 432nd NSC meeting (with respect to African leadership), both Ann Whitman File, NSC Series, DDE Library; July 21, 1960, memorandum re: 452nd NSC meeting, p. 16 (emphasis added).

73. Smith Hempstone, *Rebels, Mercenaries, and Dividends: the Katanga Story* (New York: Praeger, 1962), pp. 89-102, 129-132; Crawford Young, *Politics in the Congo: Decolonization and Independence* (Princeton, NJ: Princeton University Press, 1965), pp. 303-305; I. Kabongo, *The Catastrophe of Belgian Decolonization*, in Gifford and Louis, eds., *Decolonization and African Independence*, pp. 395-399; October 6, 1960, memorandum re: 462nd NSC meeting, p. 11; August 4, 1960, memorandum re: 454th NSC meeting, p. 19; July 28, 1960, memorandum re: 453rd NSC meeting, p. 5; see, e.g., *FRUS 1958-1960, vol. XIV*, July 18, 1960, cable from Leopoldville (Clare Timberlake) to State Department (relaying Lumumba-Kasavubu threat to Ralph Bunche that if the United Nations will not force the Belgians out of the Congo, they will ask the Soviet Union to do so), pp. 322-323; van Lierde, ed., *Lumumba Speaks*, pp. 279-285 (regarding the prime minister's July 22, 1960, national radio address stating that though his government wanted "nothing to do with imported doctrines," it may have no choice but to ask the Soviet Union to intervene militarily to oust the Belgian forces). With regard to the American rejection of Lumumba's requests, see, e.g., *FRUS, 1958-1960, vol. XIV*, July 27, 1960, Memorandum of Conversation between Lumumba and Herter, pp. 359-366.

74. Namikis, "Battleground Africa," p. 154.

75. Carole Collins, "Fatally Flawed Mediation: Cordier and the Congo Crisis," *Africa Today* (3rd Quarter, 1992), pp. 12, 16; November 8, 1954, letter from Dwight Eisenhower to Edgar Eisenhower, Ann Whitman File, DDE Diary Series, DDE Library.

76. August 4, 1960, memorandum re: 454th NSC meeting, Ann Whitman File, NSC Series, DDE Library, pp. 15-16; see also July 22, 1960, Joint Chiefs of Staff memorandum for the Secretary of Defense, "Possible U.S. Courses of Action Relative to the Contingency of Unilateral Sino-Soviet Bloc Military Intervention in the Republic of the Congo," White House Office, National Security Council Staff Papers, Disaster File, Box #44, DDE Library, pp. 2-4.

77. *FRUS, 1958-1960, vol. XIV*, August 30, 1960, memorandum from Hare to Herter and September 9, 1960, memorandum from Satterthwaite to Herter (regarding contingency planning done by the joint State-Defense departments Working Group), pp. 449-450; see also *FRUS 1958-1960, vol. XIV*, September 2, 1960, memorandum from the Joint Chiefs of Staff (Burke) to Gates and September 9, 1960, memorandum, pp. 453-455 and 468-471, respectively.

78. Collins, "Fatally Flawed Mediation," pp. 7-8; Gibbs, *The Political Economy of Third World Intervention*, pp. 78, 84-85; Hempstone, *Rebels, Mercenaries, and Dividends*, pp. 22-23, 30-41, 98.

79. Gibbs, *The Political Economy of Third World Intervention*, pp. 85-89; Hempstone, *Rebels, Mercenaries, and Dividends*, pp. 120-127; see generally, Alan James, *Britain and the Congo Crisis, 1960-63* (Houndmills: Macmillan, 1996).

80. See, e.g., March 21, 1958, OCB Progress Report on NSC 5719/1, p. 6; August 8, 1958, memorandum re: 375th NSC meeting, p. 11-13; Namikis, "Battleground Africa,"

pp. 120 (regarding the deployment of the USS *Wasp* and the alert status of two companies in West Germany in July 1960), pp. 121-122.

81. Harold K. Jacobson, "The Changing United Nations," in Roger Hilsman and Robert C. Good, eds., *Foreign Policy in the Sixties: The Issues and the Instruments—Essays in Honor of Arnold Wolfers* (Baltimore, MD: Johns Hopkins University Press, 1965), pp. 67-89; Kalb, *The Congo Cables*, pp. 7-14, 17-24.

82. See, e.g., September 22, 1960, Secretary of State Memorandum of Conversation between Eisenhower, Herter, and Nkrumah, pp. 2-3.

83. See, e.g., September 15, 1960, memorandum re: 459th NSC meeting, p. 9, and September 21, 1960, memorandum re: 460th NSC meeting, p. 14; see also Kalb, *The Congo Cables*, pp. 85-88.

84. See, e.g., August 25, 1960, memorandum re: 457th NSC meeting, p. 13, and Alleged Assassination Plots, p. 58; with respect to the fear of Egyptian radicalism, see August 23, 1957, memorandum re: 335th NSC meeting, p. 9, January 7, 1958, memorandum re: 350th NSC meeting, pp. 2-3, December 2, 1960, memorandum re: 468th NSC meeting, p. 17, and January 5, 1961, memorandum re: 473rd NSC meeting, p. 9 [all from Ann Whitman File, NSC Series, DDE Library]; Nwaubani, "Eisenhower, Nkrumah, and the Congo Crisis," pp. 611-619.

85. See, e.g., September 22, 1960, memorandum of Coversation during the meeting between Eisenhower, Herter, and Nkrumah.

86. February 26, 1959, memorandum re: 397th NSC meeting, Ann Whitman File, NSC Series, DDE Library, p. 12; see also Kevin Danaher, *50 Years Is Enough: The Case Against the World Bank and the International Monetary Fund* (Boston: South End Press, 1994).

87. See March 24, 1960, memorandum re: 438th NSC meeting, p. 9; Namikis, "Battleground Africa," pp. 130, 163, 216-217, 225-228; see also April 7, 1960, memorandum re: 440th NSC meeting, Ann Whitman File, NSC Series, DDE Library, p. 19.

88. August 25, 1960, memorandum re: 456th NSC meeting, p. 8.

89. July 18, 1960, memorandum re: 451st NSC meeting, p. 6, and July 21, 1960, memorandum re: 452nd NSC meeting, p. 15-16; Kalb, *The Congo Cables*, pp. 13-14, 18-19; August 4, 1960, memorandum re: 454th NSC meeting, p. 18.

90. Namikis, "Battleground Africa," p. 170; Collins, "Fatally Flawed Mediation," p. 17.

91. Kalb, *The Congo Cables*, pp. 104-127; Gibbs, *The Political Economy of Third World Intervention*, pp. 97-98; Namikis, "Battleground Africa," p. 197.

92. Namikis, "Battleground Africa," pp. 217, 226-227 (where the author details the creation of the U. N. Conciliation Commission for the Congo in November 1960); Kalb, *The Congo Cables*, pp. 95-96, 139; August 4, 1960, memorandum re: 454th NSC meeting, pp. 16-17; Gibbs, *The Political Economy of Third World Intervention*, p. 96; Kelly, *America's Tyrant*, pp. 50-55; Collins, "Fatally Flawed Mediation," pp. 16 (where the author writes that Cordier's authorization of a $1 million payment to Mobutu, money provided by Washington under the instructions that Mobutu be given credit for securing it, was pivotal in the cultivation of Mobutu and the cementing of his reputation among other soldiers and factions within the Congo) and 17 (regarding Cordier's disdain for the Congolese parliament and a potential reconciliation between Lumumba and Kasavubu); October 18, 1960, memorandum re: 462nd NSC meeting, p. 10; October 24, 1960, memorandum re: 464th NSC meeting, p. 16; see also Nwaubani "Eisenhower, Nkrumah, and the Congo Crisis," pp. 613-618.

93. Namikis, "Battleground Africa," pp. 158-161; Gibbs, *The Political Economy of Third World Intervention*, p. 96.

94. August 25, 1960, memorandum re: 456th NSC meeting, p. 12; October 24, 1960, memorandum re: 464th NSC meeting, pp. 16-17.

95. January 13, 1961, memorandum re: 474th NSC meeting, Ann Whitman File, NSC Series, DDE Library, p. 23.

96. *FRUS 1958-1960, vol. XIV*, May 1, 1960, memorandum from American Embassy, Brussels (Freeman) to State Department, p. 272 (in which the embassy personnel recommended using a strengthened *Force Publique* to counteract possible Communist incursions); van Lierde, ed., *Lumumba Speaks*, pp. 229-236; see also Kelly, *America's Tyrant*, pp. 24-25.

97. See, e.g., July 9, 1958, OCB Progress Report on NSC 5615/1, OSANSA Records, NSC Series, Policy Papers Sub-series, DDE Library, pp. 3-4, and August 25, 1960, memorandum re: 456th NSC meeting, p. 12; see also January 19, 1960, NSC 6001 "U.S. Policy Toward South, Central, and East Africa," White House Office, National Security Council Staff Papers, Disaster File, Box #44, DDE Library, p. 5.

98. NSC 6001, pp. 6, 9-10.

99. See, e.g., Cynthia G. Fleming, *Soon We Will Not Cry: The Liberation of Ruby Doris Smith Robinson* (Lanham, MD: Rowman and Littlefield, 1998), pp. 49-68 (with regard to the Sit-Ins and other protests against racially segregated facilities, the emergence of the Student Nonviolent Coordinating Committee, and the presence of African nationalist leaders on Black college campuses, among other things).

100. See March 15, 1960, PCIAA meeting notes, OSANSA Records, Sprague Committee File, Meeting Minutes series, DDE Library, p. 1; see also Collins, "Fatally Flawed Medation," p. 8 (regarding the media).

101. See, e.g., March 15, 1960, PCIAA meeting notes, OSANSA Records, Sprague Committee Files, Meeting Minutes Series, DDE Library, p. 1; Collins, "Fatally Flawed Mediation," p. 8 (regarding the media); see also August 25, 1960, memorandum re: 456th NSC meeting, p. 10; see also August 2, 1960, memorandum from J. I. Coffey to Waldemar Nielsen regarding the PCIAA's report to the president, OSANSA Records, Sprague Committee File, "Ten Major Points" subseries, DDE Library, paragraph 8.

102. November 5, 1959, memorandum re: 423rd NSC meeting, Ann Whitman File, NSC Series, DDE Library, p. 7; February 12, 1960 NSC briefing note on NSC 6001 "US Policy Toward South, Central, and East Africa," OSANSA Records, NSC briefing notes series, DDE Library, pp. 1-2.

103. Collins, "Fatally Flawed Mediation," p. 8; Nwaubani, "Eisenhower, Nkrumah, and the Congo Crisis," pp. 608-611; Namikis, "Battleground Africa," p. 114 (where the author notes that General Mile Janssens scribbled onto an Army blackboard the phrase "before independence = after independence" as a symbolic way of reinforcing the Belgian expectation of African subordination).

104. August 4, 1960, memorandum re: 454th NSC meeting, p. 18; see also Namikis, "Battleground Africa," p. 166 (regarding U.N. officials' dismay at Congolese soldiers' outbursts against White U.N. soldiers and staffers).

105. August 16, 1960, memorandum re: 455th NSC meeting, p. 12; August 25, 1960, memorandum re: 457th NSC meeting, p. 5.

106. Namikis, "Battleground Africa," pp. 45, 117, 125, 159, 162; Collins, "Fatally Flawed Mediation," p. 16.

107. Namikis, "Battleground Africa," pp. 189, 217, 240-241, 243.

108. July 26, 1960, letter from Mansfield Sprague to PCIAA members re: draft letter to president of PCIAA recommendations for "early action on a number of matters concerning Africa," OSANSA Records, Sprague Committee Files, Africa Series, DDE Library, p. 3 of draft letter.

109. 1960 PCIAA Report to the President, Appendix I: Supplementary Recommendations, OSANSA Records, Sprague Committee Files, Presidential Report Series, DDE Library, p. 9.

110. For an interesting Caribbean corollary, see July 21, 1960, memorandum re: 452nd NSC meeting, Ann Whitman File, NSC Series, DDE Library, pp. 8-9 (where the discussants entertain, then dismiss, the idea of having the Haitian military participate in the U.N. peacekeeping force in the Congo; they preferred leaving the Haitian military at home because of the growing political instability on that island).

111. Teshale Tibebu, *The Making of Modern Ethiopia: 1896-1974* (Lawrenceville, NJ: Red Sea Press, 1995), p. 51.

112. March 29, 1958, journal entry, Clarence Randall Journal of 1958 Trip to Africa, Clarence Randall Papers, Box #11, Public Policy Papers, Department of Rare Books and Special Collections, Seeley G. Mudd Library, Princeton University, pp. 1-4.

113. See, e.g., Catherine Coquery-Vidrovitch, *African Women: A Modern History*, trans. Beth G. Raps (Boulder, CO: Westview Press, 1997), pp. 63-64. See also Patricia Hill Collins, *Black Feminist Thought: Knowledge, Consciousness, and the Politics of Empowerment* (Boston: Unwin Hyman, 1990), and Yanick St. Jean and Joe R. Feagin, *Double Burden: Black Women and Everyday Racism* (Armonk, NY: M. E. Sharpe, 1999).

114. Coquery-Vidrovitch, *African Women*, pp. 39-44; David Sweetman, *Women Leaders in African History* (London: Heinemann Books, 1984), pp. 48-54, 91-97.

115. Audrey Wipper, "Riot and Rebellion Among African Women: Three Examples of Women's Political Clout," in Jean F. O'Barr, ed., *Perspectives on Power: Women in Africa, Asia, and Latin America* (Durham, NC: Duke University Press, 1982), p. 50.

116. Ibid., pp. 51-70.

117. Ibid., p. 52 (emphasis added).

118. Coquery-Vidrovitch, *African Women*, pp. 184-187.

119. Namikis, "Battleground Africa," pp. 48, 97.

120. See, e.g., William J. Taylor Jr., Eric T. Olson, and Richard A. Schrader, eds., *Defense Manpower Planning: Issues for the 1980s* (New York: Pergamon Press, 1981).

121. Martha Chamallas, *Introduction to Feminist Legal Theory* (Gaithersburg, MD: Aspen Law & Business Publishers, 1999), p. 18.

122. Coquery-Vidrovitch, *African Women*, pp. 143, 150-158.

123. See *FRUS, 1955-1957: Africa, Vol. XVIII*, July 5, 1956, memorandum of Conversation, pp. 785-786; March 29, 1958, Clarence Randall journal entry, Clarence Randall Papers, Box #11, Seeley G. Mudd Library, Princeton University, pp. 2-3.

124. Coquery-Vidrovitch, *African Women*, pp. 59-64, 76-80, 119-120, 124-125; Lapchick and Urdang, *Oppression and Resistance*, pp. 17-85.

# Chapter Seven

1. Borstelmann, *Apartheid's Reluctant Uncle*, p. 8.

2. See, e.g., January 25, 1956, presidential diary entry, Ann Whitman File, DDE Diary Series; see also undated pre-press conference briefing, Ann Whitman File, ACW Diary Series, both from DDE Library.

3. See March 22, 1956, Eisenhower letter to Rev. Graham, Ann Whitman File, DDE Diary Series, DDE Library.

4. June 18, 1959, memorandum regarding 410th NSC meeting, Ann Whitman File, NSC Series, DDE Library, pp. 3, 5-6.

5. *FRUS, 1958-1960, vol. XIV*, February 6, 1958, memorandum from the Secretary of State's Special Assistant (Holmes) to Secretary of State Dulles, pp. 2, 8-10.

6. See, e.g., November 5, 1959, memorandum regarding 423rd NSC meeting, Ann Whitman File, NSC Series, DDE Library.

7. See, e.g., Cress-Welsing, *The Isis Papers*, p. 33.

8. See, e.g., Michael Crowder, *West Africa Under Colonial Rule* (Evanston, IL: Northwestern University Press, 1968), p. 166.

9. See, e.g., July 29, 1960, briefing note for August 1, 1960, NSC meeting, Ann Whitman File, NSC Series, NSC Briefing Notes subseries, DDE Library.

10. Jan N. Pieterse and Bhikhu Parekh, "Shifting imagniaries: decolonization, internal decolonization, postcoloniality," in Jan N. Pieterse and Bhikhu Parekh, eds., *The Decolonization of the Imagination: Culture, Knowledge, and Power* (London: Zed Books, 1995), p. 14.

11. See Margaret M. Russell, "Race and the Dominant Gaze: Narratives of Law and Inequality in Popular Film," 15 *Legal Stud. F.* 243, 245 (1991).

12. Marion O'Callaghan, "Continuities in Imagination," in Pieterse and Parekh, eds., *The Decolonization of Imagination*, p. 22.

13. Ibid, p. 25.

14. Cress-Welsing, *The Isis Papers*, pp. 176-177.

15. See generally, Frantz Fanon, *The Wretched of the Earth*, trans. by Constance Farrington (New York: Grove Press, 1968).

16. See PCIAA #37, "Themes," OSANSA Records, Sprague Committee File, PCIAA Papers, DDE Library; July 26, 1960, Waldemar Nielsen, "Ten Major Points" memorandum to PCIAA, OSANSA Records, Sprague Committee File, Ten Major Points series, DDE Library.

17. See, e.g., Kenneth B. Clark, *Dark Ghetto: Dilemmas of Social Power* (New York: Harper and Row, 1967); Arnold R. Hirsch, *Making the Second Ghetto: Race and Housing in Chicago, 1940-1960* (Cambridge: Cambridge University Press, 1983); Morrow, *Black Man in the White House*; Von Eschen, *Race Against Empire*, pp. 124, 135, 167.

18. NSC 5719/1, p. 7.

19. Kelly, *America's Tyrant*, pp. 32-33.

20. Ibid., p. 35.

21. Amos N. Wilson, *The Falsification of Afrikan Consciousness: Eurocentric History, Psychiatry, and the Politics of White Supremacy* (New York: African World InfoSystems, 1993), pp. 70-77.

22. Ibid., p. 34.

23. Noer, *Cold War and Black Liberation*, pp. 12-15, 34-60.

24. Rodney, *How Europe Underdeveloped Africa*, p. 107.

25. August 25, 1960, memorandum regarding 456th NSC meeting, p. 9.

26. Henry Jackson, *From the Congo to Soweto: U.S. Foreign Policy Toward Africa Since 1960* (New York: William Morrow, 1982), pp. 169-201.

27. See Rodney, *How Europe Underdeveloped Africa*, p. 26.

28. Patrick Brantlinger, "'Dying Races': Rationalizing Genocide in the Nineteenth Century," in Pieterse and Parekh, eds., *The Decolonization of Imagination*, pp. 44-49; Reginald Horsman, *Race and Manifest Destiny: The Origins of American Racial Anglo-Saxonism* (Cambridge, MA: Harvard University Press, 1981), pp. 122-124, 129-137.

29. *FRUS 1958-1960, vol. XIV*, February 6, 1958, Holmes memo to Dulles, pp. 9-10.

30. The phrase and, in part, the idea are taken from Samir Amin, *Delinking: Towards a Polycentric World* (London: Zed Books, 1990); see also Rodney, *How Europe Underdeveloped Africa*, p. 26.

31. See August 25, 1960, memorandum regarding 456th NSC meeting; see also August 30, 1960, Staff Notes # 828, Ann Whitman File, DDE Diary Series, Toner Notes Series, DDE Library; see also Noer, "The New Frontier and African Neutralism," p. 63.

32. August 25, 1960, memorandum regarding 456th NSC meeting, p. 10.

33. See, e.g., Jackson, *From the Congo to Soweto*, p. 18; see also Peter Schraeder, "Speaking with Many Voices: Continuity and Change in U.S. Africa Policies," *The Journal of Modern African Studies* 29, no. 3 (1991), pp. 374-375.

34. *FRUS, 1958-1960, vol. XIV*, February 6, 1958, Holmes memorandum to Dulles, pp. 1-2, 5, 8-9.

35. See, e.g., Thomas Freidman, "World War III," *New York Times*, September 13, 2001; Thomas Friedman, "We Are Alone," *New York Times*, October 26, 2001.

36. See, e.g., "Defending Civilization: How Our Universities Are Failing America, and What Can Be Done About It," a report by the American Council of Trustees and Alumni, which can be viewed at www.goacta.org.

37. February 6, 1958, Holmes memo to Dulles, pp. 2,7.

38. See, e.g., Robert F. Burk, *The Eisenhower Administration an Black Civil Rights* (Knoxville: University of Tennessee Press, 1984), pp. 138-139.

39. See July 7, 1953, Eisenhower letter to Sen. Ralph Flanders, Ann Whitman File, DDE Diary; February 2, 1954, Eisenhower telephone conversation with Gen. Smith regarding Ho Chi Minh and the military situation in Indo-China, Ann Whitman File, DDE Diary, both from DDE Library.

40. O'Callaghan, "Continuities in Imagination," in Pieterse and Parekh, eds., *The Decolonization of Imagination*, p. 32.

41. Fuller, *The United Independent Compensatory Code/System/Concept*, p. 31.

42. See, e.g., Davidson, *African Civilization Revisited* (Trenton, NJ: Africa World Press, 1991); Stanley Lane-Poole, *The Moors in Spain* (London: T. Fisher Unwin, 1912); and Ivan Van Sertima, *They Came Before Columbus* (New York: Random House, 1976).

43. See, e.g., Basil Davidson, *African Civilization Revisited*, pp. 229-238; Richard L. Greaves et al., eds., *Civilizations of the World: The Human Adventure* 2nd edition (New York: HarperCollins, 1993), pp. 495-535, 657-670; J. A. Rogers, *World's Great Men of Color, vol. I* (New York: Touchstone edition, 1996), pp. 247-250; Fuller, *United Independent Compensatory Code/System/Concept*, p. 207.

44. McCormick, *America's Half-Century*, p. 118 (where the author discusses the Bandung Conference and the members' use of the term "Third World" as an articulation of their desire to remain aloof from the Western bloc-Soviet bloc struggle).

# SELECTED BIBLIOGRAPHY

## Manuscript Collections

### Dwight D. Eisenhower Presidential Library, Abilene, Kansas

*Ann Whitman File, ACW Diary Series*
*Ann Whitman File, DDE Diary Series*
*Ann Whitman File, International Series*
*Ann Whitman File, National Security Council Series*
*Christian Herter Papers*
*Christian Herter Papers, CAH Telephone Calls Series*
*Christian Herter Papers, Chronological File*
*Council on Foreign Economic Policy, Office of the Chairman Records, Randall Series*
*Council on Foreign Economic Policy, Policy Papers Series*
*Council on Foreign Economic Policy, Report Series*
*Dwight D. Eisenhower, Papers as President File, Cabinet Series*
*E. Frederick Morrow Papers, Special Projects Series*
*John Foster Dulles Papers, Telephone Call Series*
*John Foster Dulles Papers, General Correspondence and Memoranda Series*
*John Foster Dulles Papers, JFD Chronological Series*
*John Foster Dulles Papers, White House Memoranda Series*
*Office of the Special Assistant to the President for Personnel Management: Records 1953-1961*
*White House Central Files, Alphabetical Files Series, Autherine Lucy*
*White House Central Files, Alphabetical File Series, Emmett Till*
*White House Central Files, Official Files Series*
*White House Central Files, Official File Series, Council on Foreign Economic Policy*
*White House Central Files, Official File Series, Negro Matters—Colored Question*
*White House Office, National Security Council Staff Papers, Disaster File*
*White House Office, National Security Council Staff Papers, Operations Coordinating Board Central Files Series*
*White House Office, National Security Council Series, Policy Papers Subseries*
*White House Office, National Security Council Staff Papers*
*White House Office, Office of the Special Assistant for National Security Affairs Records*
*White House Office of the Staff Secretary Cabinet Series*
*White House Staff Files, Fred Morrow Papers*

## National Archives and Records Administration
*Miscellaneous Records of the Bureau of Public Affairs, U.S. Department of State*

## Seeley G. Mudd Library, Princeton University
*John Foster Dulles Oral History Collection*
*Clarence Randall Papers*
*Adlai Stevenson Papers*

# Books

Adams, Ephraim, *Great Britain and the American Civil War* (New York: Russell & Russell, 1958).

Agbodeka, Francis, *African Politics and British Policy in the Gold Coast 1868-1900* (Evanston, IL: Northwestern University Press, 1971).

Agee, Phillip, *Inside the Company: CIA Diary* (New York: Stonehill, 1975).

Agyeman, Opoku, *Nkrumah's Ghana and East Africa: Pan-Africanism and African Interstate Relations* (Cranbury, NJ: Associated University Press, 1992).

"Alleged Assassination Plots Involving Foreign Leaders," *An Interim Report of the Senate Select Committee to Study Governmental Operations with Respect to Intelligence Activities*, United States Senate (Washington, DC: U.S. Government Printing Office, 1975).

Allen, Robert L., *The Port Chicago Mutiny: The Story of the Largest Mass Mutiny Trial in U.S. Naval History* (New York: Amistad Press, 1993).

Aluko, Olajide, *Ghana and Nigeria 1957-70: A Study in Inter-African Discord* (New York: Barnes and Noble Books, 1976).

Ambrose, Stephen E., *Rise to Globalism: American Foreign Policy Since 1938* (New York: Penguin Books, 4th edition, 1985).

Amin, Samir, *Eurocentrism* (New York: Monthly Review Press, 1989).

———, *Delinking: Towards a Polycentric World* (London: Zed Books, 1990).

Ani, Marimba, *Yurugu: An African-Centered Critique of European Cultural Thought and Behavior* (Trenton, NJ: Africa World Press, 1994).

Aptheker, Herbert, *John Brown: American Martyr* (New York: New Century Publishers, 1960).

Astor, Gerald, *And a Credit to His Race: The Hard Life and Times of Joseph Louis Barrow, a.k.a. Joe Louis* (New York: E. P. Dutton, 1974).

Avey, Elijah, *The Capture and Execution of John Brown: A Tale of Martyrdom* (Chicago: Afro-Am Press, 1969).

Awoonor, Kofi, *The Breast of the Earth: A Survey of the History, Culture and Literature of Africa South of the Sahara* (Garden City, NY: Anchor Press, 1975).

Barlow, William, "Commercial and Noncommercial Radio," in Janette L. Dates and William Barlow, eds., *Split Image: African Americans in the Mass Media* (Washington, DC: Howard University Press, 1990).

Barrett, James, *Work and Community in the Jungle: Chicago's Packinghouse Workers, 1894-1922* (Urbana: University of Illinois Press, 1990).

Bell, Derrick, *Race, Racism and American Law* (Boston, MA: Little, Brown & Company, 2nd edition 1980).

Bell, Derrick A., *And We Are Not Saved* (New York: Basic Books, 1987).

———, *Faces at the Bottom of the Well: The Permanence of Racism* (New York: Basic Books, 1992).

Bell, Sidney, *Righteous Conquest: Woodrow Wilson and the Evolution of the New Diplomacy* (Pt. Washington, NY: National Universities Publications, 1992).

Bennett, Lerone, *Before the Mayflower: A History of Black America* (New York: Penguin Books, 5th edition, 1982).

Berat, Lynn, *Walvis Bay: Decolonization and International Law* (New Haven, CT: Yale University Press, 1990).

Berlin, Ira, and Ronald Hoffman, eds., *Slavery and Freedom in the Age of the American Revolution* (Charlottesville: University of Virginia Press, 1983).

Berry, Mary F., *Military Necessity and Civil Rights Policy* (Port Washington, NY: Kennikat Press Corp., 1977).

Berwanger, Eugene, *The British Foreign Service and the American Civil War* (Lexington: University of Kentucky Press, 1994).

Besteman, Catherine, "Out Migration," in Helen K. Henderson and Ellen Hansen, eds., *Gender and Agricultural Development: Surveying the Field* (Tucson: University of Arizona Press, 1995).

Blum, William, *The CIA: A Forgotten History* (London: Zed Books, 1986).

Bogle, Donald L., *Blacks in American Films and Television: An Illustrated Encyclopedia* (New York: Simon & Schuster, 1989).

Borstelmann, Thomas, *Apartheid's Reluctant Uncle: The United States and Southern Africa in the Early Cold War* (New York: Oxford University Press, 1993).

Bowie, Robert, and Richard Immerman, *Waging Peace: How Eisenhower Shaped an Enduring Cold War Strategy* (New York: Oxford University Press, 1998).

Boyer, Richard O., *The Legend of John Brown: A Biography and A History* (New York: Alfred A. Knopf, 1973).

Brack, Gene, *Mexico Views Manifest Destiny, 1821-1846: An Essay on the Origins of the Mexican War* (Albuquerque: University of New Mexico Press, 1975).

Brands, H. W., *India and The United States: The Cold Peace* (Boston, MA: Twayne Publishers, 1990).

Brown, Dee, *Bury My Heart At Wounded Knee: An Indian History of the American West* (New York: Washington Square Press, 1981).

Brown, Elaine, *A Taste of Power: A Black Woman's Story* (New York: Doubleday, 1992).

Brown, Elsa B., "To Catch the Vision of Freedom: Reconstructing Southern Black Women's Political History, 1865-1880," in Ann D. Gordon et al., eds., *African American Women and the Vote, 1837-1965* (Amherst: University of Massachusetts Press, 1997).

Burton, David H. *Theodore Roosevelt, American Politician: An Assessment* (Teaneck, NJ: Fairleigh Dickinson University Press and Associated University Presses, 1997).

Burton, David, *Theodore Roosevelt: Confident Imperialist* (Philadelphia: University of Pennsylvania Press, 1968).

Calhoun, Frederick S., *Uses of Force and Wilsonian Foreign Policy* (Kent, OH: Kent State University Press, 1993).

Cecelski, David, and Timothy B. Tyson, eds., *Democracy Betrayed: The Wilmington Race Riot of 1898* (Chapel Hill: University of North Carolina Press, 1998).

Chafe, William H., *Civilians and Civil Liberties: Greensboro, North Carolina and the Black Struggle for Freedom* (Oxford: Oxford University Press, 1981).

Chamallas, Martha, *Introduction to Feminist Legal Theory* (Gaithersburg, MD: Aspen Law & Business Publishers, 1999).

Chamberlain, Greg, "Up by the Roots: Haitian History Through 1987," in Diedre McFayden et al., eds., *Haiti: Dangerous Crossroads* (Boston: South End Press, 1995).

Chancy, Myriam J. A., *Framing Silence: Revolutionary Novels By Haitian Women* (New Brunswick, NJ: Rutgers University Press, 1997).

Chester, Edward, *Clash of Titans: Africa and U.S. Foreign Policy* (Maryknoll, NY: Orbis Books, 1974).

Chideya, Farai, *Don't Believe the Hype: Fighting Cultural Misinformation About African Americans* (New York: Plume Books, 1995).

Chinweizu, *The West and the Rest of Us: White Predators, Black Slavers, and the African Elite* (New York: Random House, 1975).

Claridge, W. Walton, *A History of the Gold Coast and Ashanti: From the Earliest Times to the Commencement of the Twentieth Century* (New York: Barnes & Noble, 1915).

Clark, E. Culpepper, *The Schoolhouse Door: Segregation's Last Stand at the University of Alabama* (New York: Oxford University Press, 1993).

Clark, Gracia, *Onions Are My Husband: Survival and Accumulation By West African Market Women* (Chicago: University of Chicago Press, 1994).

Clark, Kenneth B., *Dark Ghetto: Dilemmas of Social Power* (New York: Harper and Row, 1967).

Clarke, John H., *Notes for An African World Revolution: Africans at the Crossroads* (Trenton, NJ: Africa World Press, 1991).

Clarke, John H., ed., *New Dimensions in African History* (Trenton, NJ: Africa World Press, 1991).

Cohen, Lizbeth, *Making A New Deal: Industrial Workers In Chicago, 1919-1939* (Cambridge: Cambridge University Press, 1990).

Cohen, William, *At Freedom's Edge: Black Mobility and the Southern White Quest for Racial Control, 1861-1915* (Baton Rouge: Louisiana State University Press, 1991).

Collier-Thomas, Betty, "Frances Ellen Watkins Harper: Abolitionist and Feminist Reformer, 1825-1911," in Ann D. Gordon et al., eds., *African American Women and the Vote, 1837-1965* (Amherst: University of Massachusetts Press, 1997).

Collin, Richard, *Theodore Roosevelt's Carribean: The Panama Canal, the Monroe Doctrine, and the Latin American Context* (Baton Rouge: Louisiana State University Press, 1990).

Cone, James, *Martin & Malcolm & America: A Dream or a Nightmare* (Maryknoll, NY: Orbis Books, 1992).

Connelley, William E., *John Brown* (Freeport, NY: New York Books for Libraries Press reprint, 1971).

Cooper, Anna J., *Slavery and the French Revolutionists (1788-1805)*, with an introduction by Frances R. Keller (Lewiston, NY: The Edwin Mellen Press, 1988).

Cottrol, Robert J., ed., *From African to Yankee: Narratives of Slavery and Freedom in Antebellum New England* (London: M. E. Sharpe, 1998).

Cover, Robert M., *Justice Accused: Antislavery and the Judicial Process* (New Haven: Yale University Press, 1975).

Crook, D. P., *The North, the South, and the Powers, 1861-1865* (New York: John Wiley & Sons, 1974).

Crow-Dog, Mary, *Lakota Woman* (New York: Harper Perennial, 1991).

Crowder, Michael, *West Africa Under Colonial Rule* (Evanston, IL: Northwest University Press, 1968).

————, *Senegal: A Study in French Assimilation Policy* (London: Methuen, 1967).

Cruse, Harold, *The Crisis of the Negro Intellectual A Historical Analysis of the Failure of Black Leadership* (New York: Quill Books reprint, 1984)

D'Orso, Michael, *Like Judgment Day: The Ruin and Redemption of A Town Called Rosewood* (New York: Boulevard Books, 1996).

Dallek, Robert, *Franklin D. Roosevelt and American Foreign Policy, 1932-1945*, (Oxford: Oxford University Press, 1979).

————, *The American Style of Foreign Policy: Cultural Politics and Foreign Affairs* (New York: Alfred A. Knopf, 1983).

Danaher, Kevin, *50 Years Is Enough: The Case Against the World Bank and the International Monetary Fund* (Boston, MA: South End Press, 1994).

Daniels, Jessie, *White Lies: Race, Class, Gender, and Sexuality in White Supremacist Discourse* (New York: Routledge, 1997).

Dash, Michael, *Haiti and the United States: National Stereotypes and the Literary Imagination* (Houndsmill, Basingstoke: Macmillan Press, 1997).

Davidson, Basil, *Let Freedom Come: Africa in Modern History* (Boston: Little Brown & Co., 1978).

————, *No Fist is Big Enough to Hide the Sky: The Liberation of Guinea-Bissau and Cape Verde* (London: Zed Press, 1981).

————, *Black Star: A View of the Life and Times of Kwame Nkrumah* (London: Allen Lane, 1973).

Davis, David B., *Slavery and Human Progress* (Oxford: Oxford University Press, 1984).

————, *The Problem of Slavery in Western Culture*, (Oxford: Oxford University Press, 1966).

de Villiers, Simon A., ed., *Otto Landsberg, 1803-1905: Nineteenth-Century South African Artist* (Cape Town: C. Struik, 1974).

De Villiers, Cas, *African Problems and Challenges* (Sandton, South Africa: Valiant, 1976).

DeConde, Alexander, *Ethnicity, Race, and American Foreign Policy: A History* (Boston: Northeastern University Press, 1992).

Degler, Carl N., *The Other South: Southern Dissenters in the Nineteenth Century* (Boston: Northeastern University Press, 1982).

Delany, Martin, *The Condition, Elevation, Emigration and Destiny of the Colored People in the United States* (Salem, NH: Ayer Co. Publishers, reprint edition, 1988).

DeLeon, Arnaldo *They Called Them Greasers: Anglo Attitudes Towards Mexicans in Texas* (Austin: University of Texas Press, 1983).

Dhada, Mustafah, *Warriors At Work: How Guinea Was Really Set Free* (Niwot: University Press of Colorado, 1993).

Dicks, Barbara A., and Eddie S. Bogle, "Sociocultural Aspects of Ethiopian Women's Contributions to Agriculture," in Valentine U. James, *Women and Sustainable Development in Africa* (Westport, CT: Praeger Publishers, 1995).

Divine, Robert A., *Roosevelt and World War II* (Baltimore. MD: Johns Hopkins University Press, 1969).

Douglass, Frederick, *Narrative of the Life of Frederick Douglass* as reprinted in Henry L. Gates and Nellie Y. McKay, eds., *The Norton Anthology of African American Literature* (New York: W. W. Norton and Co., 1997).

Drago, Edmund L., *Black Politicians and Reconstruction in Georgia: A Splendid Failure* (Athens: University of Georgia Press, 1992).

Duberman, Martin, *Paul Robeson: A Biography* (New York: The New Press, 1989).

DuBois, Ellen C., *Feminism and Suffrage: The Emergence of an Independent Women's Movement in America, 1848-1869* (Ithaca, NY: Cornell University Press, 1978).

DuBois, W. E. B., *The Souls of Black Folk* (New York: Signet Classic Series, 1982).

———, W. E. B., *Black Reconstruction in America, 1860-1880* (New York: Atheneum edition, 1992).

———, W. E. B., *John Brown* (Millwood, NY: Kraus-Thomson Organization, 1973).

Dudziak, Mary, *Cold War Civil Rights: Race and the Image of American Democracy* (Princeton, NJ: Princeton University Press, 2000).

Duignan, Peter, and L.H. Gann, *The United State and Africa: A History* (Cambridge: Cambridge University Press, 1984).

Dunn, D. Elwood, *The Foreign Policy of Liberia During the Tubman Era, 1944-1971* (London: Hutchinson Books, 1979).

Dupuy, Alex, *Haiti in the New World Order: The Limits of the Democratic Revolution* (Boulder, CO: Westview Press, 1997).

Dyer, Thomas G., *Theodore Roosevelt and the Idea of Race* (Baton Rouge: Louisiana State University Press, 1980).

Dyson, Walter, *Howard University, The Capstone of Negro Education: A History, 1867-1940* (Washington, DC: Howard University Press, 1941).

Eisen, Jonathan, *The Age of Rock: Sounds of the Cultural Revolution; a Reader* (New York: Random House, 1969).

Eisenhower, Dwight D., *Waging Peace: The White House Years; A Personal Account 1956-1961* (Garden City, NY: Doubleday, 1965).

Ekrich, Arthur A. Jr., *Ideologies and Utopias: The Input of the New Deal on American Thought* (Chicago, IL: Quadrangle Books, 1969).

Ellsworth, Scott, *Death in a Promised Land: The Tulsa Race Riot of 1921* (Baton Rouge: Louisiana State University Press, 1982).

Escott, Colin, *All Roads Lead to Rock: Legends of Early Rock and Roll* (New York: Schrimer Books, 1999).

Esedebe, P. O., *Pan-Africanism: The Idea and Movement, 1776-1963* (Washington, DC: Howard University Press, 1982).

Fage, J. D., *Ghana: A Historical Interpretation* (Madison: University of Wisconsin Press, 1959).

Fahim, Hussein M., *Egyptian Nubians: Resettlement and Years of Coping* (Salt Lake City: University of Utah Press, 1983).

Fanon, Frantz, *Black Skin, White Masks* (New York: Grove Weidenfeld, 1967).

Fass, Simon, *Political Economy in Haiti: the Drama of Survival* (New Brunswick, NJ: Transaction Books, 1990).

Feagin, Joe R., "Old Poison in New Bottles: The Deep Roots of Modern Nativism," in Juan F. Perea, ed., *Immigrants Out! The New Nativism and the Anti-Immigrant Impulse in the United States* (New York: New York University Press, 1997).

Fehrenbacher, Don E., ed., *Slavery and Its Consequences: The Constitution, Equality, and Race* (Washington, DC: American Enterprise Institute for Public Policy Research, 1988).

Feis, Herbert, *Churchill, Roosevelt, Stalin: The War They Waged and The Peace They Sought* (Princeton, NJ: Princeton University Press, 1957).

Fenelon, James, *Culturicide, Resistance, and Survival of the Lakota (Sioux Nation)* (New York: Garland Publishing, Inc., 1998).

Fieldhouse, David K., *Black Africa, 1945-1980: Economic Decolonization and Arrested Development* (London: Allen & Unwin, 1986).

———, *The West and the Third World: Trade, Colonialism, Dependence, and Development* (Oxford: Blackwell, 1999).

———, *Merchant Capital and Economic Decolonization: the United Africa Company, 1929-1987* (Oxford: Clarendon Press; New York: Oxford University Press, 1994).

———, "Arrested Development in Anglophone Black Africa?" in Prosser Gifford and William Roger Louis, eds., *Decolonization and African Independence: The Transfers of Power, 1960-1980* (New Haven, CT: Yale University Press, 1988).

Finkleman, Paul, ed., *His Soul is Marching On: Responses to John Brown and the Harper's Ferry Raid* (Charlottesville: University of Virginia Press, 1995).

———, *Dred Scott v. Sandford: A Brief History with Documents* (Boston, MA: Bedford Books, 1997).

Fite, Emerson, *Social and Industrial Conditions in the North During the Civil War* (New York: Unger reprint edition 1963).

Foner, Eric, *Reconstruction: America's Unfinished Revolution, 1863-1877* (New York: Harper & Row, 1989).

*Foreign Relations of the United States, 1958-1960: Volume XIV, Africa* (Washington, DC: United States Government Printing Office, 1989).

*Foreign Relations of the United States, 1955-1957: Volume XVIII, Africa* (Washington, DC: United States Government Printing Office, 1989).

Fox, Stephen R., *The Guardian of Boston: William Monroe Trotter* (New York: Atheneum, 1970).

Franck, Thomas and John Carey, *The Legal Aspects of the United Nations Action in the Congo* (Dobbs Ferry, NY: Oceana Publications, Inc., for the Association of the Bar of the City of New York, 1963).

Fredrickson, George M., *The Arrogance of Race: Historical Perspectives on Slavery, Racism, and Social Inequality* (Middletown, CT: Wesleyan University Press, 1988).

———, *White Supremacy: A Comparative Study in American and South African History*, (Oxford: Oxford University Press, 1981).

Friedenberg, Robert V., *Theodore Roosevelt and the Rhetoric of Militant Decency* (New York: Greenwood Press, 1990).

Frommer, Harvey, *Rickey and Robinson* (New York: Macmillan, 1982).

Gaddis, John, *Strategies of Containment: A Critical Appraisal of Postwar American National Security Policy* (Oxford: Oxford University Press, 1982).

Galeano, Eduardo, *Open Veins of Latin America: Five Centuries of the Pillage of Latin America* (New York: Monthly Review Press, 1973).

Gatewood, William B. Jr., *Theodore Roosevelt and the Art of Controversy: Episodes of the White House Years* (Baton Rouge: Louisiana University Press, 1970).

Genovese, Eugene D., *Roll, Jordan, Roll: The World the Slaves Made* (New York: Vintage Books, 1976).

George, Nelson, *The Death of Rhythm and Blues* (New York: Plume Books, 1988).

Gibbs, David N., *The Political Economy of Third World Intervention: Mines, Money and U.S. Policy in the Congo Crisis* (Chicago: University of Chicago Press, 1991).

Gilmore, Al-Tony, *Bad Nigger! The National Impact of Jack Johnson* (Port Washington, NY: Kennikat Press, 1975).

Glatthaar, Joseph T., *Forged In Battle: The Civil War Alliance of Black Soldiers and White Officers* (New York: Meridian Books, 1990).

Greaves, Richard L., et al., *Civilizations of the World: The Human Adventure* (HarperCollins College Publishers, 2nd edition, 1993).

Gutman, Herbert G., *Work, Culture, and Society in Industrializing America* (New York: Knopf, 1977).

Guyer, Jane I., "Women in the Rural Economy: Contemporary Variations," in Margaret J. Hay and Sharon Stichter, *African Women South of the Sahara* (London: Longman Group, 1984).

Hale, Grace E., *Making Whiteness: The Culture of Segregation in the South, 1890-1940* (New York: Vintage Books, 1999)

Haley, Alex, and Malcolm X, *The Autobiography of Malcolm X* (New York: Ballantine Books, 1973).

Hall, Michael R., *Sugar and Power in the Dominican Republic: Eisenhower, Kennedy, and the Trujillos* (Westport, CT: Greenwood Press, 2000).

Halliburton, R., *The Tulsa Race War of 1921* (San Francisco: R & E Research Associates, 1975).

Hamilton, Alexander, John Jay, and James Madison, *The Federalist* (New York: Random House, 1932), pp. 53-69 (encompassing federalist papers # 10 and 11).

Hamilton, Charles V., *Adam Clayton Powell, Jr.: The Political Biography of an American Dilemma* (New York: Atheneum, 1991).

Harding, Vincent, *There Is a River: The Black Struggle for Freedom in America* (New York: Harcourt, Brace, Jovanovich, 1981).

Harley, Sharon, and Rosalyn Terborg-Penn, *The Afro-American Woman: Struggles and Images* (Port Washington, NY: Kennikat Press, 1978).

Harris, Robert L. Jr., "Racial Equality and the United Nations Charter," in Michael Krenn, ed., *Race and U.S. Foreign Policy During the Cold War* (New York: Garland Publishers, 1998).

Heald, Morrell, and Laurence S. Kaplan, *Culture and Diplomacy: The American Experience* (Westport, CT: Greenwood Press, 1977).

Healy, David, *Gunboat Diplomacy in the Wilson Era: The U.S. Navy in Haiti, 1915-1916* (Madison: University of Wisconsin Press, 1976).

Heater, Derek, *National Self-Determination: Woodrow Wilson and His Legacy* (New York: St. Martin's Press, 1994).

Heinrichs, Waldo, *Threshold of War: Franklin D. Roosevelt and American Entry into World War II* (New York: Oxford University Press, 1988).

Hempstone, Smith, *Rebels, Mercenaries, and Dividends: The Katanga Story* (New York: Praeger Publishers, 1962).

Henri, Florette, *Black Migration: Movement North, 1900-1920* (New York: Anchor Press, 1975).

Henrickson, Alan K., "Mental Maps," in Michael Hogan and Thomas Paterson, eds., *Explaining the History of American Foreign Relations* (Cambridge: Cambridge University Press, 1991).

Hietala, Thomas, *Manifest Design: Anxious Aggrandizement in Late Jacksonian America* (Ithaca, NY: Cornell University Press, 1985).

Higginbotham, A. Leon, *In the Matter of Color: Race and the American Legal Process; The Colonial Period* (Oxford: Oxford University Press, 1977).

Higginbotham, Evelyn B., *Righteous Discontent: The Women's Movement in the Black Baptist Church, 1880-1920* (Cambridge, MA: Harvard University Press, 1993).

Hilliard, David, *The Autobiography of David Hilliard and the Story of the Black Panthers* (Boston, MA: Little, Brown & Co., 1993).

Hine, Darlene C., "Black Migration to the Urban Midwest: The Gender Dimension, 1915-1945," in Joe W. Trotter, ed., *The Great Migration in Historical Perspective: New Dimensions of Race, Class, and Gender* (Bloomington: Indiana University Press, 1991).

Hine, Darlene C., et al., eds., *Black Women in America: An Historical Encyclopedia* (Brooklyn, NY: Carlson Publishing, Inc.)

Hofstadter, Richard, *Anti-Intellectualism in American Life* (New York: Vintage Books, 1963).

Holmes, Alexander, "What Was the Nationalism of the 1930's in Ghana?" in Paul Jenkins et al., eds., *Akyem Abuakwa and the Politics of the Inter-war Period in Ghana* (Basler: Afrika Bibliographien, 1975).

Holt, Thomas, *Black Over White: Negro Political Leadership in South Carolina During Reconstruction* (Urbana: University of Illinois Press, 1979).

hooks, bell, "Overcoming White Supremacy: A Comment," in *Talking Back: Thinking Feminist, Thinking Black* (Boston: South End Press, 1989).

———, *Teaching to Transgress: Education as the Practice of Freedom* (New York: Routledge, 1994).

Hoopes, Townsend, and Douglas Brinkley, *FDR and the Creation of the U.N.* (New Haven: University Press, 1997).

Horne, Gerald, *Black Liberation/Red Scare: Ben Davis and the Communist Party* (Newark: University of Delaware Press, 1994).

Hoskyns, Catherine, *The Congo: A Chronology of Events, January 1960-December 1961* (Oxford: Oxford University Press, 1962).

House-Midamba, Bessie and Felix K. Ekechi, eds., *African Market Women and Economic Power: The Role of Women in African Economic Development* (Westport, CT: Greenwood Press, 1995)

Hunt, Michael, *Ideology and U.S. Foreign Policy* (New Haven, CT: Yale University Press, 1987).

Hunter, Tera W., "Domination and Resistance: The Politics of Wage Household Labor in New South Atlanta," in Darlene C. Hine et al., eds., *We Specialize in the Wholly Impossible: A Reader in Black Women's History* (Brooklyn, NY: Carlson, 1995).

Hurston, Zora N., "Blacks, Whites, and Work," in David R. Roediger, ed., *Black on White: Black Writers On What It Means to Be White* (New York: Schocken Books, 1998).

Ignatiev, Noel, *How the Irish Became White* (New York: Routledge, 1995).

Iliffe, John, *Tanganyika Under German Rule, 1905-1912* (London: Cambridge University Press, 1969).

Jackson, Henry, *From the Congo to Soweto: U.S. Foreign Policy Toward Africa Since 1960* (New York: William Morrow, 1982).

Jacobson, Harold K., "The Changing United Nations," in Roger Hilsman and Robert C. Good, eds., *Foreign Policy in the Sixties: The Issues and the Instruments-Essays in Honor of Arnold Wolfers* (Baltimore, MD: Johns Hopkins University Press, 1965).

Jalata, Asafa, *Oromo Nationalism and the Ethiopian Discourse: The Search for Freedom and Democracy* (Lawrenceville, NJ: The Red Sea Press, Inc. 1998).

James, Alan, *Britain and the Congo Crisis, 1960-63* (Houndmills and London: Macmillan, 1996).

James, C. L. R., *The Black Jacobins; Toussaint L'Ouverture and the San Domingo Revolution* (New York: Vintage Books, 2nd revised edition, 1963).

Jenkins, Wilbert, *Seizing the New Day: African Americans in Post-Civil War Charleston* (Bloomington: Indiana University Press, 1998).

Johnson, Jack, *Jack Johnson is a Dandy* (New York: Chelsea House Publishers reprint, 1969).

Johnstone, Frederick A., *Class, Race and Gold: A Study of Class Relations and Racial Discrimination in South Africa* (London: Routledge & K. Paul, 1976).

Jones, Howard, *Union in Peril: The Crisis Over British Intervention in the Civil War* (Chapel Hill: University of North Carolina Press, 1992).

Jones, Jacqueline, *Labor of Love, Labor of Sorrow: Black Women, Work and the Family, From Slavery to the Present* (New York: Vintage Books, 1985).

Jordan, Winthrop D., *White Over Black: American Attitudes toward the Negro, 1550-1812* (Chapel Hill: University of North Carolina Press, 1968).

Jordanova, Ludmilla, *Sexual Visions: Images of Gender In Science and Medicine Between the Eighteenth and Nineteenth Centuries* (Madison: University of Wisconsin Press, 1989).

Juckes, Tim, *Opposition in South Africa: The Leadership of Z. K. Matthews, Nelson Mandela, and Stephen Biko* (Westport, CT: Praeger Publishers, 1995).

Kahin, Audrey R., and George McT., *Subversion as Foreign Policy: the Secret Eisenhower and Dulles Debacle in Indonesia* (New York: New Press, 1995).

Kalb, Madeline, *The Congo Cables: The Cold War in Africa—From Eisenhower to Kennedy* (New York: Macmillan, 1982).

Karis, Thomas, and Gwendolen M. Carter, eds., *From Protest to Challenge: a Documentary History of African Politics in South Africa, 1882-1964* (Stanford, CA: Hoover Institution Press, 1972).

Katz, Robert, *Black Indians: A Hidden Heritage* (New York: Atheneum, 1986).

Keller, Allen, *Thunder at Harper's Ferry* (Englewood Cliffs, NJ: Prentice-Hall, 1958).

Kelley, Robin D. G., *Hammer and Hoe, Alabama Communists During the Great Depression* (Chapel Hill: University of North Carolina Press, 1990).

Kelly, Sean, *America's Tyrant; The CIA and Mobutu of Zaire: How the United States Put Mobutu in Power, Protected Him from His Enemies, Helped Him Become One of the Richest Men in the World and Lived to Regret It* (Washington, DC: The American University Press, 1993).

Kenan, Randall, "Let the Dead Bury the Dead," as excerpted in Herb Boyd and Robert A. Allen, eds., *Brotherman: The Odyssey of Black Men in America—An Anthology* (New York: Ballantine Books, 1995).

Kimball, Warren F., *Forged In War: Roosevelt, Churchill and the Second World War* (New York: William Morrow, 1997).

———, *The Juggler: Franklin Roosevelt As Wartime Statesman* (Princeton, NJ: Princeton, University Press, 1991).

———, "US Economic Strategy in World War II: Wartime Goals, Peacetime Plans," in Warren F. Kimball, ed., *American Unbound: World War II and the Making of a Superpower* (New York: St. Martin's Press, 1992).

King, Martin L. Jr., *Letter From Birmingham City Jail* (Philadelphia: American Friends Service Committee, 1963).

Kiwanuka, M. Semakula, "Colonial Policies and Administrations in Africa: The Myth of Contrast," in Gregory Maddox, ed., *The Colonial Epoch in Africa* (New York: Garland Publishing, 1993), pp. 1-21.

Kluger, Richard, *Simple Justice: The History of Brown v. Board of Education and Black America's Struggle for Equality* (New York: Vintage Books, 1977).

Knock, Thomas J., *To End All Wars: Woodrow Wilson and the Quest For a New World Order* (New York and Oxford: Oxford University Press, 1992).

Knupfer, Anne M., *Toward a Tenderer Humanity and a Nobler Womanhood: African American Women's Clubs in Turn-of-the-Century Chicago* (New York: New York University Press, 1996).

Kolko, Gabriel, *Confronting the Third World: U.S. Foreign Policy, 1945-1980* (New York: Pantheon Books, 1988).

Koning, Hans, *Columbus: His Enterprise* (New York: Monthly Review Press, 2nd edition, 1991).

Kurland, Phillip B., and Gerhard Casper, eds., *Landmark Briefs and Arguments of the Supreme Court of the United States: Constitutional Law*, vol. 49 (Bethesda, MD: University Publications of America, 1975).

Kusmer, Kenneth, *A Ghetto Takes Shape: The Making of Black Cleveland, 1870-1930* (Urbana: University of Illinois Press, 1976).

Lane, Ann J., *The Brownsville Affair* (Pt. Washington, NY: Kennikat Press, 1971).

Langston, Thomas S., *Ideologues and Presidents: From the New Deal to the Reagan Revolution* (Baltimore, MD: Johns Hopkins University Press, 1992).

Lapchick, Richard E., and Stephanie Urdang, *Oppression and Resistance: The Struggle of Women in Southern Africa* (Westport, CT: Greenwood Press, 1982).

Lebsock, Suzanne, *The Free Women of Petersburg: Status and Culture in a Southern Town* (New York: W.W. Norton, 1984).

Leffler, Melvyn, *A Preponderance of Power: National Security, the Truman Administration, and the Cold War* (Stanford, CA: Stanford University Press, 1992).

Lewis, David L., *W. E. B. DuBois: Biography of a Race, 1868-1919* (New York: Henry Holt, 1993).

Lewis, Herbert S., "The Development of Oromo Political Consciousness from 1958 to 1994," in P. T. W. Baxter, Jan Hutlin, and Alessandro Triulzi, eds., *Being and Becoming Oromo: Historical and Anthropological Enquiries* (Lawrenceville, NJ: The Red Sea Press, Inc., 1996).

Lewis, Ronald, *Black Coal Miners in America: Race, Class, and Community Conflict, 1780-1980* (Lexington: University of Kentucky Press, 1987).

Link, Arthur S., ed. and trans., *The Deliberations of the Council of Four: Notes of the Official Interpreter*, vol. I and II (Princeton, NJ: Princeton University Press, 1992).

———, *The Higher Realism of Woodrow Wilson and Other Essays* (Nashville, TN: Vanderbilt University Press, 1971).

Lipsitz, George, *The Possessive Investment in Whiteness: How White People Profit From Identity Politics* (Philadelphia: Temple University Press, 1998).

Little, Tom, *Modern Egypt* (New York: Praeger, 1967).

Litwack, Leon, *Been in the Storm So Long: The Aftermath of Slavery* (New York: Vintage Books, 1979).

———, Leon, *North of Slavery: The Negro in the Free States, 1790-1860* (Chicago: University of Chicago Press, 1961).

Liu, Xiaoyuan, *A Partnership for Disorder: China, the United States, and Their Policies for the Postwar Disposition of the Japanese Empire, 1941-1945* (New York: Cambridge University Press, 1996).

Lobban, Richard, and Marilyn Halter, *Historical Dictionary of the Republic of Cape Verde* (Metuchen, NJ: The Scarecrow Press, 2nd edition, 1988).

Logan, Rayford W., *The Diplomatic Relations of the United States with Haiti, 1776-1891* (Chapel Hill: University of North Carolina Press, 1941).

———, *Haiti and the Dominican Republic* (New York: Oxford University Press, 1968).

———, *The Betrayal of the Negro: From Rutherford B. Hayes to Woodrow Wilson* (New York: Da Capo Press, 1997).

Louis, Joe, *Joe Louis, My Life* (New York: Harcourt, Brace, Jovanovich, 1978).

Louis, William R., *Imperialism At Bay, 1941-1945: The United States and the Decolonization of the British Empire* (New York: Oxford University Press, 1978).

Louis, William R. and Ronald Robinson, "The United States and the Liquidation of the British Empire in Tropical Africa, 1941-1951," in Prosser Gifford and William Roger Louis, eds., *The Transfer of Power in Africa: Decolonization, 1940-1960* (New Haven, CT: Yale University Press, 1982).

Lugard, Frederick D., *The Dual Mandate in British Tropical Africa* (Hamden, CT: Archon Books, reprinted 1965).

Lumumba, Patrice, *Congo, My Country* (New York: Praeger Publishers, 1962).

Lundahl, Mats, *Politics or Markets? Essays on Haitian Underdevelopment* (London: Routledge Press, 1992).

Luthuli, Albert, *Let My People Go* (New York: McGraw-Hill, 1962).

Lynd, Staughton, *Class Conflict, Slavery, and the United States Constitution: Ten Essays* (Indianapolis, IN: Bobbs-Merrill Publishers 1967).

MacDonald, J. Fred, *Blacks and White TV: African Americans in Television Since 1948* (Chicago: Nelson-Hall Publishers, 1992).

Maddox, Gregory, ed., *African Nationalism and Revolution* (New York: Garland Publishing, 1993).

Magubane, Bernard, "The Evolution of the Class Structure in Africa," in P. C. W. Gutkind and Immanuel M. Wallerstein, eds., *The Political Economy of Contemporary Africa* (Beverly Hills, CA: Sage Publications, 1976).

———, *The Making of a Racist State: British Imperialism and the Union of South Africa, 1875-1910* (Trenton, NJ: Africa World Press, 1996).

Manning, M. M., *Slave in a Box: the Strange Career of Aunt Jemima* (Charlottesville: University Press of Virginia, 1998).

Marcum, John A., *The Angolan Revolution* (Cambridge, MA: MIT Press, 1978).

Marcus, Harold, *Ethiopia, Great Britain, and the United States, 1941-1974: The Politics of Empire* (Berkeley: University of California Press, 1983).

Marks, Frederick W. III, *Velvet on Iron: The Diplomacy of Theodore Roosevelt* (Lincoln: University of Nebraska Press, (1979).

Marquard, Leo, *The Peoples and Policies of South Africa* (London: Oxford University Press, 1969).

Martelli, George, *Leopold to Lumumba: A History of the Congo, 1877-1960* (London: Chapman & Hall, 1962).

Martin, Tony, *Race First: The Ideological and Organizational Struggles of Marcus Garvey and the Universal Negro Improvement Association* (Dover, MA: The Majority Press, 1986).

Martin, Waldo, "Frederick Douglass: Humanist as Race Leader," in Leon Litwack and August Meier, eds., *Black Leaders of the Nineteenth Century* (Urbana: University of Illinois Press, 1988).

Martin, Eveline, *The British West African Settlements: A Study in Local Administration* (London: Pub. for the Royal Colonial Institute, 1927).

Massey, Douglas S., and Nancy A. Denton, *American Apartheid: Segregation and the Making of the Underclass* (Cambridge, MA: Harvard University Press, 1993).

May, Ernest R., ed., *American Cold War Strategy: Interpreting NSC 68* (Boston, MA: Bedford Books of St. Martin's Press, 1993).

McClintock, Anne, "The Very House of Difference: Race, Gender, and Politics of South African Women's Narrative in *Poppie Nongena*," in Dominick LaCapra, ed., *The Bounds of Race: Perspectives on Hegemony and Resistance* (Ithaca, NY: Cornell University Press, 1991).

McCorklin, James, *Garde d'Haiti, 1915-1934: Twenty Years of Organization and Training by the United States Marine Corps* (Annapolis, MD: U.S. Naval Institute, 1956).

McCormick, Thomas J., *America's Half Century: United States Foreign Policy in the Cold War* (Baltimore, MD: Johns Hopkins University Press, 2nd printing, 1991).

McLuhan, T. C., ed., *Touch the Earth: A Self-Portrait of Indian Existence* (New York: Touchstone Books, 1971).

McPherson, James, *Battle Cry of Freedom: The Civil War Era* (New York: Ballantine Books, 1988).

Mellinger, Philip J., *Race and Labor in Western Copper: The Fight for Equality, 1896-1918* (Tucson: University of Arizona Press, 1995).

Meredith, H., *Account of the History of the Gold Coast* (London: Longman, 1812).

Mikell, Gwendolyn, "Pleas for Domestic Relief: Akan Women and Family Courts," in Mikell, ed., *African Feminism: The Politics of Survival in Sub-Saharan Africa* (Philadelphia: University of Pennsylvania Press, 1997).

Minter, William, *King Solomon's Mines Revisited: Western Interests and the Burdened History of Southern Africa* (New York: Basic Books, 1986).

Mitchell, George W., *The Question Before Congress* (Philadelphia: The AME Book Concern, 1918).

Moore, Shirley A., "Getting There, Being There: African-American Migration to Richmond, California, 1910-1945," in Joe W. Trotter, ed., *The Great Migration in Historical Perspective: New Dimensions of Race, Class, and Gender* (Bloomington: University of Indiana Press, 1991).

Mullin, Gerald W., *Flight and Rebellion: Slave Resistance in Eighteenth-Century Virginia* (New York: Oxford University Press, 1972).

Musambachime, Mwelwa C., "Military Violence Against Civilians: The Case of the Congolese and Zairean Military in the Pedicle, 1890-1988," in Gregory Maddox, ed. *African Nationalism and Revolution* (New York: Garland Publishing, Inc., 1993).

Musisi, Nakanyike B., "Baganda Women's Night Market Activities," in Bessie House-Midamba and Felix K. Ekechi, eds., *African Market Women and Economic Power*.

Mwase, George S., *Strike a Blow and Die: A Narrative of Race Relations in Colonial Africa* (Cambridge, MA: M.I.T. Press, 1967).

Nash, Gary B., *Red, White, and Black: The Peoples of Early America* (Englewood Cliffs, NJ: Prentice-Hall, 2nd edition, 1982).

Nash, Gary B., and Jean Soderland, *Freedom By Degrees: Emancipation in Pennsylvania and Its Aftermath* (New York: Oxford University Press, 1991).

Nelson, Truman, *The Old Man: John Brown at Harper's Ferry* (New York: Holt, Rinehart and Winston, 1973).

Neverdon-Morton, Cynthia, *Afro-American Women of the South and the Advancement of the Race, 1895-1925* (Knoxville: University of Tennessee Press, 1988).

Newton, Huey P., *Revolutionary Suicide* (New York: Harcourt, Brace, Jovanovich, 1973).

Niebuhr, Rhienhold, *The Nature and Destiny of Man*, vol. 1 (New York: Charles Scribner's Sons, 1937).

Nkrumah, Kwame, *Challenge of the Congo* (London: Panaf Books, 1967).

————, *Consciencism: Philosophy and Ideology for Decolonization* (New York: Monthly Review Press, 1964).

Novak, William J., *The People's Welfare: Law and Regulation in Nineteenth-Century America* (Chapel Hill: University of North Carolina Press, 1996).

Novick, Peter, *That Noble Dream: The Objectivity Question and the American Historical Profession* (Cambridge: Cambridge University Press, 1988).

Null, Gary, *Black Hollywood: The Black Performer in Motion Pictures* (Secaucus, NJ: The Citadel Press, 1975).

Nye, Joseph, *Pan-Africanism and East African Integration* (Cambridge, MA: Harvard University Press, 1966).

O'Reilly, Kenneth, *Racial Matters: The FBI's Secret File on Black America, 1960-1972* (New York: Free Press, 1989).

————, *Black Americans: The FBI Files* (New York: Carrol & Graf Publishers, 1994).

Oakes, James, *Slavery and Freedom: An Interpretation of the Old South* (New York: Vintage Books, 1990).

Obadele, Imari A., *Free The Land* (Washington, DC: The House of Songhay, 1987).

Ojo, Olatunde, D. K. Orwa, and C. M. B. Utete, *African International Relations* (London: Longman Group, 1985).

Osirim, Mary J., "Trade, Economy and Family in Urban Zimbabwe," in Bessie House-Midamba and Felix K. Ekechi, eds., *African Market Women and Economic Power.*

Ostereicher, Richard, *Solidarity and Fragmentation: Working People and Class Consciousness in Detroit, 1875-1900* (Urbana: University of Illinois Press, 1989).

Owen, Leslie H., *This Species of Property: Slave Life and Culture in the Old South* (New York: Oxford University Press, 1977), pp. 7-8.

Owsley, Frank, *King Cotton Diplomacy: Foreign Relations of the Confederate States of America* (Chicago, IL: University of Chicago Press, 1931).

Painter, Nell, *Exodusters: Black Migration to Kansas After Reconstruction* (New York: Knopf, 1976).

———, *Soul Murder and Slavery: Toward a Fully Loaded Cost Accounting* (Charles Edmondson Historical Lectures Series, 15) (Waco, TX: Baylor University Press, 1998).

Pakenham, Thomas, *The Scramble for Africa: White Man's Conquest of the Dark Continent From 1876 to 1912* (New York: Avon Books, 1991).

Parekh, Bhikhu, "Liberalism and Colonialism: A Critique of Locke and Mill," in Jan Pieterse and Bhikhu Parekh, *The Decolonization of Imagination: Culture, Knowledge, and Power* (London: Zed Books, 1995).

Parker, Albert, "The March on Washington," in C. L. R. James, ed. *Fighting Racism in World War II* (New York: Pathfinder Books, 1980).

Paterson, Thomas G., *On Every Front: The Making of the Cold War* (New York: W. W. Norton, 1979).

Patterson, James T., Brown v. Board of Education: *A Civil Rights Milestone and Its Troubled Legacy* (New York: Oxford University Press, 2001).

Patterson, Orlando, *Slavery and Social Death: A Comparative Study* (Cambridge, MA: Harvard University Press, 1982).

———, *Freedom, Vol. 1: Freedom In the Making of Western Culture* (New York: Basic Books, 1991).

Patterson, Thomas, *On Every Front: The Making of the Cold War* (New York: W. W. Norton, 1979).

Patterson, William L., ed., *We Charge Genocide: The Historic Petition to the United Nations for Relief from a Crime of the United States Government Against the Negro People* (New York: International Publishers, 1970).

Perlmann, Joel, *Ethnic Differences: Schooling and Social Structure Among the Irish, Italians, Jews and Blacks in an American City, 1880-1935* (Cambridge: Cambridge University Press, 1988).

Phillips, Wendell, *The Constitution: A Pro-Slavery Compact* (New York: Negro Universities Press reprint edition, 1969).

Pieterse, Jan, *White On Black: Images of Africa and Blacks in Western Popular Culture* (New Haven CT: Yale University Press, 1992).

Pieterse, Jan N., and Bhikhu Parekh, "Shifting Imagniaries: Decolonization, Internal Decolonization, Postcoloniality," in Pieterse and Parekh, eds., *The Decolonization of the Imagination: Culture, Knowledge, and Power* (London: Zed Books, 1995).

Plummer, Brenda, G., *Haiti and the Great Powers, 1902-1915* (Baton Rouge: Louisiana State University Press, 1988).

————, *Haiti and the United States: the Psychological Moment* (Athens: University of Georgia Press, 1992).

————, *Rising Wind: Black Americans and U.S. Foreign Affairs, 1935-1960* (Chapel Hill: University of North Carolina Press, 1996).

Poelchau, Warner, ed., *White Paper Whitewash: Interviews with Phillip Agee on the CIA and El Salvador* (New York: Deep Cover Books, 1981).

Polinkov, Leon, *The Aryan Myth: A History of Racist and Nationalist Ideas In Europe* (New York: New American Library, trans. Edmund Howard, 1974).

Presley, Cora A., *Kikuyu Women, The Mau Mau Rebellion, and Social Change in Kenya* (Boulder, CO: Westview Press, 1992).

*Progress Through Separate Development: South Africa in Peaceful Transition* (New York: Information Service of South Africa, 4th edition, 1973).

Purdue, Theda, *Slavery and the Evolution of Cherokee Society, 1540-1866* (Knoxville: University of Tennessee Press, 1979).

Quarles, Benjamin, ed., *Black On John Brown* (Urbana: University of Illinois Press, 1972).

Range, Willard, "FDR—A Reflection of American Idealism," in Warren F. Kimball, ed., *Franklin D. Roosevelt and the World Crisis, 1937-1945* (Lexington, MA: D. C. Heath & Co., 1973).

Rawick, George P., *From Sundown to Sunup: The Making of the Black Community* (Westport, CT: Greenwood Press, 1972).

Ray, Donald I., *Ghana: Politics, Economics and Society* (Boulder, CO: Lynne Rienner Publishers, 1986).

Ray, Ellen, et al., eds., *Dirty Work 2: The CIA in Africa* (Secaucus, NJ: Lyle Stuart, 1979).

Reyher, Rebecca H., *Zulu Woman: The Life Story of Christina Sibiya* (New York: First Feminist Press, 1999).

Roberts, Dorothy, *Killing the Black Body: Race, Reproduction, and the Meaning of Liberty* (New York: Pantheon Books, 1997).

Robertson, Claire C., *Sharing the Same Bowl: A Socioeconomic History of Women and Class in Accra, Ghana* (Bloomington: Indiana University Press, 1984).

Robinson, Jackie, *I Never Had It Made* (New York: G. P. Putnam's Sons, 1972).

Rodney, Walter, *How Europe Underdeveloped Africa* (Washington, DC: Howard University Press, 1982).

Roediger, David R., *The Wages of Whiteness: Race and the Making of the American Working Class* (London: Verso, 1991).

Rogin, Michael P., *Fathers and Children: Andrew Jackson and the Subjugation of the American Indian* (New Brunswick, NJ: Transaction Publishers, 2nd printing, 1995).

Roosevelt, Elliot, *As He Saw It* (New York: Duell, Sloan & Pearce, 1946).

Rosenberg, Emily S., *Spreading the American Dream: American Economic and Cultural Expansion, 1890-1945* (New York: Hill and Wang, 1982).

Rotter, Andrew J., *The Path to Vietnam: Origins of the American Commitment to Southeast Asia* (Ithaca, NY: Cornell University Press, 1987).

Rudwick, Elliot, *Race Riot at East St. Louis, July 2, 1917* (Carbondale: Southern Illinois University Press, 1964).

Russell, Margaret M., "Race and the Dominant Gaze: Narratives of Law and Inequality in Popular Film," in Richard Delgado, ed., *Critical Race Theory: The Cutting Edge* (Philadelphia, PA: Temple University Press, 1995).

Said, Edward, *Beginnings: Intentions and Method* (New York: Basic Books, 1975).

Sanders, Robert M., *In Search of Woodrow Wilson: Beliefs and Behaviors* (Westport, CT: Greenwood Press, 1998).

Saunders, Christopher, *Historical Dictionary of South Africa* (Metuchen, NJ: The Scarecrow Press, 1983).

Schraeder, Peter J., *United States Foreign Policy Toward Africa: Incrementalism, Crisis and Change* (Cambridge: Cambridge University Press, 1994).

Schulzinger, Robert D., *The Wise Men of Foreign Affairs: The History of the Council on Foreign Relations* (New York: Columbia University, 1984).

———, Robert D., *United States Diplomacy Since 1900* (New York: Oxford University Press, 4th edition, 1998).

Schwab, John C., *The Confederate States of America, 1861-1865: A Financial and Industrial History of the South During the Civil War* (New York: Burt Franklin Publishers, 1968).

Scott, Anne F., *Natural Allies: Women's Associations in American History* (Urbana: University of Illinois Press, 1991).

*Second Annual Report of the American High Commissioner of Haiti to the Secretary of State, December 31, 1923* (Washington, DC: Government Printing Office, 1924).

Shakur, Assata, *Assata: An Autobiography* (London: Zed Books, 1987).

Shapiro, Herbert, *White Violence and Black Response: From Reconstruction to Montgomery* (Amherst: University of Massachusetts, 1988).

Shaw, Timothy M., "The Non-Aligned Movement and the New International Division of Labour," in Ralph I. Onwuka and Timothy M. Shaw, eds., *Africa in World Politics: Into the 1990s* (Houndmills: Macmillan, 1989).

Shiva, Vandana, and Maria Miles, *Ecofeminism* (Halifax, Nova Scotia: Fernwood, 1993).

Shoup, Laurence, and William Minter, "Shaping A New World Order: The Council on Foreign Relations' Blueprint for World Hegemony," in Holly Sklar, ed., *Trilateralism: The Trilateral Commission and Elite Planning for World Management* (Boston, MA: South End Press, 1980).

Sims-Wood, Janet, "The Black Female: Mammy, Jemima, Sapphire, and Other Images," in Jessie C. Smith, ed., *Images of Blacks in American Culture* (New York: Greenwood Press, 1988).

Sitkoff, Harvard, *A New Deal For Blacks*, vol. 1 (Oxford: Oxford University Press, 1978).

Sivanandan, Ambalavaner, *A Different Hunger: Writings on Black Resistance* (London: Pluto Press, 1982).

Snyder, Margaret C., and Mary Tadesse, *African Women and Development: A History: The Story of the African Training and Research Centre for Women of the United Nations Economic Commission for Africa* (London: Zed Books, 1995).

Soocher, Stan, *They Fought the Law: Rock Music Goes to Court* (New York: Schrimer Books, 1999).

Spear, Allan H., *Black Chicago: The Making of a Negro Ghetto, 1890-1920* (Chicago: University of Chicago Press, 1967).

Stampp, Kenneth, *The Peculiar Institution* (New York: Alfred A. Knopf, 1965).

Standing Bear, Luther, *My People The Sioux* (Lincoln: University of Nebraska Press, 1975).

Staniland, Martin, *American Intellectuals and African Nationalists, 1955-1970* (New Haven, CT: Yale University, 1991).

Sterling, Dorothy, ed., *We Are Your Sisters: Black Women in the Nineteenth Century* (New York: W. W. Norton and Co., 1984).

Stockwell, John, *In Search of Enemies: A CIA Story* (New York: Norton, 1978).

Stuckey, Sterling, "A Last Stern Struggle: Henry Highland Garnet and Liberation Theory," in Leon Litwack and August Meier, eds., *Black Leaders of the Nineteenth Century* (Urbana: University of Illinois Press, 1988).

Stuessy, Joe, *Rock and Roll: Its History and Stylistic Development* (Englewood Cliffs, NJ: Prentice Hall, 1970).

Sundiata, Ibrahim K., "The Roots of African Despotism: The Question of Political Culture," in Gregory Maddox, ed., *African Nationalism and Revolution* (New York: Garland Publishers, 1993).

Surkin, W. A. E., ed., *African Political Thought: Lumumba, Nkrumah, and Toure* (Denver, CO: University of Denver, 1968).

Swanson, Timothy, *The International Regulation of Extinction* (London: The MacMillan Press, 1994).

Taylor, William J. Jr., Eric T. Olson, Richard A. Schrader, eds., *Defense Manpower Planning: Issues for the 1980s* (New York: Pergamon Press, 1981).

Taylor, Wayne C., *The Firestone Operations in Liberia* (Washington, DC: National Planning Association, 1956).

Terborg-Penn, Rosalyn, *African American Women in the Struggle for the Vote, 1850-1920* (Bloomington: Indiana University Press, 1998).

Thomas, Brook, ed., *Plessy v. Ferguson: A Brief History with Documents* (Boston: Bedford Books, 1997).

Thompson, W. Scott, *Ghana's Foreign Policy, 1957-1966: Diplomacy, Ideology, and the New State* (Princeton, NJ: Princeton University Press, 1969).

Tibebu, Teshale, *The Making of Modern Ethiopia, 1896-1974* (Lawrenceville, NJ: Red Sea Press, 1995).

Tilchin, William, *Theodore Roosevelt and the British Empire: A Study in Presidential Statecraft* (New York: St. Martin's Press, 1997).

Trafzer, Clifford E., *Death Stalks the Yakama* (East Lansing: Michigan State University Press, 1997).

Trelease, Allen, *White Terror: The Ku Klux Klan Conspiracy and Southern Reconstruction* (Westport, CT: Greenwood Press, 1979).

Trotter, Joe W., *Black Milwaukee: The Making of an Industrial Proletariat, 1915-1945* (Urbana: University of Illinois Press, 1985).

Trotter, Joe W., and Earl Lewis, eds., *African Americans in the Industrial Age: A Documentary History* (Boston, MA: Northeastern University Press, 1996).

Tuttle, William M., *Race Riot: Chicago in the Red Summer of 1919* (New York: Atheneum, 1972).

*United Nations Mission of Technical Assistance to Haiti* (Lake Success, NY: United Nations, 1949).

van Lierde, Jean, ed., *Lumumba Speaks: The Speeches and Writings of Patrice Lumumba, 1958-1961* (Boston: Little, Brown and Co., 1972).

Vanauken, Sheldon, *The Glittering Illusion: English Sympathy for the Southern Confederacy* (Washington, DC: Regnery Gateway, 1989).

Vogt, John, *Portuguese Rule on the Gold Coast, 1469-1682* (Athens: University of Georgia Press, 1979).

Wala, Michael, *The Council on Foreign Relations and American Foreign Policy in the Early Cold War* (Providence, RI: Berghahn Books, 1994).

Walker, Margaret, "Reflections On Black Women Writers," in Maryemma Graham, *On Being Female, Black and Free: Essays by Margaret Walker, 1932-1992* (Knoxville: University of Tennessee Press, 1997).

Walker, Walter, *The Bear at the Back Door: The Soviet Threat to the West's Lifeline in Africa* (Sandton, Republic of South Africa: Valiant Publishers, 1978).

Wallerstein, Immanuel M., *The Modern World-System: Capitalist Agriculture and the Origins of the European World-Economy in the Sixteenth Century* (New York: Academic Press, 1974).

Ward, W. E. F., *A History of Ghana* (New York: Praeger, 1958).

Warren, Nagueyalti, "From Uncle Tom to Cliff Huxtable, Aunt Jemima to Aunt Nell: Images of Blacks in Film and the Television Industry," in Jessie C. Smith, ed., *Images of Blacks in American Culture* (New York: Greenwood Press, 1988).

Washington, Booker T., *Up From Slavery: An Autobiography* (Garden City, NY: Doubleday, 1946).

Washington, E. Davidson, *Selected Speeches of Booker T. Washington* (Garden City, NY: Doubleday, Doran & Co., 1932).

Watson, Richard L. Jr., *The Development of National Power: The United States, 1900-1919* (Boston: Houghton Mifflin Co., 1976).

Weber, David J., "Scarce More Than Apes: Historical Roots of Anglo-American Stereotypes of Mexicans in the Border Region," in Michael Krenn, ed., *Race and U.S. Foreign Policy in the Ages of Territorial and Market Expansion, 1840 to 1900* (New York: Garland Publishing, 1998) .

Wedell, Marsha, *Elite Women and the Reform Impulse in Memphis, 1875-1915* (Knoxville: University of Tennessee Press, 1991).

Weisbrot, Robert, *Freedom Bound: A History of America's Civil Rights Movement* (New York: Plume Books, 1991).

Weiss, Nancy J., *Farewell to the Party of Lincoln: Black Politics in the Age of FDR* (Princeton, NJ: Princeton University Press, 1983).

Wharton, Vernon, *The Negro in Mississippi, 1865-1890* (Chapel Hill: University of North Carolina Press, 1947).

White, Walter F., *A Man Called White: The Autobiography of Walter White* (New York: Viking Press, 1948).

Whitehead, Ann, "Wives and Mothers: Female Farmers in Africa," in Aderanti Adepoju and Christine Oppong, eds., *Gender, Work, and Population in Sub-Saharan Africa* (Portsmouth, NH: Heinemann Publishers, 1994).

Whitman, Mark, ed., *Removing a Badge of Slavery: The Record of Brown v. Board of Education* (Princeton, NJ: Markus Wiener Publishing, 1993).

Wickman, Patricia R., *The Tree That Bends: Discourse, Power, and the Survival of the Maskoki People* (Tuscaloosa: University of Alabama Press, 1999).

Wildman, Stephanie et al., *Privilege Revealed: How Invisible Preference Undermines America* (New York: New York University Press, 1996).

Williams, Eric, *Capitalism and Slavery* (Chapel Hill: University of North Carolina Press, 1944).

Williams, Lee E., and Lee E. Williams II, *Anatomy of Four Race Riots: Racial Conflict in Knoxville, Elaine (Arkansas), Tulsa, and Chicago, 1919-1921* (Hattiesburg: University and College Press of Mississippi, 1972).

Williams, William A., *The Tragedy of American Diplomacy* (New York: W. W. Norton, 1972).

Williamson, Joel, *After Slavery: The Negro in South Carolina During Reconstruction, 1861-1877* (Hanover, NH: University Press of New England, 1990).

Wilson, Amos N., *The Falsification of Afrikan Consciousness: Eurocentric History, Psychiatry and the Politics of White Supremacy* (New York: African World InfoSystems, 1993).

Wilson, Clint C. II, and Felix Gutierrez, *Race, Multiculturalism, and the Media: From Mass to Class Communication* (Thousand Oaks, CA: Sage International Publishers, 1995).

Wilson, Joseph T., *The Black Phalanx* (New York: Arno Press, 1968).

Wimer, Kurt, "Woodrow Wilson and World Order," in Arthur S. Link, ed., *Woodrow Wilson and A Revolutionary World, 1913-1921* (Chapel Hill: University of North Carolina Press, 1982).

Wipper, Audrey, "Riot and Rebellion Among African Women: Three Examples of Women's Political Clout," in Jean F. O'Barr, ed., *Perspectives On Power: Women in Africa, Asia, and Latin America* (Durham, NC: Duke University Press, 1982).

Woods, Forrest, *The Arrogance of Faith* (New York: Alfred A. Knopf, 1990).

Woodson, Carter G., *A Century of Negro Migration* (New York: Russell and Russell Publishers, 1918).

Woodward, C. Vann, *The Strange Career of Jim Crow* (New York: Oxford University Press, 1974).

World Conference for Action Against Apartheid, *Report of the World Conference for Action Against Apartheid, Lagos, Nigeria*, 2 vols. (New York: United Nations, 1977).

Wright, Bobby E., *The Psychopathic Racial Personality and Other Essays* (Chicago: Third World Press, 1984).

Wyaco, Virgil, *A Zuni Life: A Pueblo Indian in Two Worlds* (Albuquerque: University of New Mexico, 1998).

Yansane, Aguibou, *Decolonization in West African States with French Colonial Legacy* (Cambridge, MA: Schenkman Publishing, 1984).

Yohannes, Okbazghi, *Eritrea, a Pawn in World Politics* (Gainesville: University of Florida Press, 1991).

Young, James C., *Liberia Rediscovered* (Garden City, NY: Doubleday, Doran, & Co., 1934).

Zinn, Howard, *A People's History of the United States, 1492-Present* (New York: HarperCollins, 1995).

Zorbaugh, Harvey W., *The Gold Coast and the Slum: A Sociological Study of Chicago's Near North Side* (Chicago: University of Chicago Press reprint, 1976).

# Articles

Abbate, E., et al., "A One-Million-Year-Old Homo Cranium from the Danakil (Afar) Depression of Eritrea," *Nature* 393 (May-June, 1998), p. 458.

Adler, Eric, "Slavery in America: What If It Had Never Existed?" *Kansas City Star*, March 7, 1999.

Afonja, Simi, "Changing Modes of Production and the Sexual Division of Labor Among the Yoruba," *Signs: Journal of Women in Culture and Society* 7, no. 2 (1981), pp. 299-313.

Ansley, Francis L., "Stirring the Ashes: Race, Class, and the Future of Civil Rights Scholarship," 74 *Cornell Law Review* 993 (1989).

Asfaw, B., et al., "Australopithecus Garhi: A New Species of Early Hominid from Ethiopia," *Science* 284 (1999), pp. 629-635.

Ben-Atar, Doran, "Nationalism, Neo-mercantilism, and Diplomacy: Rethinking the Franklin Mission," *Diplomatic History* 22, no. 1 (Winter 1998), pp. 101-114 .

Brewer, Charles C., "African American Sailors and the Unvexing of the Mississippi River," *Prologue: The Journal of the National Archives* 30, no. 4 (1998), pp. 278-286.

Brooks, Alison S., "What's New in Early Human Evolution," *Journal of the National Museum of Natural History* 18, no. 2 (Spring 1996) (online version).

Burgess, Norma J., and Hayward D. Horton, "African American Women and Work: A Socio-Historical Perspective," *Journal of Family History* 18, no. 1, p. 55.

Capeci, Dominic J. Jr., and Jack C. Knight, "Reactions to Colonialism: The North American Ghost Dance and East African Maji-Maji Rebellions," *Historian* 52, no. 4 (1990), pp. 584-600.

Captain, Gwendolyn, "Enter Ladies and Gentlemen of Color: Gender, Sport, and the Ideal of African American Manhood and Womanhood During the Late Nineteenth and Early Twentieth Century," *Journal of Sport History* 18, no. 1 (Spring 1991), p. 100.

Cho, Sumi, "Redeeming Whiteness in the Shadow of Internment: Earl Warren, Brown, and a Theory of Racial Redemption," 19 *Boston College Third World Law Journal* 73 (Fall 1998).

Cottrol, Robert, and Raymond Diamond, "The Second Amendment: Toward An Afro-Americanist Reconsideration," 80 *Georgetown Law Review* 309, 323-324 (December 1991).

Danaher, Kevin, "Educational Inequality in South Africa and Its Implications for U.S. Foreign Policy," *Harvard Educational Review* 54, no. 2, (May 1984), pp. 166-174.

Dudziak, Mary, "Desegregation As A Cold War Imperative," 41 *Stanford Law Review* 61 (1988).

Elman, Phillip, "The Solicitor General's Office, Justice Frankfurter, and Civil Rights Litigation, 1946-1960, An Oral History," 100 *Harvard Law Review* 817 (1987).

Fitzgerald, Charlotte D., "The Story of My Life and Work: Booker T. Washington's Other Autobiography," *Black Scholar* 21, no. 4 (1991), pp. 35-40.

Geiger, Susan, "Women in Nationalist Struggle: TANU Activists in Dar Es Salaam," *International Journal of African Historical Studie* 20 (1987).

George, Christopher T., "Mirage of Freedom: African Americans in the War of 1812," *Maryland Historical Magazine* 91, no. 4 (1996), pp. 426-450.

Gitlin, Jay, "Private Diplomacy to Private Property: States, Tribes, and Nations in the Early National Period," *Diplomatic History* 22, no. 1, (Winter 1998), pp. 85-99.

Hardin, Einar, "The Integration of Women Into Professional Personnel and Labor Relations Work," *Industrial and Labor Relations Review* 44, no. 2, (1991), pp. 229-240.

Harris, Cheryl I., "Whiteness As Property," 106 *Harvard Law Review* 1707 (1993).

Hays, Christopher K., "The African American Struggle for Equality and Justice in Cairo, Illinois, 1865-1900," *Illinois Historical Journal* 90, no. 4 (1997).

Higginbotham, A. Leon Jr., and Barbara K. Kopytoff, "Property First, Humanity Second: The Recognition of the Slave's Human Nature in Virginia Civil Law," 50 *Ohio State Law Journal* 511 (Summer 1989).

Hill-Collins, Patricia, "The Meaning of Motherhood in Black Culture and Black Mother/Daughter Relationships," *Sage* 4, no. 2 (1987), p. 4.

Hoskins, Linus, "Review Article: Independence, Political Economy and U.S. Policy in Africa," *A Current Bibliography on African Affairs* 23, no. 3 (1991-1992), p. 249.

Krenn, Michael, "Unfinished Business: Segregation and U.S. Diplomacy at the 1958 World's Fair," *Diplomatic History* 20, no. 4 (Fall 1996), pp. 591-612.

LaFeber, Walter, "Roosevelt, Churchill, and Indochina, 1942-5," *American Historical Review* 80, (December 1985), pp. 1277-95.

Lansdale, John, "Mau Maus of the Mind: Making Mau Mau and Remaking Kenya," *Journal of African History* 31 (1990), pp. 393-421.

Lockett, James D., "Abraham Lincoln and Colonization: An Episode That Ends in Tragedy at Lile a Vache, Haiti, 1863-1864," *Journal of Black Studies* 21, no. 4 (1991), pp. 428-444.

Marable, Manning, "The Racial Contours of the Constitution," unpublished course material.

Matthewson, Tim, "Jefferson and the Non-Recognition of Haiti," *Proceedings of the American Philosophical Society* 140, no. 1 (1996), pp. 22-48.

Maxwell, Kenneth, "The Portugese Colonies and Decolonization," *Africana Journal* 15 (1990), pp. 59-73.

Mayer, Michael S., "With Much Deliberation and Some Speed: Eisenhower and the *Brown* Decision," *Journal of Southern History* 52 (1986), pp. 43-76.

McHenry, Elizabeth, "Dreaded Eloquence: The Origins and Rise of African American Literary Societies and Libraries," *Harvard Library Bulletin* 6, no. 2 (1995), pp. 32-56.

Modell, John, and Duane Steffey, "Waging War and Marriage: Military Service and Family Formation, 1940-1950," *Journal of Family History* 13, no. 2 (1988), pp. 195-218.

Muir, Donal E., and C. Donald McGlamery, "Trends in Integration Attitudes on a Deep-South Campus During the First Two Decades of Desegregation," *Social Forces* 62, no. 4 (June 1984), pp. 963-972.

Noer, Thomas, "The New Frontier and African Neutralism: Kennedy, Nkrumah and the Volta River Project," *Diplomatic History* 8, no. 1 (1984), pp. 61-79.

Onuf, Peter S., "A Declaration of Independence for Diplomatic Historians," *Diplomatic History* 22, no. 1 (Winter 1998), pp. 71-83.

Painter, Nell, "Representing Truth: Sojourner Truth=s Knowing and Becoming Known," *Journal of American History* 81 (September 1994), pp. 461-492.

Perkins, Linda M., "The Impact of the Cult of True Womanhood on the Education of Black Women," *Journal of Social Issues* 39, no. 3 (1983), p. 18.

Portwood, Shirley J., "The Alton School Case and African American Community Consciousness, 1897-1908," *Illinois Historical Journal* 91, no. 1 (Spring 1998), pp. 5-13.

Prost, Charlene, "Adam's Mark Hotels: Troubled Relations With Blacks," *St. Louis Dispatch*, December 17, 1999, p. A12.

Reid, Maree-Anne, "Kiss the Boys Goodbye: Clare Boothe Luce's Appointment As United States Ambassador to Italy," *Australasian Journal of American Studies* [New Zealand] 16, no. 2 (1997), pp. 45-67.

Roca, Steven L., "Presence and Precedents: The USS *Red Rover* During the American Civil War, 1861-1865," *Civil War History* 44, no. 2 (1998), pp. 91-110.

Ross, Thomas, "The Rhetorical Tapestry of Race: White Innocence and Black Abstraction," 32 *William & Mary Law Review* 1 (Fall 1990).

Rung, Margaret C., "Paternalism and Pink Collars: Gender and Federal Employee Relations, 1941-1950," *Business History Review* 71, no. 3 (1997), pp. 381-416.

Russell, Margaret M., "Race and the Dominant Gaze: Narratives of Law and Inequality in Popular Film," 15 *Legal Stud. F.* 243, 245 (1991).

Schraeder, Peter, "Speaking with Many Voices: Continuity and Change in U.S. Africa Policies," *The Journal of Modern African Studies* 29, no. 3 (1991), pp. 374-375.

Sheller, Mimi, "Sword-Bearing Citizens: Militarism and Manhood in Nineteenth-Century Haiti," *Plantation Society in the Americas* 4, no. 2 (1997), pp. 233-278.

Shesgreen, Diedre, "Justice Department Sues Adam's Mark Chain," *St. Louis Dispatch*, December 17, 1999, p. A1.

Singer, Barret, "A New Model Imperialist In French West Africa," *Historian* 56, no. 1 (Autumn 1993), pp. 69-86.

Sofka, James R., "The Jeffersonian Idea of National Security: Commerce, the Atlantic Balance of Power, and the Barbary War, 1786-1805," *Diplomatic History* 21, no. 4 (Fall 1997), pp. 519-544.

Thornton, John K., "African Dimensions of the Stono Rebellion," *American Historical Review* 96 (1991), pp. 1108-1113.

Torres, Gerald, and Kathryn Milun, "Frontier of Legal Thought III: Translating Yonnondio by the Precedent and Evidence: The Mashpee Indian Case," 1990 *Duke Law Journal* 660 (September 1990), pp. 664-686.

Wise, Tim, "Racism and Preferential Treatment by the Numbers," *Z Magazine—Znet Commentary*, March 13, 1999, pp. 4-5.

# INDEX

# ABOUT THE AUTHOR

**George White Jr.** is a native of Knoxville, Tennessee and teaches American History and Africana Studies at the University of Tennessee. He received B.A.'s in History and Political Science from Southern Methodist University in 1984. In 1987, he earned a J.D. from Harvard Law School. A few years later, he returned to school and received a Ph.D. in History from Temple University in 2001. George is married to his law-school sweetheart, Deseriee Kennedy. Together, they are the proud parents of three children, Noelle, Noah, and Nolani.

## DATE DUE

| | | | |
|---|---|---|---|
| | | | |
| | | | |
| | | | |
| | | | |
| | | | |
| | | | |
| | | | |
| | | | |
| | | | |
| | | | |
| | | | |
| | | | |
| | | | |
| | | | |
| | | | |
| | | | |
| | | | |
| | | | |